DEVELOPMENT WITH HUMAN TOUCH

Edited by
D.VASUDEVA RAO
S.VIJAYA KUMAR

ATLANTIC PUBLISHERS AND DISTRIBUTORS

Published by
ATLANTIC PUBLISHERS AND DISTRIBUTORS
B-2, Vishal Enclave, Opp. Rajouri Garden, New Delhi-27
Phones : 5413460, 5429987

Sales Office :
4215/1, Ansari Road, Darya Ganj, New Delhi-110 002
Phones : 3273880, 3285873, 3280451
Fax : 91-11-3285873
e-mail : info@atlanticbooks.com
web site : www.atlanticbooks.com

ISBN 81-7156-894-7

Typeset at
APD Computer Graphics, Delhi
Printed in India at
Nice Printing Press, Delhi-51

IN LOVING MEMORY OF OUR BELOVED COLLEAGUE

DR. C. CHAKRAPANI
(1956-1998)

FOREWORD

In India, Human Development is a very important and multifaceted continuous process throwing up challenges, from time to time, to the planners and administrators. The angle of development shifts/varies with the target group, *i.e.*, infants, children, girls, women, unemployed, aged, destitutes, etc. Till recently, the development was considered/viewed narrowly to be improving the economic status of masses, through various self-employed programmes. But of late the development is viewed to go hand in hand with human dignity. The all-round development is no more confined only to providing adequate calories for the masses but also equal access to social opportunities to one and all alike.

Prof. Amartya Sen, the Indian Noble Laureate, opines that development should have the human and dignity. It should provide equal and better access for both men and women to the very little available health, nutrition and education opportunities. He advocates that empowerment of masses, specially woman, will go a long way for the sustainable development in the third world countries.

Many books have come, in the recent times, on Human Development with special focus on a single area. This Volume brought out by two senior and seasoned academicians comprehensively covers almost all the important and current topics like Rural Development (Poverty Alleviation, Thrift and Credit), People's Participation, Women Empowerment, Food Security and Environmental Improvement. I congratulate the editors who made an earnest effort to bring the latest topics under one cover.

Both the editors deserve appreciation for their sincere gesture, to immortalise the memories of their beloved colleague late Dr. C. Chakrapani through this valuable Volume.

C.S. RAMALAKSHMI
SPECIAL COMMISSIONER
RURAL DEVELOPMENT, HYDERABAD

PREFACE

During 80's the poor, across wider areas, have gained in political awareness, economic aspirations and readiness to mobilise. From government side also the poor have received policy support for their growth and empowerment.

The poverty scenario has undergone a major change during 90's. That the poor and under-previlaged, it is recognised by planners and polity, won't live by bread alone but aspire for secular, just the equitable socio-economic order. A shift in the paradigm of the economic reforms is a good beginning : economic reforms can be politically sustained in a democracy if balanced by social justice. In the early days of reforms, the social costs of structural adjustments appear to have exceeded the benefits accruing to the poor.

Also it is noticed that the critical variable affecting the poor would be the viability and cohesiveness of the policy regimes in bringing growth with equity and sustainability.

In spite of the activation of Panchayati Raj Institutions (73rd Amendment) a smaller, slower, weaker and scattered processes of group formations among rural poor is taking place. The standing examples in Andhra Pradesh are : Joint Forest Management Committees (Vana Samrakshana Samithi), Zilla Saksharata Samithi, DWCRA/DWCUA groups, thrift and credit (women) groups, Water Users Associations, etc. Thus, the policy making has moved from a Holistic Approach (based on ideological foundation) to Pragmatic Approach (providing immediate help and support to the poor).

The very compulsions of changing society forced the poor to acquire change in attitudes, behaviour and group action helping them to adjust to the emerging conditions.

In this Volume a humble attempt has been made to touch

many aspects relating to human development. It is well known that "Development" has no meaning without human dignity — a prerequisite in a civil society — where people are no more passive beneficiaries but are active participants/stakeholders. Their pro-active involvement not only keeps the programmes run efficiently and effectively but also develops 'identification with the cause' : thereby bringing self-dignity to individuals.

We thank each author for his/her valuable contribution on topics of their specialisation. We are beholden to Council for Social Development, Hyderabad for the valuable support extended to us in this endeavour.

Dr. K.R. Gupta of M/s Atlantic Publishers and Distributors, New Delhi, deserves our profound thanks for having readily agreed to bring out this book, so neatly and efficiently.

D. VASUDEVA RAO
S. VIJAYA KUMAR

ACKNOWLEDGEMENTS

This Volume would not have been possible without the voluntary and valuable contributions from our friends, who are well known academicians in their respective fields. All of them have appreciated the idea of bringing out a Commemorative Volume in the memory of our common friend and readily cooperated with us by sparing their precious time and a paper. We whole heartedly thank each one of them for making our endeavour a great success.

We are highly grateful to Smt. C.S. Rama Lakshmi, I.F.S., Special Commissioner, Rural Development, Government of Andhra Pradesh who has readily agreed to give us the Foreword to this Volume.

We thank Dr. K.S. Bhat, Regional Director, Council for Social Development, Hyderabad for his constant encouragement in our effort. Our thanks are also due to Prof. V. Eswara Reddy for his valuable guidance.

We thank Shri Y.S.S. Prasad, Ms. Preeti Deshpande and Shri P. Kumar who have entered the manuscript painstakingly on the computer and thereafter another couple of drafts as a homage to our departed colleague.

We are grateful to Dr. K.R. Gupta, Managing Director, M/s Atlantic Publishers and Distributors, New Delhi for bringing out our efforts nicely in the form of this volume.

HYDERABAD

D.V. RAO
S. VIJAYA KUMAR

CONTENTS

LIST OF CONTRIBUTORS

1. **DR. S. VIJAYA KUMAR**, Fellow, C.D. Deshmukh IMPART Centre, Council for Social Development, Southern Regional Office, O.U.B. No. 1, Osmania University Campus, HYDERABAD-500 007.
2. **DR. M. LAKSHMINARASAIAH**, Associate Professor, Department of Economics, S.K. University, ANANTAPUR-515 003.
3. **DR. M. GOPINATH REDDY**, Associate Fellow, Centre for Economic and Social Studies, Nizamia Observatory Campus, Begumpet, HYDERABAD-500 016.
4. **DR. INDIRA DEVI**, Associate Professor and Head, Department of Sociology, Andhra University, VISAKHAPATNAM-530 003.
5. **MRS. VANAJA RANI**, Senior Research Fellow, Department of Sociology, Andhra University, VISAKHAPATNAM-530 003.
6. **DR. V.V. RAMANA**, Secretary and Project Director, ARDAR, (Association for Rural Development and Action Research), VISAKHAPATNAM-530 003.
7. **DR. P. VENKATA RAO**, Associate Professor, Department of Anthropology, University of Hyderabad, HYDERABAD-500 046.
8. **DR. G. SREEDHAR**, Associate Professor and Head, Department of Rural Development and Social Work, Srikrishnadevaraya University, ANANTAPUR-515 003.
9. **MR. RAVINDRA BABU**, Research Scholar, Department of Rural Development and Social Work, Srikrishnadevaraya University, ANANTAPUR 515 003
10. **DR. (MRS.) P.V.L. RAMANA**, Research Associate, Department of Sociology, Andhra University VISAKHAPATNAM-530 003.
11. **DR. (MRS.) SUSAN VERGHESE**, Associate Professor, Department of Sociology, Andhra University, VISAKHAPATNAM-530 003.

12. DR. (MRS.) B. MEENA RAO, Associate Professor, Department of Politics and Public Administration, Andhra University, VISAKHAPATNAM-530 003.

13. DR. (MRS.) D.VIJAYALAKSHMI, Assistant Professor, Gitam Institute for Foreign Trade, VISAKHAPATNAM-530 003.

14. LATE DR. K. RANGA RAO, Ex-Professor, U.G.C. Emeritus, Fellow, Department of Sociology Andhra University, VISAKHAPATNAM-530 003.

15. DR. M. VENKATA REDDY, Registrar, Institute for Social and Economic Change, Nagarbhavi, BANGALORE-560 072

16. DR. D. SUNDARAM, Professor and Head, Department of Sociology, University of Madras, CHENNAI-600 005.

17. DR. A. THANDEESWARAN, Research Scholar, Department of Sociology, University of Madras, CHENNAI-600 005.

18. DR. C. RAMACHANDRAIAH, Faculty Member, Centre for Economic and Social Studies, Begumpet, HYDERABAD-500 016.

19. MS. B. JANAKI, Senior Engineer, Environment, Nagarjuna Fertilisers and Chemicals Limited, Panjagutta, HYDERABAD- 500 082.

20. MR. D. SUNDER RAJ, Faculty Member, C.D. Deshmukh, IMPART Centre, Council for Social Development, Southern Regional Office, O.U.B. No. 1, Osmania University Campus, HYDERABAD-500 007.

21. DR. P.S. DIXIT, Associate Professor, Department of Social Work, Andhra University, Rajiv Gandhi Marg, VISAKHAPATNAM-530 003.

22. DR. B.S. VASUDEVA RAO, Project Officer, Department of Adult and Continuing Education, Andhra University, Rajiv Gandhi Marg, VISAKHAPATNAM-530 003.

23. DR. S.D.A. JOGA RAO, Associate Professor, Department of Philosophy, Andhra University Rajiv Gandhi Marg, VISAKHAPATNAM-530 003.

24. DR. D. VASUDEVA RAO, Senior Fellow, Council for Social Development, Southern Regional Office, O.U.B. No. 1, Osmania University Campus, HYDERABAD-500 007.

25. MR. P. PRABHAKAR VARMA, Regional Manager, Action Aid (India), SECUNDERABAD.

26. MS. T.S. RAJA KUMARI, Doctoral Fellow, Department of Sociology, Andhra University, Rajiv Gandhi Marg, VISAKHAPATNAM-530 003.

27. DR. (MRS.) S. UMA DEVI, Assistant Professor, Centre for Technology Forecasting, Department of E.C.E., College of Engineering, Andhra University, VISAKHAPATNAM-530 003.

Introduction

Human Development has been a complex and continuous process which requires constant attention. In the beginning of our country's planning, the planners thought of "top to bottom" models to be suitable for the Indian context. After two or three Five Year Plans, with the help of quick evaluations and mid-term evaluations, it has been found that there is need for a new approach, *i.e.* from "bottom to top". In this new experience many procedures and processes have been tested. For example, to identify people below poverty line economic parameters considered were per capita expenditure on consumption. But due to constantly changing inflation that method did not yield expected results. Next food intake in terms of calories was considered as a tool for determining people below the poverty line. Even then this indicator was not fool-proof as the calories can be derived from various types of food with difference in quality and price. Of late new theories have been profounded by International economists, the prominent one among them being Prof. Amartya Sen, Nobel Laureate of 1998, that filling up the belly is not the only criteria by which a government can wash off its hands and thereby uplift many people from below poverty line. The state's response does not end by providing enough number of calories to the individual in the society but it should also simultaneously provide equal social opportunities to the underprivileged to have access to health, education, nutrition, safe drinking water, and basic civic amenities. With this welfare concept catching up in all societies, development with human face and dignity is the new paradigm of the 21st century. Even the International funding institutions like World Bank, IMF, DFID, UNICEF, etc., have changed their focus from providing calories to the total well-being of the man kind in their projects. The human development needs multi faceted approaches to be adopted simultaneously so that no sector lags behind the other. Because the all-round development demands all these sectors to be developed with different rates, so that at one point of time they converge and then proceed with equal growth rate.

For translating these activities more of participatory approaches, are advocated these days — be it may in the education, health, thrift, empowerment, resource mobilisation and utilisation (like forest and water). Not only participating but sequencing all the programmes has also gained importance.

In terms of human development, Indian states exhibit striking disparities and this could be due to the long standing socio, economic, political and cultural variations. Thus, India registered its position at 139th rank in the World Human Development Index. Among the states, for instance, Kerala ranks first with an HDI value of 0.603 whereas Uttar Pradesh and Madhya Pradesh figured at the bottom of the scale. This does not mean that, in its 50 years of independence, nothing was achieved by India. Considerable progress is clearly visible. However, still it has to achieve its goals and for this a systematic planning is required. First and foremost, it should address 'Human Poverty' which is the root cause for all failures. Next, knowledge, information, communication and technology has to be developed.

Human capabilities have to be strengthened, and bureaucratic indifferences and political instability has to be wiped off. Finally, India must learn certain lessons from the development chapters of developed countries. By referring the UNDP document, Vijaya Kumar has given a brief note on progress, deprivations and human poverty in India.

Development means change, not only in the volume of production, but in the composition of output and the conditions under which it is produced. This is the argument made by Lakshminarasaiah in his article on Poverty in India and the Lessons Learned. He further stressed that to overcome poverty, poor producers should also be given equal importance on par with other categories of producers in terms of development programmes. In other words, technology, credit and market systems should be made equally accessible to all categories of the producers.

With 75 per cent agrarian population, India need to focus much emphasis on rural development and administration. Even though several development and welfare programmes are now in operation, progress at required level is yet to be achieved. The reasons are obviously ineffective decentralisation, proliferation of special agencies, bureaucratic apathy, lack of people's participation in planning and administration and inadequacy of institutional involvement. Elaborating all these issues, Gopinath Reddy in his article suggested that involvement of stakeholders at all levels could only be possible way to achieve substantial and sustainable rural development in India.

It is evident that (UNDP-HDR, 1998) in terms of Gender Related Development Index and Gender Empowerment Measure, India ranks 128 and 90 respectively. Critics say that this is due to the long standing gender discrimination. Recognising this basic fact, Government of India has launched several special programmes and also guaranteed one-third representation to women in all local bodies through 73rd and 74th Constitutional Amendments. Meena Rao and Vijayalakshmi in their article — Women and Democratic Development — evaluated the status of women in India and stressed the importance of giving equal status and opportunities to women in all spheres to achieve social development.

On similar lines in their article — Human Values, Feminism and Social Change — Ranga Rao and Ramana discussed about the human rights with special reference to women's rights. To protect the women's rights, according to the authors, political will and social legislations are essential.

Poverty and Unemployment are the two basic evils affecting millions of people in developing countries and being a developing country, India is in this matter hosting about 40 per cent of below poverty line people inhabiting in rural areas. If the government would be able to address the unemployment problem properly, then automatically the situation of poverty will get reduced. In this direction Government of India launched several programmes such as National Rural Employment Programme (1972/80), Rural Landless Employment Guarantee Programme (1983) and later on as the prime objectives of these two programmes were similar, these two were merged into single programme known as Jawahar Rozgar Yojana (in 1989). In their empirical study on JRY, Sreedhar and Ravindra Babu suggest that, though JRY is successful to some extent, several short falls in the programme have to be dealt with. For instance, proper awareness about JRY among the rural youth, developing effective management information system at the district level to implement and monitor the programme at village panchayat level are some of the essential issues to be given priority.

In the process of development, thrift and credit are the newly emerged concepts and were given highest priority and propaganda. In fact these two concepts were developed by the Non-governmental agencies in making the people self sufficient and sustainable. In this process, how an NGO involved is elaborately described by Ramana. In the situation analysis, author concluded that the initiation and advancement of women thrift groups acted as a base for overall development and change within the family and in the community.

Considering the socio-economic backwardness of tribal communities, Indian government has brought couple of Constitutional Amendments and provided certain financial allocations in the five year plans. However, during the past 50 years, tribal development has fallen short of expectations and is not commensurate with the efforts made so far. This is the critical argument put forth by Venkata Rao in his article "Structural and Organisational Factors in Tribal Development".

Globalisation has brought several changes both positive and negative on Indian economy and though the term "globalisation" is used as a new concept in new economic policy, in India, it is one form or the other existing since decades. The impact of globalisation on coastal economy in general, and on women of fishing community in particular is discussed by Indira Devi and Vanaja Rani in their Case Study at Visakhapatnam, a harbour city of Andhra Pradesh. Their argument ends up with a conclusion that mechanisation of fishing has forced majority of the fishing community to survive in a situation of diminishing work opportunities for men and increasing work load for women against low returns and less fall back position. This in turn resulted in increase child labour, shift in traditional occupation and disintegration of the family.

"Working women in slums are deprived and dehumanised" say Ramana and Susan Vergheese in their case study conducted at selected slums of Visakhapatnam city. They suggest that to overcome this, high priority should be given to slum women in income generating programmes. This will enable them to improve their living standards and also help in over all development of their families.

In his paper on "Sociology of Major Irrigation in India", Venkata Reddy has discussed the need for handing over the management of major irrigation schemes to the beneficiaries themselves for deriving better results and guaranteed project sustenance. Many a time the major irrigation projects are manned by technocrats, bureaucrats and social scientists with intended results of attaining higher yields, but leaving the cultivator far behind. The pity is the water owner is the government and the water user is the farmer. Most of the times there is a big communication gap between the provider and the user resulting in losses (of time, water, fertiliser, human labour, crops). Due to lack of communication the farmers prepare their lands in advance for raising a crop of their choice, but the Engineers plan it in a different way and the water is released at a wrong time in insufficient quantities. Thus, the farmer loses faith on the Engineer-managed-water-distribution. Even among the cultivators raising crops under one distributary, there are differences in the caste, landholding size, location and crop pattern. Generally the head reach and upper caste farmers tend to take advantage of a less realistically planned water distribution system. They enjoy more than a fair share in the available water supply leaving little or some times no water to the tailenders. Added to this, the irrigation bureaucracy have not been successful enough to ensure equitable supply of water across space and between farmers because of the less realistic localisation pattern. Due to inadequate water supply and the location of the plot, some farmers get lesser yields for the same crop. The process of income inequalities set in, where the social gulf between the rich and the poor with its attendant problems tend to increase. Since the government is the owner of the irrigation water, it would be more appropriate and meaningful to introduce water rationing system with hour as a unit of measurement in proportion to land owned by a farmer. The Warabandi system — water sharing among the farmers equitably under one distributary based on land holding size — if implemented properly would be good enough to solve the problem of inequality. This would not only provide water for the crop on equitable terms to the disadvantageously located tailend farmers, but frees them from humiliation they undergo on different counts. In this direction well planned and organised farmers committees at different locations would, in all probability, limit exploitation by dominant and influential farmers. Thus, Reddy advocates land development and use of irrigation waters with human dignity through his illustrious narration.

Sundaram and Thandeeswaran have taken brief for the farmers participation in the irrigation management transfer as an important step towards social action research and diffusion process. They profess the concept of use of water for irrigation with a management domination wherein self-employment, participatory management and administration transfer are being used. They also, like Reddy, advocated for equitable distribution of irrigation water for all the farmers through farmers participation and voluntary social action. As a process they suggest farmers as groups and the changing nature of interest groups with focus on irrigation need to be incorporated into the participatory social action in the irrigation. They have gone a step ahead and suggested that the formalisation of water users associations in irrigation must be started on a big way and should be interoven within the frame work of interest groups. As a pre-succour to the interest group concept, motivation of the farmers to organise themselves in the management transfer programme is discussed in detail in the paper. The motivation can bear fruit if only the farmers perceive that the on farm development benefits to them are obvious. The need for management transfer from government to the actual users has raised in the recent past because water, though a natural resource, is also a common property. Water for irrigation is not a consumption product, not an input, but it is getting commoditised fast and then becomes consumption product/input. The role and importance of opinion leaders is stressed and presented in right perspective and their role is specified as spread agents and are extension workers. The authors felt that they only can act as catalysts and provide men, source of information about the management transfer process to the farming community. In conclusion, the authors suggested that the mechanisms of institution suggest, farmer's associations or water users associations need to be viewed as a policy measure by social scientists within the framework as their role is second to none in bringing farmers and the technocrats together to ensure equity, efficiency and maximum profits.

In their article on "Urban Water Crisis and the Need for Rain Water Harvesting", Ramachandraiah and Janaki reviewed the present situation of the shrinking fresh water resources for the people living in Hyderabad and the future scenario where people may not get even adequate water if they do not care for conserving and replenishing the ground water now. Otherwise drinking water had to be imported and transported from long distances making huge investments in the process. The present surface water sources like rivers are getting highly polluted in our country. Simultaneously most of the urban centres do not have adequate treatment facilities for sewage, industrial affluents resulting in polluted water, if at all it is available. The share of harvest water is around 73 per cent in class I cities as against 23 per cent by ground water. More or less their percentages are in equal proportions in Class II cites and downwards. Supplying of water through tanks has become flourishing activity in many cities during February to June of every year. If the same trend continues for years together with heavy extraction of ground water without sufficient recharge, a day will come when urban areas will turn into deserts. The experiences in the neighbouring Asian countries can be taken as a forewarning and we must prepare ways and means to conserve the only source of fresh water available, *i.e.*, the rain water. The rain water harvesting measures assume tremendous significance for future groundwater resources in urban areas. The process involves capturing opinion of the urbanites and local catchments, capturing fresh flood water from local streams and conserve water through watershed management. Specially in the urban areas where there are no other source of fresh water such measures will help in providing drinking water and replenish ground water. Due to reckless wastage of available water, which is brought from miles to the cities the natural *baghs* (gardens) have also disappeared in the city of Hyderabad; the Kundanbagh, Jambagh, Basheerbagh, Bagh Lingampally have disappeared and in their places the steel towers have emerged. Even Hussain Sagar, Meer Jumla Tank, Ibrahimpatnam Tank, Meer Alam Tank, Jalpally Tank, Masab Tank, etc., which were built 300 to 400 years back were storing rain water and help to recharge ground water. Even Osman Sagar, Himayat Sagar and Manjira channels year after year are getting silted and their capacity is getting reduced year after year. Thus, even in good rain fall areas, the people of Hyderabad city are not able to get drinking water in all the days of an year. Thus, the only alternative for people in Hyderabad to get water for survival is to resort to rain water harvesting. Most of the public institutions which are located in high level places can go in for ground water recharge pits which will help to harvest rain water and helped in recharge of ground water so that the water table does not go down rapidly. Thus, the authors have very successfully advocated for the people's participation in harvesting the rain water for the common good of the entire population of Hyderabad. This experience in the opinion of the authors will go a long way to provide continuous ground water and least wastage of the available rain water because people are involved in harvesting the rain water.

In his paper on "Rural Development and People's Participation", Sunder Raj advocated the recent thrust by the government on the need and importance of participatory aspect, which is hitherto missing in all the programmes. He pointed out that the participation of the people keep them united and responsible in the development programmes and also accelerate economic growth of the nation. He stresses the participatory aspect more so in the context of rural development in view of the latest 73rd Amendment of the Constitution. To substantiate his point of view, he has reviewed the planning and development policies of the government for the eradication of the poverty specially in the rural India. He has mentioned that most of the target based developmental programmes have performed poorly and in addition increased the burden on nation's exchequer because there was no involvement of the people in these programmes. He cited four "A's" as the root cause for the failure or poor results of the programmes. They are lack of Awareness, Accessibility, Availability and Adoptability. Consequently it was felt by the government operating at Block, District and State levels, that no programme can be successful without the involvement of the people. The participation should also be substantial standard and compulsory. Otherwise the sustenance for the longer period is in doubt. The Janmabhoomi programme has given as a reference in point. To secure people's participation, he has given 14 points like motivating people, consulting community leaders, problem identification by the people and prioritisation by themselves, involvement of local voluntary organisations, empowering people, encouraging participation at all levels, and intensive extension work. In conclusion the author says that a sense of belonging and sharing should be created among the rural people by bringing them together thereby translate the noble purposes of plans and policies into sustainable actions.

In their article, Dixit, Vasudeva Rao and Joga Rao stressed the role and need of literacy for the people's participation in developmental activities. Free India, as authors mentioned, has inherited from the British rule the most important obstacles like problem of illiteracy, ignorance, inertia, poverty, ill health and over population. But the Government of India has not given importance to eradicate illiteracy and ignorance confronted by the majority of the people, right from the beginning. As these fields were not tackled in the beginning, they have grown out of proportion inspite of 50 years of planning. Thus, resulting in failure of many programmes specially the women illiteracy has become a major hurdle for many developmental programmes.

The social and economic institutions of user areas dominated the lives of the people and made them more lethargic. But now lot of stress is given to literacy programmes to attain cent per cent literacy. The literacy programmes aimed at eradicating illiteracy specially among women and weaker sections so that in course of time, empowerment and capacity building can be inculcated among them. As a consequence they will send their children to the schools. This will reduce the burden and responsibility of the government in future. The authors concluded their paper that by making literacy movement as a social action programme with total people's participation as the only solution for the success of the programme. They are afraid that in the absence of such measures national programmes may lose their direction and could not be implemented systematically.

In his paper on "Food Security to Food Scarcity" D. Vasudeva Rao has quoted two incidents in the history : the great famine in China (1958-61) and the West Bengal famine as often quoted by the noble laureate Prof. Amartya Sen. The lack of purchasing power makes people to starve rather than lack of foodgrain availability. The food production has touched 194 million tonnes and it is advocated to feed 100 million population of the country at macro level. But at micro level (household level) many people are not able to get their minimum 500 gms. per head per day inspite of the functioning of PDS in different forms. Food security should ensure that all the people at all times should have both physical and economic access to the basic food they need. But due to faulty distribution channels most of the people are not able to get their food requirement throughout the year. Especially in the rural areas for half of the year most of the people do not get work but yet they have survived. Hence, they pledge their time with the money lenders and landlords in advance for a few packets of grains under unfavourable terms and helpless conditions. Thus, they are walking into the debt trap without respite. These people can be helped by the state through appropriate strategies and interventions. To substantiate his arguments, the author has quoted results from an household survey conducted on a larger scale in two districts of North-Coastal Andhra Pradesh. The data showed that half of the respondents are agricultural labourers depending on daily wages, and for nearly 60 per cent of them work is available for half of the year. For only 9 per cent of the respondents food stocks are available for one year or beyond. The data has also showed the yawning gap between food availability and the food requirement at household levels specially beyond 5 quintals per year per family (while the standard norm prescribed by the ICMR requires 18 Quintals per year per family). Food scarcity also varied between seasons where the rainy season has the least food scarcity. The present PDS has proved to be of not much assistance to many households because apart from non users (17 per cent) majority of the households are making use of their targeted rice quantity from the ration shops. Neither wheat nor kerosene nor palmolive oil are provided in sufficient quantities and on time to these people. The study has recommended to widen the net of items through PDS so that the marginalisation of the poor at the retail end of buying can be reduced thereby their real incomes can go up. As observed in the recent past the ration shops have broaden the items in the time of emergency like onions, chillies, tur dal and edible oil. Another suggestion made by the study was to make available the items throughout the month on small quantities so that the poor people can survive with their meagre incomes. The recommendation of the study is that in the present context of acute poverty, unemployment for millions of people, subsidies are both unavoidable and essential. Thus, the author has stressed the need for food security to millions which is the stepping stone for any development programme with the government and the people as partners.

Continuing the same topic of household food security, Varma has demonstrated his experiences of changes in cropping pattern through a case study of dry land South Indian village. The study has its own important angle of documenting efforts made by the people in the dry land to attach themselves to the changes in the cropping pattern unlike in the irrigated regions. Specially for the small and marginal farmers who are growing crops in dry conditions, any change in the cropping pattern means a threat to their food security. The results of the study are also expedited to develop appropriate mechanism to ensure food security specially during the scarce periods. The paper discusses the theoretical and empirical issues, methodology and major findings along with the policy implications. The study was done in 264 households covering a population of 1200. The tribals continue to cultivate their land under Podu system. The people are growing cotton which is suitable for the black alluvial soil of that region. Also the price of cotton in the market is another guiding factor. In addition maize, jowar, black gram are also grown. The trend also showed a shift from mixed crop to mono crop, resulting in decline in varieties of foodgrains. Due to improper implementation of crop raising methods, the cost of cultivation has unnecessary gone up and the profits are drastically reduced. Added to that the agricultural labour availability is also reduced to 170 days per an year. The small and marginal farmers have to necessarily seek employment outside specially during December to May. Even during those days of employment, the casual wages have reduced their accessibility to food and subsequently the food insecurity has increased. As observed in the earlier paper, this paper also has narrated the food shortage by the people for 8 months in a year and thereby they borrow from landlords or money lenders for consumption purposes. During summer the availability of animals from the forest and other forest produce has been reduced drastically driving the people to the level of insecurity. Under these circumstances the Rs. 2 a kilo rice scheme seems to be the cushion on which most of the tribals depended for their food security. The study suggested that apart from depending on the government for food security, the people can take up judicious mix of natural manures and fertilisers which will retain the soil fertility and increase the productivity. The people must also search for irrigation sources which will improve their ability to raise the second crop and provide work for landless and marginal farmers. Formation of grain banks to ensure food security during scarce periods is being suggested and implemented in a few villages. Thus, the paper has brought out the ills of total dependency on government welfare programmes, mono cropping. The suggestions came out from the paper stress the need for people to involve themselves in the programmes for continuous food security including summer.

So far the papers have discussed on the readily available natural resources like water, and food. The authors have also listed their experiences on how to get better results from out of the existing system through people's participation. But in the following papers, the authors have taken up the most relevant and important topic of environmental protection. Unless the present day people take adequate care against environmental degradation, the future generations can not have a safe and sound life. This requires proper motivation to the younger generations who would be living in a safe environment of tomorrow. Though every citizen is responsible in the environmental protection, the voluntary agencies have to play a more responsible role in motivating and training people as a group.

Susan Vergheese and Raja Kumari in their paper on "Environmental Protection for Sustainable Development : Role of Voluntary Agencies" have shown how the children if motivated properly can become environment conscious. The young children have an important role to play to create a sustainable development in future. If they are trained on limiting the harmful impact of today's human activities on tomorrow's natural environment, the future generations needs will not be jeopardised. In a city like Visakhapatnam in Andhra Pradesh the rapid urbanisation, industrialisation, population explosion, falling of trees, erosion of soil, rapid depletion of ground water, ever increasing number of vehicles and factories have polluted the environment sufficiently thus causing serious concern for the people living there.

An humble attempt has been made by grossroot level activists and organisations in Visakhapatnam to arose environmental awareness in the people and bring about changes in attitudes and practices of the people. For this study, two schools were selected by Green Vision (an NGO). In one school environment education is given to the students studying 8th and 9th standards. The environmental issues included in the education are standards of cleanliness, air, water, noise, food pollution, protection of flora and fauna and the need to conserve renewable and non-renewable resources. A total of 71 questions were asked on the above issues. The results showed that the children who were given environmental education scored higher scores. In the school where the environmental education was not given, the performance was not bad, which indicates that the school curriculum and present mass movement have helped them to have that level of awareness. The authors concluded the need for grass root level action groups to play significant role in bringing about environmental awareness among the younger generation. By doing so the authors feel that the groups can bring about a steady but silent social revolution. The networking of the groups in the larger interest with the cause will further bring out better results on a sustainable basis.

Uma Devi continued the earlier topic on "Environment and Development : The Future Scenario". The perception that man lives in close relationship with all living things and animals is quite old. The word "environment" is given an additional meaning to express the broader concept of interaction of human activities on the ecological system and impact of eco-system changes on man actions. The destructive impact of development like industrial revolution, upgradation of consumerism have led to degradation of environment. Growth can be physically destructive, for example, huge irrigation and industrial projects may provide man only of their life but in the long run they disturb the ecology of that area so much without clean water and air and food cannot be taken for granted. A paradigm shift in the approach to the development is called for to avoid development becoming environmentally destructive and socially obstructive. Besides chemicals, industrial effluents, other toxic substances thrown into rivers are raising their ugly heads now and then. Both renewable and non-renewable sources are being exploited without similar stress on their harvest. The poor people are the first and most beneficial from environment degradation. In their struggle for survival they cut bushes and trees and over graze pastures. They are also most vulnerable to the catastrophe like earth quakes, floods and famines. Indirectly the unprecedented population growth affects future generations with inadequate food, housing, medical care, education and employment opportunities. Planning for development recognises the unity of nature and man. Therefore, in our country's planning effective service and rationale on natural resources, protection and importance of human environment are very viable. The social costs and benefits may be used as a yard stick rather than provide gains and losses. While bio-technology has made greater strides in meeting the food supply to the growing population, they are more vulnerable to stress, floods and drought. Water shortage aggravated by population will cause new dimensions. Demographic pressures will cause migration and urbanisation will be the root cause for political stability. Thus, the dangerous ecological trends should be restricted at the local level. Therefore, the saying *think globally and act locally* has gained currency. Local or regional action is to be initiated to correct environmental imbalances to set in the process of development in the right path. For the success of the environmental policies, there should be a consensus between political leadership and the people of the community. We must educate the people to create awareness and responsibility in them. Individuals and groups must be related to environment through their perception. The people cooperate only when they get benefit from various developments. The leadership should be able to motivate people and obtain their cooperation by actual participation whenever possible. Thus, Uma Devi stresses the importance of people's participation and their larger role in protecting the environment while simultaneously marching in the path of environment. Unless the political leader and the people go together in this direction, the future scenario would be dark and bleak.

SECTION 1
RURAL DEVELOPMENT ISSUES
(POVERTY ALLEVIATION THROUGH THRIFT ETC.)

1
Human Development : An Overview

—Dr. S. Vijaya Kumar

Having a rich cultural, social, ethnic and religious diversity, India is a developing country with underdeveloped economy. In terms of human development it exhibits lots of striking internal disparities. UNDP document of 1997 says that in India, certain states report levels of human development similar to those of leading industrialised countries and certain states achievement levels are worse than the average of the poorest countries. This imbalance and long-standing socio-economic disparities could be attributed to the lack of sufficient knowledge on local resources and their utilisation, untimely plan schedules, failure in resource saving and using low cost technologies for agricultural production and perhaps the huge burden of subsidies.

Nevertheless, certainly India is having a scope for development with sustainability and for this there is an immediate need to identify the grey areas and has to address them comprehensively. Stating the India's position in the human development, here I tried to discuss some of the grey areas in the development and finally concluded with certain strategies to be thought about.

In terms of Human Development, India ranks 139 (HDR,

1998). Thus, confining India's position in the countries of low human development category. Some of the neighbouring countries such as Pakistan (138), Sri Lanka (90), and Maldives (95) are exhibiting better progress and the later two countries are grouped under medium human development category. This variation could possibly because of better access to (1) information and communication, (2) education, (3) credit system, (4) high level of production and consumption.

Among the Indian States Kerala ranks first with an HDI value of 0.603, which is more or less comparable to that of China. At the same time Uttar Pradesh (HDI of 0.348) and Madhya Pradesh (HDI of 0.349) figured at the bottom of the scale and these ranks are similar to that of Madagascar, Nepal, Rwanda which are ranked at the lowest levels of Human Development (Shiv Kumar, 1991). In terms of Gender related Development Index and Gender Empowerment Measure India ranks 128 and 90 respectively and in these two categories India is below to Sri Lanka and Maldives. If we take Gender-related Development Index for Indian States, gender inequalities and countries poor performance are clearly visible. Here again Kerala tops the list with a GDI value of 0.565 and Uttar Pradesh is at the bottom with a GDI value of 0.293 (Shiv Kumar, 1996). With this lowest GDI value Uttar Pradesh can be ranked after Benin in the GDI countries list.

India had an infant mortality rate of 73 deaths per 1000 live births where as Sri Lanka's IMR is 17 and Maldives 54. Among the Indian States Kerala's IMR of 16 can be compared with the average IMR of the 14 among industrialised countries. Whereas Orissa state's IMR of 103 is equivalent to the average of all least developed countries and for that matter it is much worse than the average IMR of 97 in sub-saharan Africa.

If we look at the other general indicators, for example, life expectancy at birth for a person in India is about 61.1 years. In this context Pakistan (62.8 years), Maldives (63.3 years) and Sri Lanka (72.5 years) are ahead than India. As per the 1989-93 data, in urban India, life expectancy at birth was 64.9 years, where as it was only 58 years in rural India. Infant mortality rate, and average literacy rates are also much more lower in rural India than urban India. Coming to the health facilities in rural India where 74 per cent of the population are living, only 18 per cent of the hospitals and beds are located.

Apart from the gender inequalities, the traditions in India divided the population into the categories and out of such categories, Scheduled Castes and Scheduled Tribes are the most disadvantaged sections of the society. Hence, the level of human development among these communities appears to be below than other communities. If we take infant mortality rate of 1992-93, among the Schedules Tribes it was 107 per 1000 live births and among Scheduled Castes it was 91 per 1000 live births. These trends are far more than the national average. Their literacy rates are also far below than the national average rates. Considering some of these aspects in its official communication (1997) Ministry of welfare has stated that "even if proportionate resources of the Central and the State Governments are earmarked and utilised for the development of these communities (*i.e.*, SCs and STs), it would take many decades before they will be able to catch up with the rest of the population. It is, therefore, essential that much higher level of resources are mobilised, including from multi-lateral and bi-lateral sources, for accelerated development of these communities".

Based on official sources (GOI 1997b; IIPS 1995 and NCAER 1996) UNDP has prepared a partial balance sheet of Human Development in India (for details see UNDP document : India The Road to Human Development). It suggests the following progress as well as deprivations :

Progress

(1) Food grain production has more than doubled between 1951 and 1991.

(2) Famines and starvation have been virtually eliminated.

(3) Per capita income has more than doubled between 1951 and 1995.

(4) Life expectancy has nearly doubled from 32 years in 1951 to 61 years in 1992.

(5) Infant mortality has been halved from 146 in 1951 to 74 deaths per 1000 live births in 1995.

(6) The member of primary health care centres and sub-centres has risen from 725 in 1951 to over 1,54,000 in 1996.

(7) Close to 50 per cent of the urban population is covered with sanitation facilities.

(8) The literacy rate has risen from 18 per cent in 1951 to 52 per cent 1991.

(9) The officially recorded primary school enrollment rate was 104.3 in 1996.

Deprivations

(1) About 53 per cent of children under four years of age, (approximately 60 million) remain under-nourished.

(2) Nearly 36 per cent (329 million) of India's population live below the poverty line.

(3) Population sex-ratio is adverse at 927 females per 1000 males.

(4) About 2.2 million infants die every year from preventable causes.

(5) The ratio of qualified doctors to para medical and nursing staff is imbalance.

(6) Only about 5 per cent of the rural population is covered with sanitation facilities.

(7) In 1991, 61 per cent of women aged seven years and above were illiterate.

(8) During 1981-91 the absolute number of illiterates has gone up by about 19 million.

(9) Nearly 36 per cent of school children drop out before completing primary school.

(10) In rural areas, about 4 per cent of children 6-14 years belong to the labour force.

These long-standing socio-economic disparities resulted from the imbalances in the flow of resources and investments. Besides, as discussed earlier, inappropriate and untimely planning, several disorders in bureaucratic administration are also some of the causative factors.

On the other side, "human poverty" is the root cause for low profile of human development in India. In general poverty is measured by the number of people living with incomes/ consumption expenditure below the poverty line. This definition does not cover several other related variables such as bonded labour, domestic violence, child prostitution, unjust employment of children, social exclusion arising out of caste and gender dissemination and environmental pollution (UNDP, 1997).

All these issues are equally relevant and important while accessing poverty line. In this direction an attempt was made by UNDP (1997). It suggests a measure of human poverty using deprivation in three essential elements — (1) longevity, represented by the percentage of people expected to die before the age 40 years (in 1990, 19.4 per cent in India); knowledge, measured by percentage of adults who are illiterate (48.8 per cent in 1994); and overall economic provisioning, represented by the percentage of people without access to health services (15 per cent in 1990-95), and to safe drinking water (19 per cent in 1990-1996),and the percentage of malnourished children (53 per cent in 1990-96). If we go by these measures Kerala's human poverty is estimated at 15 per cent compared to Rajasthan and Bihar where it is more than 50 per cent.

Here it is important to note that UNDP (1997) provided a useful conception of poverty from the human development perspective. Accordingly human poverty (1) is multidimensional, taking into account, along with income and consumption, other aspects of human life that are basic to human existence; (2) human poverty is people cêntered, focusing on the well-being of people rather than or the availability of material possessions; (3) want of material means is often the consequence of lack of opportunity for improving skills and knowledge, for maintaining good health, for having access to public resources, and having a say in decisions affecting people's lives and (4) it is more relevant for policy purposes as it focuses on causes, not symptoms.

Having been inspired by the development plans of some of the industrialised and developed countries, India has reaffirmed its commitment to eradicate poverty by the year 2005. Some of the important setbacks are identified and were incorporated in the long term goals. They are (1) to maintain an annual average growth rate in GDP of 7.8 per cent over the next decade and (2) ensure adequate provision of basic minimum services, *viz.*, safe drinking water; coverage of primary health care, universalisation of primary education, public housing assistance to shelterless poor families; mid-day meals for school children, road connectivity to all villages and habitations and provision of subsidised food to poor families through the public distribution system.

If we look into our five year plans similar goals were spelled out, however could not achieve our targets. This is of course due to the lack of coordination between ministries, bureaucratic indifference and to some extent political instability. However, gradually the Indian policy makers realised the importance of above said aims and framed certain important policies to enable positive environment to sensitise the process of growth to human poverty reduction which ultimately leads to human development. Among such policy measures 73rd and 74th Constitutional Amendments are worth mentioning. These two important amendments have opened up new opportunities for decentralised management and people's participation in the development process.

The concept planning from below/bottom to top planning will certainly give better results in the direction of development, however, to achieve this very basic objective local governments have to be strengthened and Centre State relations have to be redrafted. Further, in this process non-governmental organizations should be involved actively in mobilizing the communities towards sustainable development.

There are certain practical hurdles before India in its road towards human development. They are lack of knowledge, inadequate information and dissemination process, serious shortfalls in human capabilities, balancing the physical infrastructure needs with social infrastructure needs, poor technological skills and inferior quality products, lack of capacity building programmes and corruption.

To overcome these, India need strong commitment, political will, transparency, international agencies cooperation and support and above all, society with consciousness. Then only we would be able to achieve a real human development.

NOTE

Most of the discussion made in this paper is drawn from UNDP document entitled — India : The Road to Human Development, prepared by a team of experts headed by Resident Representative, Hans C. Vou Spoueck and R. Sudarshan. Author acknowledge the information provided by UNDP and the World Bank.

REFERENCES AND USEFUL READINGS

Datt G., 1997, *Poverty in India and Indian States : An Update,* Washington D.C., IFPRI.

Dreze. J & Sen A.K., 1995, *Economic India : Development and Social Opportunity,* Delhi : Oxford University Press.

Dreze. J & Sen A.K. (eds.), 1996, *Indian Development : Selected Regional Perspectives,* Oxford : Oxford University Press.

Government of India, 1997, Official Communication of Ministry of Welfare, New Delhi.

Government of India, 1997, Report of the Working Group on Elementary Education, Non-Formal Education, Early Childhood Education for the Ninth Five Year Plan, Ministry of Human Resource Development, Department of Education, New Delhi.

International Institute for Population Sciences, 1995, *National Family Health Survey,* 1992-93, Bombay.

National Council of Applied Economic Research, 1996, Human Development Profile of India, Inter-State and Inter-Group Differentials, Selected Indicators, New Delhi.

Parikh K.S. and R. Sudarshan (eds.), 1993, *Human Development and Structural Adjustment,* Madras : MacMillan.

Sainath. P., 1996, *Everybody Loves a Good Drought : Stories from India's Poorest Districts,* New Delhi : Penguin Books India.

Shiva Kumar, 1991, UNDP's Human Development Index : A Computation for Indian States, *Economic and Political Weekly* (October 12).

Shiva Kumar, 1996, UNDP's Gender Related Development Index : A Computation for Indian States, *Economic & Political Weekly* (April 6).

United Nations Development Programme, 1998, Human Development Report, Delhi : Oxford University Press.

United Nations Development Programme, 1997, India : The Road to Human Development, New Delhi : UNDP.

UN System in India, 1996, India Towards Population and Development Goals, New Delhi.

World Bank Report, 1998/99, Knowledge for Development, New York : Oxford University Press.

World Bank, 1997, *Poverty in India, Report No. 16483-IN,* Washington D.C.

2

Overcoming the Poverty in India and the Lessons Learned

—M. Lakshminarasaiah

Basic elements in the struggle against poverty in India are the provision of the economic services and assets which the poor have tended not to receive in the past as a result of oversight or design. The emphasis on economic services and assets is just because the mass of the rural poor are self-employed, and it is upon the improvement in the means of production directly accessible to them that their prosperity depends. Health and education are very important, but offer more if combined with the material means of making a living — of putting body and mind to work. These assets and services include land, water, technology, commercial services, handling output and inputs and credit-provided within an economic policy framework conductive to their optimal exploitation.

This list is hardly new. It corresponds to the requirements of any producer. The basic points to be made in this regard are : firstly, that the general requirements of poor producers are precisely the same as those of other producers and that measures to alleviate poverty that fall short of recognising the full range of such requirements are doomed to failure and secondly, that these assets and services are not typically provided in a form accessible to the poor. India has made important progress in providing a more effective framework for agricultural production "in general", this framework has not properly embraced small and poor producers. They are as follows : Access to Land and Water.

In the case of access to land, for example, land reform efforts in India has frequently involved major loop-holes, allowing the socially powerful to minimize *de facto* improvements in the condition of the poor. In the critical area of land rights, registration processes have been so complex and costly relative to the resources of the poor that land regularization programmes have, sometimes unintentionally, become virtual characters for legalizing the eviction of the poor and the actual loss of their traditional rights. Irrigation without specific measures to defend the interests of existing occupants of areas exposes them to expulsion — and, moreover, has tended to be concentrated in large-scale schemes benefiting already high potential areas in which the better-off predominate. While huge sums have been spent on large-scale irrigation schemes, little has been spent on water conservation and the sort of small-scale developments that are more likely to be of relevance to marginal small-scale producers.

Technology Transfer

In the area of technology, attention has been focused on technologies (such as the Green Revolution) requiring extensive access to water and fertilizers, neither of which are generally available among the poor. In fact, research almost every-where has concentrated on larger-scale production in areas of relatively high resource endowment. In contrast to this, research relevant to small-scale producers in marginal soil and rainfed areas in India has been shockingly deficient. As in other fields, this is partly explicable in terms of a frequently unproved belief that large-scale production is more efficient. It is also explicable in terms of the fact that it is the powerful who set the research agenda, not the poor. Taking its inspiration from highly specialized, large-scale agricultural units of production, research has tended to dwell separately on individual crops rather than on the interaction between crops, which is of much greater relevance to small-scale producers engaging in highly complex systems of production to maximize food self-sufficiency and minimize risks.

Commercial Services

In the area of handling of output and inputs, organised services (not infrequently under public control in the past) have tended to concentrate in the proximity of large-scale producers and users of input in relatively well-endowed areas. In India the poor have had to incur the extraordinary costs of handling their own transport of goods to and from service points — frequently over long and deficient line of communication. The alternative has been to resort to private intermediaries offering goods, and buying products, at prices very different from those enjoyed by larger producers. In effect, the better-off and the poor have confronted different sets of prices — with the poor paying more for what they buy, and receiving less for what they sell.

Credit

In the area of credit, the situation has been disastrous. It is generally recognised that productive improvement needs a change in means of production — new tools, improved seeds, fertilisers, etc. Such a change everywhere is typically effected on the basis of credit. Yet rural credit schemes in India have usually not extended support to small farmers and the poor. Credit has been concentrated among richer farmers with collateral, and with demand for larger loans. In order to improve their productivity, the poor have been forced to seek credit from informal money lenders — at virtually confiscatory rates. Again, the cost of modernization has been much higher for the poor than for the better-off. The inevitable result has been a lower rate of change — and the consolidation, rather than the reduction of poverty.

The Victims Blamed

Although vast amounts of money have been invested in rural development in India, very little of it has reached the poor. The poor have been left to their own devices, while the better-off have received a wide range of assistance — not infrequently allowing them to encroach further upon the land of the poor. Support for agricultural expansion has not led to rural development, and it has not eliminated rural poverty. The relatively undynamic performance of many small-scale farmers under these circumstances is frequently taken as "proof" that they are a poor investment. This is a variant of "blaming the victim". In fact, the poor have fared badly, not because they could not efficiently use support, but because they did not get it.

In other words, the failure of the poor to benefit from agricultural sector investments has not reflected an economic failure among the poor themselves. Rather, it has involved policy and institutional failures. On the policy level, it has tended to reflect an unwillingness to restrain the socially influential from seeking to monopolize scarce resources to their own benefit — and, perhaps, a lack of awareness of the incompatibility between apparently "neutral" criteria for support (*e.g.*, the demand for land title as collateral for credit) and the particular circumstances of poor and small farmers (*e.g.*, involvement in traditional forms of land tenure). On the institutional level, it has involved both unwillingness to give weight to the requirements of the poor, and a lack of initiative in solving real problems in providing services to the poor such as the high cost of providing services on an individual basis to a large number of small and often dispersed "clients". While there has been a great deal of lamentation about poverty in India, remarkably little has been done to change it at the level of economic systems — perhaps because social welfare activities are much easier to implement than real policy and institutional changes. It is possible to do very much better — not by simply pouring in more resources (in channels which at times do not even ultimately reach the poor), but by changing the framework of investment, *i.e.*, the instruments of development.

LESSONS LEARNED

Targeting of Resources

The fundamental lessons learned are that investment resources must be targeted at the poor. In a world of competition for scarce resources, investments in rural development tend to be captured by those with national and local power — a group which rarely encompasses the rural poor. The first step in delivering resources to the poor is establishing strict criteria for eligibility for assistance. Indicators of wealth in India vary according to the nature of the local economy — in some cases it is extent of land ownership, in others size of cattle herds, in yet others ownership of draught animals — but the principle remains the same : investment in those with the least assets. In some cases, for example, where women represent a significant proportion of actual producers, this may give rise to entirely new patterns of investment.

Reorienting Institutions

The intention to distribute resources to the poorest is not always accompanied by actual performance. Among the reasons for this is the inappropriateness of delivery mechanisms. Put simply, institutions long oriented to the non-poor have tended to develop operating procedures and structures which reflect the nature of their *de facto* clientele and which hinder them from serving a new target group. In the area of credit, for example, insistence upon collateral in land may be an absolute obstacle to participation by the poor — just as a limited banking network may represent an obstacle to delivery to the poor, for whom the costs of communicating with a bank at considerable distance might well add significantly to the real cost of credit. Effectively channeling resources to the poor, therefore, means the elaboration of institutional means of delivery consistent with their circumstances.

However, it must be recognised that there are exceptional institutional costs associated with providing services to (and among) the poor — costs arising from the fact that there are many individuals involved, and that their individual requirements tend to be quite small. The costs of government services in, for example, agricultural credit, are necessarily higher if this involves a very large number of small producers than if it involves a small number of large producers. Administration costs in banking tend to be much higher relative to loan volume if it involves a myriad of individual small loans. These factors have often been adduced as reasons for "impossibility" of serving the poor. Effective Service appears financially impossible, especially the context of widespread retrenchment in public expenditure under structural adjustment programmes. The poor are often willing to pay the actual costs of services — especially if the alternative is no service at all, or supply by local informal monopolists. On the other hand, there are proven ways of reducing costs of service supply to the poor — by involving the poor themselves. Everywhere in India poor people overcome some of the obstacles involved in their individual poverty through cooperation and joint action. While such organisation typically develops in the absence of formal service organisations and markets, it can also develop in association with formal organisations. In effect, the organised small farmers can help shoulder the cost of services through organising local level distribution and administration themselves.

People's Participation

People's participation is, therefore, not only a "social" concept. It is an eminently economic concept, involving cost sharing. It is fundamental to the sustainability of improvements. The long-term solution is not to throw money at the problems of the poor, but to help them to organise to overcome them themselves. One of the happy externalities of this approach is not only lower cost services, but services more likely to be in harmony with what small farmers perceive themselves as needing.

Balanced Development

Development means change, not only in the volume of production, but in the composition of output and the conditions under which it is produced. What is argued is that the pursuit of development without the inclusion of the mass of small-scale producers and the poor has important structural drawbacks, and that their inclusion offers the basis for more sustainable long term development. Some small holder groups have a vast unutlised potential for expansion. Others have much more modest prospects.

Even those with the poorest assets and possibilities, however, can be helped to improve their condition. While the direct economic benefits of this may be relatively slender, the side-effects may be great. An eventual shift of those groups to other areas and systems of production might be inevitable if aspirations for a better life are to be satisfied, but it is essential that this shift be orderly necessitating that support be given in the transitional period. This support can be either a direct welfare transfer or an investment in productive capacity. In many cases the latter may be the least-cost alternative.

The issue, then, is neither the "rich way" nor the "poor way". What is required is : an unprejudiced evaluation of the capacities and possibilities of poor and small-scale producers, and their potential role in the overall scheme of national development; allocation of investment resources according to potential and within an institutional framework ensuring delivery and profitable use; and a more balanced view of the overall social costs and benefits of alternative means of addressing transitional states. The belief is that the outcome of this will involve a reappraisal of the role of the poor in economic development, and a major improvement in the state of the rural poor throughout India.

The poor are many, their productive potential is great, but in few places is the exploitation of this potential an explicit focus of policy concern and action — although everywhere it is concern of the poor themselves. While concrete evidence of the efficacy of systematic policy of support to the poor is sparse (simply because it has so rarely been tried), the evidence of its effectiveness on the local level is abundant.

3

Rural Development Administration and the Poor : Some Emerging Issues

—*M. Gopinath Reddy*

Introduction

Issues in rural development administration need to be discussed with reference to objectives and scope of rural development. Rural development, in a country of India's size and diversity is obviously massive and complex process. Before discussing the issues in rural development administration/organisation, the concept of rural development need to be elaborated.

The importance of rural development in a country like India, which is predominantly rural, cannot be over-emphasized. There are 74.3 crores of inhabitants living in rural areas and only 25.7 crores of inhabitants live in urban regions (C.S.O., 1993). Besides, the sharp incidence of poverty in the countryside rather than in urban areas emphasizes the supreme need for an accelerated rural development. According to latest official estimate, 39 per cent of rural population is estimated to live below the poverty line (Hag, 1997). Unless the concrete and time bound programmes are formulated and executed to deal directly with the problems of rural poverty, the outflow of rural poor is likely to grow, creating more slums and posing more problems for urban development.

Rural Development and Its Scope

Rural development for a quite long time was equated with just agricultural growth. The rationale behind this was that the benefits of growth would trickle down to the poorer communities. In other words, growth in agricultural produce would itself take care of distributional aspect. However, the expected "trickling down" did not actually take place. Much of the hope on "percolation effect" in India as well as in other developing countries seems to have faltered. In this regard the following observation of the Planning Commission 'Task force on Integrated Rural Development' is pertinent :

"After careful consideration, we have belatedly decided to talk what might be considered a rather restricted view of the expression 'rural development'. We have chosen to equate it with agricultural development in the widest sense so as to embrace besides crop husbandry. All the allied activities" (Planning Commission, 1975). Here the word "allied activities" encompasses not only agriculture but also all types of development activity intended to improve the quality of life in the country side.

Concept and Definition

The concept of rural development has changed gradually from a mere agricultural growth to a comprehensive development of the rural life. It is process directed essentially towards improving the living standard of the rural poor. In this context, the World Bank's definition of rural development is precise and comprehensive. The Bank's paper says : "Rural Development is a strategy designed to improve the economic and social life of a specific group of people — the rural poor. It signifies extending the benefits of development to the poorest among those who seek a livelihood in the rural area. The group includes small scale farmers, tenants and landless" (World Bank, 1975). It is mentioned in the same World Bank paper that the provision of improved food supplies and nutrition, together with basic services such as health and education, contribute not only to the physical well-being of the rural people but also raise their productivity and their capacity to contribute to the national economy. In other words, the general framework of rural development does not cover increasing agriculture production alone. This includes generating new employment, improving health and education, providing housing facilities etc. Thus, the World Bank defines rural development in terms of an improvement in the economic and social life of the rural poor.

The essence rural development lies in creating the capacity of the people, especially of the rural poor, for sustained self-development. Uma Lele, an expert in the field of rural development, writes that such development effort has three basic features (Lele, 1975).

(a) Mobilisation and allocation of resources so as to reach desirable balance over time between the welfare and productive services available to the subsistence rural sector;

(b) Mass participation to make sure that resources are allocated to the target group and that the productive and social services actually reach the groups and

(c) Making the development process self-sustaining in terms of development of appropriate skills and implementing capacity of institutions at different levels to ensure effective use of existing resources and foster mobilisation of additional financial and human resources.

Rural development has been similarly conceived by the Sixth Plan Document. It says : "The aim of agricultural and rural development will be growth for social justice, achievement of full employment in the rural areas in a period of ten years and removal of poverty".

Some Socio-Economic Aspects of Rural Structure

After having dealt with concept and definitions of rural development, some understanding of the basic features of rural socio-economic structure in the countryside is necessary.

Since 1951 census, rural population continues to account between 75 to 80 per cent of the total population which shows a meagre inflow of population to urban areas. Agriculture continues to be the major source of livelihood of the majority of the total national work force. Inspite of the development of the large scale manufacturing and infrastructure sectors, the share of agriculture in the total work force has not diminished at all.

The rural areas, of around 9.5 crore families, 30 per cent

are agricultural labourers with almost no land, sometimes not even a house site. The number of agricultural labourers is increasing. Between 1961 and 1991, the percentages of agricultural labourers went by 50 per cent.

The employment situation in the rural areas has been deteriorating fast as new entrants join the labour force annually and there is virtual non-implementation of the minimum wage provisions. In India, one important feature is the preponderance of unorganised sector which sustains most of the total work force (nearly 90 per cent). In the unorganised sector, again it is agriculture which absorbs most.

Land which is the main productive asset in the rural areas is skewly distributed and it continues to be in the possession of an influential minority of the landed gentry. Rural poverty shows no sign of decline in terms of actual number of persons below the poverty line. While various estimates indicate a progressive decline in the percentage of population below the poverty line from 54.93% in 1973-74 to 35.97% in 1993-94, in a period of two decades, the number of persons below the poverty line, however, remains almost the same at about 320 million (S.R. Sankaran, 1997). This situation is alarming and this reflects the failure of plan process.

On the social front not much has changed since the attainment of independence. Social inequalities that have been there since centuries continue to exist. The status of scheduled castes and schedule tribes continue to be inferior to other upper castes. The position of backward castes remain more or less the same. The Schedule Castes for centuries, have been the most oppressed section of our population. They form a little more than 15 per cent of the country's population. Eighty per cent of the SCs are dependent on agriculture of which more than 60 per cent are agriculture labourers and the rest are marginal holders. A large proportion lives below the poverty line. Many are engaged in the so called unclean vocations such as scavengers, sweepers, flayers and tanners. Many of them are still treated as untouchables and all are vulnerable to social oppression.

The situation of scheduled tribes is no better. There is no widening of the resource base for the tribals. On the other hand, forest produce and forest land which were available in abundance earlier are dwindling day by day.

Overview of the Rural Development Administration

After attainment of Independence, the shift from regulatory functions such as law and order to developmental functions has necessitated the creation of various administrative agencies/ organisations to effectively implement the rural development programmes. Bureaucracy in the changed socio-economic environment has assumed a significant role in the background of the magnitude of the problems in the rural areas. It is expected to play a catalyst role in the process of social and economic transformation. As mentioned above various organisational efforts have been made since Independence to cope with the rural problems. An overview of these efforts is given below :

The strategy of rural development has shifted gradually from macro to micro or area-based and clientele specific development. In 1952 the Community Development (CD) Programme has started and it was very general in scope and specifically production oriented. It was beset with serious internal contradictions and as a result, Government of India appointed a Committee namely the Balwantrai Mehta Committee, to study the working of the CD programme. The Committee recommended a three-tier system of local Government named as Panchayati Raj in 1957. The difficult situation on food front subsequently led to a search for directly production oriented programmes. This situation led to the formulation in the early 60s of a number of programmes such as Intensive Agricultural District Programme (IADP) and Intensive Agricultural Area Programme (IAAP) to accelerate agricultural production in selected regions which were endowed with good soil and better irrigation facilities (Bhattacharya 1978). Administrative machinery was created specially at Centre, State levels for supervising and guiding the programme. A designated district functionary was made in charge of programme administration at district level. At the block level, the normal CDP staff was strengthened by providing additional staff.

In 70s the emphasis shifted to the target group approach. A number of clientele specific programmes were launched to improve the economic conditions of small and marginal farmers and the landless agricultural labour. An autonomous agency registered under the Registration of Societies Act of 1860 was established at the district level to implement SFDA/MFAL programmes. In 1972 another special programme was launched for the development of the chronically drought affected areas called Drought Prone Area Programme (DPAP). In addition, a variety of special programme have been launched to deal with specific areas and problems such as command areas, hill areas, desert areas etc. From the beginning of 80's the most ambitious programme for removal of poverty and unemployment called Integrated Rural Development Programme (IRDP) has been launched. The administrative structure proposed for the implementation of IRDP was District Rural Development Agency (DRDA), an Autonomous Registered society headed by the District Collector/District Development Officer. The Chief Executive of the DRDA is designated as Project Officer/Director (Government of India 1980).

Main Issues in Rural Development Administration

There was general agreement that the failure of numerous rural development projects to achieve their major objectives of reaching the poorest section could be attributed to administrative inadequacy. It was felt that affluent and vested minority in the rural areas has gained most from the way development had been conceived and implemented in the past. In large measure the blame for failure is attributed to development administration and its personnel.

Several inadequacies in administrative structure and functioning were increasingly coming to light as governmental functions expanded to include the activities designed to assist the poor, particularly in the rural areas.

It was becoming clear now that forms as well norms of the administrative apparatus would need to be modified substantially to enable it to cope with the emerging issues of managing a variety of projects scattered over a large rural area.

The following are the important issues that emerges from the study of rural development administration and organisation. The important issues being fragmentation of field administration, ineffective decentralisation, proliferation of special agencies, bureaucratic apathy, lack of people's participation in the planning and administrative and inadequacy of institutional involvement in dealing with the problem of rural poor. An elaboration of each issue is attempted below :

(i) **Regulatory Administration *versus* Development Administration.** The first characteristic of the Indian administrative system was its orientation towards revenue functions and collection taxes imposed by the Government. In other words, revenue administration has in fact been synonymous with public administration in the past. Even after attainment of Independence in 1947 the basic functional orientation and structural alignment had remained more or less static and alternative ethos has not been emerged (ESCA) 1979). The emergence of a number of programmes for rural development necessitated the drafting of revenue functionaries for developmental work. The result is that the revenue work was being neglected or undermined. In our country wide ranging rural development projects and programmes have been launched without creating necessary delivery systems at State, District and Village levels. For several decades the people in rural India had become accustomed to the administrative presence of a chain of revenue functionaries and the key middle level revenue functionary namely the District Collector has been made the pivot of rural development administration. The District Collector had traditionally functioned as all purpose representative of the government, in addition to performing the revenue functions. The development planners had sought to utilise the esteem and efficiency of the collector for revenue and regulatory work for purposes of 'rural development' through a number of statutory and executive devices. The collector had, therefore, been designated as District Development Officer (DDO) and public functionaries engaged in development work at or below the district level had been placed under his administrative control and coordination. This realignment of converting Collector into District Development Officer resulted in undermining the importance of the Collector's revenue functions. Further, the policy of treating the collector as District Development Officer was ad-hoc because this decision had not been extended to Tehsildars and Patwaris, with the result that these key revenue functionaries had been totally kept out of the ongoing development programmes, thereby making the collector preside over two parallel hierarchies — regulatory administration and rural administration.

As already mentioned the blending of revenue and development functions in the office of the Collector proved more counterproductive when the increasing tempo of development work had resulted in the revenue work being assigned a low priority. The land reform (enactment and enforcement of ceilings on holdings) was only one example of the development policy which could have been better implemented had the revenue departments not been assigned secondary importance. More recently, the developmental importance of the revenue functions was being increasingly realised in the execution of schemes relating to farm forestry, development of village waste land etc.

The strategy of utilising the Collector as the head of rural development pyramid without restructuring the revenue machinery and establishing new administrative agencies had resulted in proliferation of public functionaries at the grass root level creating confusion in the minds of rural people (ESCAP, 1979). The key problem, therefore, lay in providing for a regular machinery for effective coordinating the field functionaries working. In this direction only worthwhile structural arrangement effected was the establishment of the office of the Block Development Officer (BDO). However the Block Level machinery was found to be quite weak for providing an appropriate and integrated delivery system. The authority of the B.D.O. as a team leader has waned. Within the block organisation there is continuous role conflict; the loyalty of Extension Officers (EOs) is divided between the B.D.O. and their superiors in parent departments. Moreover, the cohesiveness of the block team is reduced due to increasing control of line departments over the block staff. Further, the staffing pattern is considerably depleted and is found insufficient to perform various tasks in the implementation of rural development programmes (Ray, 1985).

From the above discussion it is clear that two important steps are to be taken on a priority basis : (a) the development administration should be delinked from maintenance and regulatory administration and (b) there is need for significant restructuring of staff at the district and block levels. There is need to augment the staff at cutting edge levels.

(ii) **Multiplicity of Functional Departments**. At the field level where development programmes are executed, multiplicity of functional departments and agencies has led to virtual balkanisation of the field. New programmes and massive investments lead to the creation of new units and agencies. The result is that over the years, the functional agencies dealing with irrigation, animal husbandry, forestry etc., have grown in scale and complexity and had their independent area of operation.

The reality is that at the ground level, functions have their natural inter-dependencies. In the absence of horizontal coordination, the functional agencies find extremely hard and difficult to serve the clientele. In other words, the major structural defect is that the administrative system is organised on a functional basis to facilitate securing the lines of command. Rural Development, particularly, Integrated Rural Development, cannot be broken up into strict functional components. It requires an integrated machinery as well as functioning by implementing agencies, especially at lower levels.

(iii) **Decentralisation of Authority and Power.** In the recent years there had been a steady erosion in the status and authority of the field staff and functional directorates. The state-level secretariats were increasingly taking on the responsibility for issuing detailed executive orders leaving little discretion to the functionaries actually engaged in development administration.

Rural development required, by definition, dispersal of field staff and deconcentration of authority but during the last four decades during which programmes had grown in magnitude, requisite delegation of authority down the line hierarchies had failed to materialise. The cast for administrative decentralisation was, in fact, for stronger than that for the political authority embodied in the concept of "democratic decentralisation".

The need for administrative adaptation to the needs of rural development was based not only on administrative factors but also for functional necessity of handling the development programmes. A number of target oriented delivery systems had, infact, been set up in recent years resulting in considerable structural changes in rural development administration. For example, DRDA (District Rural Development Agency) had been given the form of registered society under the Registration of Societies Act.

Decentralisation of rural development management was, therefore, accepted as an administrative canon in most developing countries. Management of rural development programmes, in other words, differed a great deal from management of other types of development programmes primarily because it could be successful only if it was decentralised in such a manner that the "over head" costs of management did not over run the actual costs of the projects themselves (ESCAP, 1979). A centralised agency could, of course, prepare a compendium of guidelines for the execution of local level projects in rural areas, but the actual projects had to be managed by the field level officials, whose daily activities could never be effectively supervised or co-ordinated from a remote centre.

(iv) **Rural Development Administration and People's Representative Institutions**. The Indian experience clearly brought out the utility of association of popular non-official leadership with the administrative of field projects in rural areas. The establishment of Panchayati Raj institutions had tended to impart a decisive momentum to the ongoing rural development programmes in the initial stages of experiment. The process could not be continued largely because regular elections of PRIs had not been held and as such leadership could not be blamed at the grass-root level. Gradually people's representative institutions have been bypassed in the planning and implementation of the various rural development programmes. Suitable institutional arrangements for effectively linking up the offices of Development Commissioners with Panchayati Raj institutions at district and block levels have to be worked out. Panchayati Raj institutions had been given statutory status and did not have explicit constitutional status despite the fact it enjoyed a non-mandatory constitutional sanctity under article 40 of the constitution. The past experience with kind of arrangement had shown that statutory sanction was not a guarantee against institutional decay and functional deterioration and many a times the powers and functions from decentralised democratic institutions in the field of rural development management had been withdrawn as and when it was found that the successful working of these grass roots institutions undermined the political base of the members of Legislative Assembly (MLAs). With the recent constitutional Amendments (73rd and 74th) mandatory constitutional status has been accorded to Panchayati Raj institutions.

(v) **Problems of Inter Institutional Linkages.** With regard to the number of institutional tiers, the key issues was whether to have only one or several tiers? The establishment of multi-tierstructure of decentralised rural development administration (namely district, Block/mandal and village) created problems of inter institutional linkages. The existing administrative systems in most situations were based upon the concept of a single line administrative hierarchy, but rural development involved simultaneous action at so many points, that administrative integration of the field projects was no longer possible in terms of the outmoded procedures of control, supervision and reporting.

The interposition of autonomous decision making institutions between administrators at one level and the others would further complicate the "chain of command" and pose intractable issues of "dual control" if the newly created democratic institutions began to erode the administrative and technical lines of control (ESCAP, 1979).

(vi) **Issues in Personnel Administration**. The shift in the administrative focus from urban to rural locations had its implications for personnel administration. The administrative class (including technocratic specialists) has been, essentially urban and elite based. The apathy and indifference of the development bureaucracy towards the rural poor is a serious constraint which obstruct the flow of developmental benefits to the target groups. There is 'cognitive distance' that separates the bureaucrat and the rural poor (Montogomery, 1986). The existing delivery system shows signs of inequality against the landless, tenants marginal farms and agricultural labourers; in several cases there is a tendency to favour certain communities and castes. In a nut shell, the administrative structure, to a large extent was remained impersonal ensuring a career with a fixed tenure and emphasis on security.

(a) *Recruitment* : There was a need for continuous improvement in the recruitment methods to ensure that talented ruralities got a fair chance of selection. So far no satisfactory formula for giving additional weight to rural orientation of candidates for various Civil service jobs had been evolved. The reorientation of bureaucracy is the immediate need of the hour.

(b) *Role of Training* : The necessity of training the development administrators to prepare productive micro-projects, infact, was a major policy issue in the context of India's programme for rural development. The role of training agencies was, to assume much greater importance than it had so far as more and more development programmes were being implemented in rural settlements. Administrators working in tribal areas located in remote villages needed, for example, intensive training in tribal customs and laws before they could go and propagate improved agricultural practices or encourage people with regard to local forestry.

At present, only a microscopic minority of the vast army of the development administrators in rural India possessed know-how regarding project formulation, project appraisal and project evaluation most of them did not infact, take an integrated view of their own activities.

(c) *Personnel Policy* : Despite the growth in the number

of development administrators operating in the rural area sufficient attention had not been devoted to evolving suitable deployment policies for the large man power engaged in rural development management. The consequences of that neglect were apparent very clearly and it was becoming very difficult to (a) attract qualified people towards rural postings and (b) ensure that functionaries who did take up rural postings stayed and performed their jobs satisfactorily. On the one hand, the Union an State Governments in India lay emphasis on local-level administrations and, on the other hand, the civil servants tried to secure assignments in metropolitan centres, large cities and big towns.

The above system calls for recasting the entire deployment policy in view of the manpower needs for sustained action in rural locations.

(vii) **Identification of Rural Poor**. The identification of the rural poor is major policy issue in rural development administration. Identification of eligible beneficiaries, an important aspect of delivery systems, has been found to be quite unsatisfactory. As a result beneficiary oriented programmes face a peculiar problem of leakages in the sense of spill over benefits from target to non-target groups (Bell and Duloy 1978). This is because of absence of systematic household surveys and non-involvement of gram sabhas in the identification process, the exact socio-economic background of households was not available in most cases. This calls for systematic data base on various indicators of poverty. This would also call for firm display of political will because the "poverty" approach would come into conflict with "Community" approach under which administrative system had been working for such long time. The division of masses into "poor" and "non-poor" and growing emphasis on preferential treatment of the poorer sections of the society would come into conflict with the interests of urban elites to whom most of the administrators belong.

In order to overcome the above obstacles efforts to revamp the administrative culture are of utmost importance. A thorough understanding and clear appreciation of the problems of the rural poor as well as genuine sympathy and concern for them are prerequisites for the programmed benefits to reach the needy.

(viii) **Proliferation of Special Agencies**. Another important feature of rural development scenario is the proliferation of special programmes, accompanied by special project organisation. Programmes like IRDP, ITDP, DPAP and CAD have these built in arrangements. The special organisation have a nuclear staff, but they depend mostly on the regular line departments for the execution of projects. Experience has shown that this kind of project organisation has neither the planning skill nor the implementation machinery. These organisations exist for funding purposes mainly and often find it hard to get their work done through the regular line departments. In consequence programme goals could not be achieved with these kind of organisational arrangements.

(ix) **Poor Monitoring and Evaluation Methods**. The absence of an effective monitoring and evaluation system also become an impediment to the efficient delivery process. An obvious weakness is that the method and monitoring and measuring the progress is still based on looking at either expenditure figures or the physical targets achieved. The excessive emphasis on the achievement of physical targets had resulted in exceeding the targets but the exact social background of the actual beneficiaries or further probing into efficient deliveries was ignored. Ultimately this has resulted in the dilution of the focus on the poorest among the poor.

(x) **People's Participation in Rural Development Programmes**. Along with the growing acceptance of the utility of decentralisation, it was also being realised by the policy makers that association of people directly in the development process is basic necessity. It is revealed in many studies that institutional representation (particularly in the grass root level Panchayati Raj Institutions) did not reflect the actual needs of the rural poor since these institutions have been dominated by oligarchic forces consisting of upper castes and classes. To overcome this distortion, the involvement of people themselves directly in the planning, implementation, monitoring and evaluation of rural development programmes is essential and sincere efforts should be made to operationalise this strategy to ensure developmental programmes reach the needy. For this to happen the rural poor had to be organised and energised so that they become active partners in the rural transformation.

REFERENCES

Bell, C.L.G. and Duloy, H. John, "Rural Target Group", quoted in Bhattacharya, Mohit, Administrative and Organisational Issues in Rural Development, Indian Journal of Public Administration, Vol. XXIV, October-November, 1978.

Bhattacharya, Mohit, "Administrative and Organisational Issues in Rural Development", Indian Journal of Public Administration, Vol. XXIV, October - November, New Delhi, 1978.

Central Statistical Organisation, Selected Socio-Economic Statistics for India, Ministry of Planning and Programmes Implementation, Government of India, 1993.

Economic and Social Commission for Asia and Pacific and Government of India, Rural Development Administration in India : Some Emerging Policy issues, New Delhi, 1979.

Government of India, Manual of Integrated Rural Development Programme (IRDP), Ministry of Rural Development, New Delhi, 1980.

Haq Mahbub Ul, Human Development in South Asia 1997, Oxford University Press, New Delhi, 1997.

Lele, Uma, The Design of Rural Development : Lessons from Africa, John Hopkins Press, Baltimore, 1975.

Montogomery, John D, "Administering to the Poor (or, if we can't help rich dictators, what can we do for the poor?)", Public Administration Review, Vol.40, No.5, September-October, 1986.

Planning Commission, Interim Report on Integrated Agricultural Development Projects in Canal Irrigated Areas by the Task Force on Integrated Rural Development, New Delhi, 1975.

Ray, Amal, "Delivery Systems for Rural Development in India : A field view of Institutional Linkages", Public Administration and Development, Vol.5, No.4, October-November, London, 1985.

Sankaran, S.R, Planning for the poor : Indian Experience, First Dr. C.D.Deshmukh Memorial Lecture, Council for Social Development, Hyderabad, April 25, 1997.

World Bank, Rural Development : Sector Policy Paper, Washington, 1975.

4

The Impact of Globalisation on Coastal Economy and its Implications for Fisherwoman : A Study of Pedda Jalaripet in Visakhapatnam*

—Dr. M. Indira Devi and Mrs. S. Vanaja Rani

Market Economy dominated by Global forces ushers in as Shiva aptly observed, "resource and energy intensive process of production, diverts resources away from survival and hence Women" (Shiva, V., 1997, 249). It also results in heavy ecological costs borne by women. Though the word 'Globalisation' as it is used in the context of New Economic Policy in India is of recent origin, globalisation in relation to fishery economy of India commenced in early 1960's with the introduction of mechanisation to exploit marine resources for exports (Kurien, J., 1978).

In this paper an attempt is being made to study the impact of mechanisation in fishing on coastal economy and its implications for women. This paper is divided into two parts. Part I presents an overview of the received knowledge on the theme. Part II presents the results of field work based on a survey of 50 fisherwomen. The focus in part II is to identify the impact of mechanisation on coastal economy as seen by fisherwomen and its implications for their survival. Attempt is also being made to identify the strategies adopted by fisherwomen to cope up with the emerging changes in coastal economy on their lives and overall well being of their families.

*Paper presented at the VIII National Conference of Women's Studies held at PUNE during 30th May-2nd June 1998.

PART-I

The adverse impact of mechanisation on coastal ecology is evident from the overfishing and consequent decline in fish catch all over the world. The total fish catch of the world has declined from 100.2 million tonnes in 1989 to 96.9 tonnes by 1991. Fish production in Japan and Russia which are among the top three nations has declined by more than a million tonnes. This decline is considered much higher in the case of U.S.A. (Joshi, 1996, 110).

On the economy front, though mechanisation facilitated augmentation of marine output and contributed to export earnings, its impact of employment and the economic well being of fishermen is considered adverse. Reflecting on the impact of entry of big business into fishing, Kurien cautioned that "Encouragement of sophisticated technology.... will certainly yield enhanced level of exploitation at present but would spell disaster for the future of both fishing and fishermen (Kurien, J., 1978, 1564).

The argument that employment generation in fish processing and export will offset the loss in employment to traditional fishing communities is the result of naive understanding of the reality and tactics of those in the Industry. Studies in the area justified the above observation. In her study on 'prawn fish Head cutters of Harora' Loening Ariane observed "exports have not helped the working women in the fishing Industry. Infact denied them access to hitherto cheaply available labour" (Ariane Loening, 1984). Nalini Nayak referred to weakening of community control over fishing, depletion of stocks, decline in women's access to space in cold storage, landing site and ability to complete, as a consequence of technological change in fishing industry (Nalini Nayak, 1991, 240).

Beena's study of fish processing industry in Kerala reveals that highest percentage of women employed in fish processing industry belong to traditionally non-fishing communities, the labour force absorbed are young, unmarried and age-specific labour force and decentralisation of processing and frequent shifts in location destroyed the bargaining strength of the work force resulting in deteriorating working conditions (Beena, 1991, 216).

In a recent study, based on a survey of 200 fishermen families in the coastal cities of Saurashtra, Joshi noted that the net impact of mechanisation on employment is not positive. Though more crew members are required in mechanised boats, compared to the traditional ones, fishermen as a group are losing their employment and income due to mechanisation. He finally observed "The number of loosing opportunities are greater than the getting opportunity of employment due to adoption of mechanisation in fishery sector". The adverse impact of mechanisation on fish catchment, income and employment of small and marginal fishermen were much more severe compared to others (Joshi, 1996, 114-15).

While studies on the mechanisation of fishing industry and its impact on the fish economy, employment and incomes have attracted the attention of scholars in the area, the problems of fisherwomen in the changed scenario have not received much attention. In a recent review of the literature on the Role and Status of Women in Indian fishing communities, Subba Rao observed that very little is known about the impact of new technology on the nature of work participation. He also noted that the indirect effects of the new technologies on fisherwomen are not clearly studied (Subba Rao, N., 1995, 22).

The limited studies on the effects of technological change on fisherwomen have brought into focus these aspects *viz.*, increase in work participation and shifts in work participation (Leela Gulati, 1982, 1983, 1984A, 1984B, Subba Rao, 1988); disappearance of traditionally diversified activities of fisherwomen except fish marketing (Subba Rao, 1988, Karuna Ambarasan, 1984); younger generation finding new avenues of non-traditional employment (Leela Gulati *op.cit.*, Beena, D., 1991). The plight of fisherwomen as a consequence of technological change are ably putforth by Leela Menon. She noted "on many days, fish vendors return home with their whole basket of fish, because the markets are glutted with 'teash fish' from trawlers and pulse-seivers. So erratic are the earning of a fish vendor that very often she has only a thin gruel to serve her family. Her children suffer from tuberculosis, heart and kidney diseases, besides chronic dysentery and diarrhoea. Families spend as much as Rs. 400 — per month on medicines digging into the small capital that fish vendors keep for trying fish (quoted by Subba Rao, N., 1995, 24).

The above evidence though limited has brought into sharp focus that globalisation and mechanisation of fishing has hit the most disadvantaged and vulnerable sections of society, namely fisherwomen. Concerns for exploitation, productivity and development have kept all other costs of economic process as invisible. Women are the most burdened by this process not only as sustainers but also because they are poorest among the poor and are also subjected to shocking discrimination by most of the basic institutions of society including family. This calls for evolving appropriate strategies, as rightly pointed out by Nandita Shaw *et al.*, "that the poor do not pay even more for a crisis which was not of their making" (Nandita Shaw *et al.*, 1994, WS, 47). Evolving supportive strategies calls for an understanding of the existing strategies being adopted by the affected for their survival. Though literature on the survival strategies of the poor and vulnerable is emerging in the recent past (Leiten G.K. *et al.*, 1989), there is hardly any information on the survival strategies adopted by the fisherwomen to overcome the economic crisis and ecological disasters unleashed by indiscriminate exploitation of marine living resources. This paper is a modest attempt to fill this void in knowledge relating to fisherwomen.

PART-II

Objective

Socio-economic changes not only impinge upon the prospects of the household but also upon the prospects of the individual members of the household (Leiten G.K. *et al.*, 1989, 8). The focus of this study is on the socio-economic changes effecting fisherwomen in the context of mechanisation of fishing industry and the survival strategies adopted by them

Survival strategy : Conceptual clarification

Survival strategies are people's responses to the emerging challenges they encountered. They are essentially defensive in nature with little potential to change the general conditions under which individuals and households survive (Nandita Shah *et al.*, 1989 WS, 46). People's responses to survival problems are diverse in nature. Some are imminent and others are long term in nature. For the purpose of this paper, responses of long-term character which agree with the specific long term connotation of the concept of strategy along are considered as survival strategies (Streetland, 1989, 28).

Area of Study

Visakhapatnam district which has a coast line of 136 kms. is one of the earliest to witness mechanisation of fishing industry. The process commended with the introduction of Pablo boats in 1962-63 and Royya type boats in 1967-68. Nearly 2860 persons are employed in mechanised boats during 1997-98. Of the 45.711 people engaged allied fishing activities, more than 52 per cent are engaged in marketing, 24 per cent in repairing of nets and around 23 per cent in the processing of fish. In April 1988, 362 mechanised fishing vessels are operating at fishing harbour of Visakhapatnam. Of the 22.71 crores worth of fish produced in the city, prawns account 84 per cent and the balance 16 per cent by fish. Thus, Visakhapatnam, with high degree of mechanization in fishing industry is considered ideal to study the impact of mechanization on coastal economy, in particular its impact on fisherwomen and the survival strategies adopted by them.

Pedda Jalaripet, one of the 7 fishermen's residential colonies in the city coast of Vizag is selected for the purpose. It has 2000 households and a population of 16,000. Total number of households owning traditional boats are 1000 and 30 households own mechanised boats. One-fourth of the households belong to other communities. They are engaged not only in occupation of fishing but also other modern occupations. The rationale for its location is in addition to many commonalities with other fishermen's colonies, it has the added advantage in the sense, that it has been exposed to research studies in the past (Subba Rao, N., 1980). These studies, it is hoped will help to throw better light on the socio-economic scenario, so that the present study can concentrate on its major theme. From this colony 50 fisherwomen were selected at random covering owners of mechanised as well as non-mechanised boats.

Methodology

A structured questionnaire to elicit socio-economic background of the sample households and to get at the changes positive and negative affecting the fisherwomen consequent upon mechanisation of fishing industry and the strategies adopted by them for socio-economic survival was prepared. However, at the time of pre-testing, this was given up in view of the tremendous time constraints it is imposing on the respondents as well, as their reluctance to answer to the questions. As such unstructured interviews were held to get at their experiences and responses to the emerging challenges. To study the survival strategies adopted by fisherwomen existing literature on the survival strategies is relied upon. Schendel Willen Van's (1989) study on rural poor in Bangladesh has classified survival strategies into five broad categories *viz.*, Economic, social, political and Demographic establishing new networks of support. Cornia also documented and classified a range of survial strategies adopted by the poor particularly women in the context of structural adjustment programme. Cornia classified strategies into three types *viz.*, strategies for creation of resources, strategies for conserving and improving the existing resources and extended family and migration strategies. Cornia's classification excludes social and political strategies noted by Schendler (quoted by Shah *et al.*, 1994, WS, 46). The results of the study on the strategies adopted by sample fisherwomen will be presented under the five fold classification advocated by Schendler.

Socio-economic profile of the sample households

The women respondents are in the age-group of 45 to 60 and many do not know even their own age let along the age details of other family members. Nearly two-thirds usually of the sample respondents reported family size in the range of

10-12 usually consisting of 8 to 10 children. Though birth of a girl child is not resented in this community, son preference is manifest. The need for hunting fish for the survival of the family and the customary division of labour *i.e.* fishing as man's job and marketing as women's role account for the phenomenon of son-preference.

Family types

With regard to family types nearly half of the sample households are joint families, while the remaining half are of nuclear type. The emerging shift from jointness to nuclearity is traced to the emerging shift from relative isolation and homogeneity to exposure to modernization and urbanization and consequent heterogeneity on the one hand and intergenerational conflicts in life styles and changing aspirations on the other. Though not spelled out by the respondents, the shift from jointness to nuclearity is a clear manifestation of the survival strategy in the changing context of increasing cost of living on the one hand and the younger generations aspirations for better quality of living despite uncertain earnings and insecurity of life due to decline in the fish stocks and catch as well as a result of glaring mechanisation.

Literacy Levels

None of the women respondents are literate. This is true of the literacy levels of majority of adult males and even children. The relatively well to do households owning mechanised boats or males employed in mechanised boats are longing to educate their children both boys and girls but their dreams are scattered for want of proper schooling facilities in their locality. There is near unanimity that their children are not taught properly and are exploited for errand jobs by the teachers in the local schools. This is the feeling among those who want to educate their children. Nearly two-thirds of the respondents strongly favoured education for their children. Around one forth of the women respondents opined that they cannot afford to wait for long term benefits of education in the midst of poverty. In these households even a three year lads are socialized in the act of hunting fish by taking them to sea.

Economic position

Around one forth of the respondent households owned mechanised boats while 50 per cent are dependent on traditional non-mechanised boats. The remaining one forth of the households could not maintain traditional boats. These people hire out their services to others but they will be paid only if there is catch on the days or days of fishing. No catch means no wage to those who hire out their services. Among the non-mecahnised boat owners families with more male members are better off compared to the others.

Impact of Mechanisation on women and the survival strategies adopted by sample households

The impact of mechanisation of fishing on women has to be seen in relation to the economic strata to which they belong. Broadly the sample respondents can be categorised into three groups *i.e.*, those belonging to households owning mechanised boats those owning traditional boats and those who do not have a boat but men hire out their services to others for fishing.

Women's Position in Households among Mechanised Boats

As mentioned earlier one forth of the sample respondents belong to this category. Economically they are well off with pucca houses with electricity in place of thatched houses, modern household facilities *viz.*, fans, tables, chairs; an array of brassware which exhibit their better economic status and for purpose of decoration in its true sense and other household utensils. Women in these households are votaries of mechanisation. With mechanisation and big catches marketing is also handled by men to the buyers at fishing harbour itself and those which cannot be sold to the big buyers is usually marketed by women or sold away to other women buyers who retail the same.

Women of the households are not worried about long spells of absence by male members nor do they feel any loss of power despite their declining role in marketing. This is largely due to the customary practice of male handing over the entire money to the housewife and consequent continuation of traditional status as financial manager of the household. One fall out of mechanised fishing on these households in particular and the fishing community in general is the emergence of the concept of dowry which was not in vogue in the pre-mechanised period.

Economic Position of Women in Households Owning Traditional Boats

Half of the sample respondents belonged to these households. Thanks to the Urban Community Development Project, taken up by the Visakhapatnam Municipal Corporation with assistance from the British Overseas Development Administration in mid 1980's, majority of these households also became owners of pucca houses like their counterparts owning mechanised boats.

Mechanisation has not bestowed any benefits to this strata of households. The dwindling of fish catch to these boats due to encroachment into their territory by the mechanised boats and trawlers added to their owes.

Women folk of this fishing community are never involved in net making operations, as such mechanisation of net making has no adverse impact on their employment. Unmarried girls are not involved in marketing of fish or any of the tasks involving going out of the house. As such there is no loss of employment to this group. Married women of the household are actively involved in drying of fish and marketing of fish both dried as well as the fresh ones. Mechanisation had hit this group of women not so much in terms of loss of working days but transforming their status from one owner marketer to that of buyers and sellers on days when there is no catch. Mechanisation and entry of big buyers into the market has increased competition in the buyers market. This has put many women to disadvantage particularly on days when the catch from the traditional boats is limited. On such days many women cannot even hope for a wage income let along profits from sale of fish.

To overcome the problem of hunger on rainy days and on days when the catch is limited, all women set aside part of their day's earning in the form of savings. They do contribute part of their earning even by cutting daily expenditure to clear loans or to contribute to the daily chits with fellow women. Cutting down consumption expenditure either by foregoing food or managing with mere gruel is another survival strategy resorted to by most of the sample respondents of this category.

Another notable feature is the entry of unmarried girls as domestic servants in the urban neighbourhood. This diversification though limited in early 1970's has intensified since mid 1980's with rise in apartments in the neighbouring colonies. Women respondents welcomed this trend as a major means of social transformation and modernisation. As domestic servants their female children will be exposed to the culture of the elite strata and better ways of living, developing positive attitude towards family planning.

The spin off benefits of unmarried girls of fisherman's families working as maid servants with elite families cannot be denied. However, the fact that even young girls of school going age are entering this profession and working on an average with 3 or 4 households as the minimum, is clear reflection of the economic compulsion of these families to send children for domestic work. Sending girl children for domestic work appears as a significant and widespread survival strategy adopted by the fishing community under study.

The shifting away of male youth from fishing to non-fishing activities like auto-driving, carpentry, rod-bending, painting, tailoring, etc., are also pointers to their disillusionment with the increase in uncertainty of incomes from fishing in the context of growing mechanisation and dwindling of fish catches.

Economic Position of Women in Households with Smaller/ No Boats

Households of this type are similar to agricultural labour households. Men of these households hire out their services mostly to fellow fishermen who have bigger boats. While agricultural labour households are assured of a wage for their work, fishermen of this category cannot hope for even a wage on days when there is no catch. Obviously, these households are at a greater disadvantage than their counterparts who own big boats. Even among these households, whole male members are employed in mechanised boats on monthly wages are better off. However, such households are rather very few. Under the U.C.D. project some households of this category also got pucca houses.

Women of these households present a pathetic picture despite owning pucca houses. Even at 6 or 7 p.m. they hand on to the houses without knowing what to cook for want of income or fish. Largely women of these households depend on man's earning for the maintenance of the households. They resort to collection of dung in the neighbourhoods for preparing dung cakes as fuel. Only a small percentage of women buy fish and market them on a limited scale for want of income. Along with unmarried girls, married women of these households also work as domestic servants.

Conclusion

Mechanisation of fishing has forced majority of the fishing community to survive in a situation of diminishing work opportunities for the man and increasing work load for women against low wages, uncertain incomes from marketing of fish and lack of opportunity to uplift their skills otherwise as individuals in their own right.

Fishing communities are also heterogeneous in nature with haves and have nots, depending upon the type of boat they own. The problem fisherwomen face and the survival strategies they adopt for the community of ways of life as rich or poor are influenced by their socio-economic position.

Among the two groups of women *i.e.*, women belonging to households own big boats of traditional type and those who own small or none, the broad strategies are more or less similar, though the hardships faced by the latter are more severe compared to the former.

Increase in child labour of girls, as domestic servants, curtailment of consumption, shifting of youth into non-traditional occupations as a cushion against uncertain incomes from fish catch are the economic strategies adopted by the two groups.

Curtailment of consumption and foregoing food on some days is more manifest among the latter compared to the former.

Splitting up of joint households into nuclear one's common to both group though more prevalent among the small boat owner households than their counterparts.

Reduction on fertility is the demographic strategy adopted by majority of the households particularly by encouraging the younger generation towards small family norm.

Economic necessity makes the poor to behave in a docile manner most of the time and the women of the area under study have not thought of any political strategy to overcome their ills. Men are used to the game of political strategies by switching of support at the time of elections but does not seem to have gained much.

The community as a group have not succeeded in establishing network of support to defend themselves. The fact that they could not save their community land for house site from encroachments by non-fishermen groups is a pointer to their vulnerability to other manoeuvring.

Their failure to evolve political strategies and establishing network of support to defend their interests can be traced to the appalling levels of illiteracy, inferiority complex and consequent dependence on outsiders. Supporting strategies for their well being have to focus attention on improving their literacy, vocational and organisational skills, to help them survive in the midst of many challenges they are encountering.

REFERENCES

Beena D., 1991, "Technological change and women workers : The case of fish processing industry in Kerala" in *Chetana Kalbah* (ed.), Women Development, Women employment and the work place, Vol. 1, New Delhi.

Joshi V. Mahesh, 1996, "Economics of Fisheries", A.P.", A.P.H. Publishing Corporation, New Delhi.

Karuna Ambaresan, 1984, "Factors influencing the role and status of fisherwomen : A Study of three villages in Chingalput District, Tamil Nadu", paper presented at the workshop on Women, Technology and Forms of Production, held on 30th and 31st October, at the Madras Institute of Development Studies, Madras.

Kurien, J., 1978, "Entry of Big Business into Fishing : Its impact on the Fish Economy", *Economic and Political Weekly,* 13(36), 1557-65.

Leela Gulati, 1984, "Fisherwomen in Kerala -The Impact of New Technology on their lives", *Manushi,* Vol. 4, No. 21, 33-39.

Loening Ariane, 1984, "Prawn fish head cutters of Harora, *Manushi,* 4(24), 36.37.

Leela Menon, 1986, "Fisherwomen's Daily Drudgery Continues", *Times of India,* 27th October.

Lieten G.K., Olga Nieuweuhuys and Loes Schenk-Sandberger, 1989, *Women, Migrants and Tribals : Survival Strategies in Asia,* Manohar Publication, New Delhi.

Nandita Shah, Sujatha Gothoskar, Nandita Gandhi and Amrita Chhachhi, 1994, "Structural Adjustment, Feminisation of Labour force and Organisational Strategies", *Economic and Political Weekly,* 29(18), WS 39-WS 48.

Nayak Nalini, 1988, "Technological change, Labour and Women's Employment in Fishing Sector", *Women in Agriculture and Rural Development,* 237-46.

Schenk-Sandberger L., 1989, "Survival without patrons and patrons : Female Domestic Servants and coolies in Kerala" in Lieten G.K., *et al.* (ed.).

Shiva, V, 1997, "Development, Ecology and Women" in Rajanikanth (ed.), *Paradigms in Economic Development,* Rawat Publications, Jaipur, pp. 243-253.

Streefland Pieter, H., 1989, "Modes of survival and survival strategies" in Lieten G.K. *et al.* (ed.).

Subba Rao, N., 1995, "Role and Status of Women in Indian Fishing Communities" *Journal of Fisheries Economics and Development,* Vol. 2, No. 1, 13-33.

Van Willem Schendel, 1989, "Self-Rescue and Survival : The Rural poor in Bangladesh" in Leiten G.K. *et al.* (ed.).

5

Thrift and Credit : Women and Household Development

—Dr. V.V. Ramana

Introduction

The poor find it difficult to improve social and economic milieu due to lack of own resources and inability to access and control over the community and institutional resources. They find it difficult to mobilise adequate and timely capital to the enhancement of income, employment and assets. They thus naturally depend on money lenders, middle traders and commission agents. The exorbitant rates of interest charged by the informal sector and the exploitative buy back arrangements of the produce at unilaterally bargained prices has further lead to poverty and dependency.

NGOs (Non Governmental Organisations) as a strategy and as a need facilitates the creation of groups. They strengthen the groups with information and trainings and made them to pay efforts to work towards development. The groups provide an opportunity to the people to participate in development efforts and in the process they are able to mobilise productive and financial resources.

This is a case study of a poorest of the poor community. It is a marine fishing community living in Vizianagaram district of Andhra Pradesh, India. ARDAR (Association for Rural Development and Action Research) is a registered NGO working with the community since 1994 in partnership with ACTIONAID, a London based funding agency that works for alleviation of poverty. The experience of the organisation in this regard is presented here as a case to show how group formation and strengthening through thrift and credit helped the community in empowerment.

Background

The marine fisherfolk in India live in oppressed, exploited and inhuman conditions. In Andhra Pradesh there is a long coast touching 9 districts. The community belongs to Voda Balija or Gangaputra or Palli castes. The community is living throughout the coast in 545 settlements or villages. In the district of the Vizianagaram, the marine fishing villages are 20 with a household size of 3.8 and a population of 22,874. A base line study was conducted in 1993 and the data on social, demographic and economic situation shows that the whole community belongs to Voda Balija marine fishing castes. Marine fishing provides the main source of livelihood and agriculture in 6 villages provides supplementary income. Most of them lack productive assets and have little control over sale of catch. They over the years exploited and marginalised by outsiders. 100 per cent of the adult population are illiterate. Women and children suffer due to inadequate health services. Access to government development initiatives and institutional credit is almost non available. A common feature in all the villages is the dependency on private money lenders for production and consumption needs. The interest charged varies from 48 per cent to 120 per cent. There is a system of "good-will" (called as Oyyam) in which the principal need not be paid but the borrower has to pledge his nets and has to sell his entire catch at rates fixed by the money lender. The system is deliberately designed so that the value of fish is not known and not received by the community. It is so vicious that it keeps them continuously in debt trap.

The community has no access to institutional credit. They are then driven to local traders cum money lenders who immerse them in increased indebtedness. The system works like this :

Thrift and Credit

ARDAR has started with organising micro credit for women in these villages by forming groups and encouraging thrift.

This is started not as an entry point activity but a felt need of the community and women in particular. The women are selected for this activity because they play crucial role in socio-economic aspects of the community. They take full responsibility of the house and deal with traders and markets : sell fish directly by taking on head to the near by villages and to the shandies.

The objective of organising thrift and credit for women in the community is for empowering the women and community. The meaning of empowerment defined here as : to see the impact on 3 levels — one at the personal level, where empowerment is about developing the sense of self (individual) confidence and capacity; second at the relationships, where empowerment is about developing the ability to negotiate and influence the nature of the relationship and decisions made within that relationship and third at the collective level, where individuals work together to have impact at the community level that influence their socio-economic environment. To achieve the above said objective the project has taken up the following activities :

* formation of small groups,
* creation of awareness to the members of the groups,
* trainings to the group leaders,
* organising exposures,
* providing opportunity to take up collective actions on local infrastructure, needs and issues.

Small neighbourhood groups with 15 to 30 membership were (one from each household) formed in all the villages. They have started thrift at Rs. 5 per week. The project has provided 50 per cent matching grant. The women utilised the amount for credit needs. The total women groups in the DA by the end of 1998 are 131 with a membership of 2334 (61 per cent).

The Awareness was imparted on the following inputs during these years.

TABLE 1

Subject of focus		Content
Concept of Group	-	Group work and cooperation
	-	Development of group norms
Access to Financial Institutions	-	Need to repay old loans to avail fresh loans
Government Schemes	-	Housing
	-	DWCRA
	-	Fishing vessels
Village Plans	-	Orientation on village plans developed by leaders during the leadership trainings
MCH	-	AN care
	-	Pre Natal
	-	Post Natal
	-	Evil practices
Child Literacy	-	Regularity of teachers and children
	-	Enrollment of eligible children into government schools
Thrift and Credit	-	Bank procedures
	-	Recording of transactions
	-	Equal loan opportunities
Marine Fishing Laws	-	Rights and obligations applicable to the community
Cooperatives	-	MAC Act of 1995
Environment	-	Save turtle nesting grounds
	-	Chemical pollutants
Disaster Preparation	-	Emergency actions

Regular meetings, held once in a month, served as a forum for imparting the above inputs.

Leadership skills were imparted to 269 members (women and men) of 13 villages in a period of 2 years through a three-phased input. The overall objective of training was three folds : understanding of their own situation; change in thinking and acting on issues/problems. The methodology for the trainings is case studies of local situations; small group analysis and thematic games. The design is election of leader for the training period; feed back; and night stay. The leadership input also dealt with their role in convening meetings, facilitating discussions and managing group dynamics (a detailed report on the inputs is available with the project). Each village is taken as a unit for imparting leadership trainings. Two leaders from each women group and 5 or 7 body members from the male group that constitute VDS (Village Development Sangha) for which leadership trainings are given. The follow up meetings were also organised. Further village level meetings were also organised covering members to orient on the village development plans.

Exposure to the leaders and members were organised to observe thrift and credit management, handling and management of issues, post harvest methods and cooperatives.

The groups were provided opportunities by linking with formal institutions and providing support to infrastructure. The process and outcomes are presented.

Process of Development

The above inputs have helped the groups to take up several development actions and in the process the people were empowered. The results of the actions are briefly presented below :

Management of Thrift and Credit

The women groups that are involved in thrift and credit have moved towards sustainability by forming women thrift cooperatives. The status of the thrift and credit is detailed as table 2.

TABLE 2

Particulars	1994	1995	1996	1997	1998
Savings and credit schemes	36	45	57	88	131
Members (female)	1081	1362	1772	1818	2334
Cumulative savings	230811	519676	872986	1270076	1951510
Matching Credit	83600	110745	135370	210915	335837
Loans in circulation	252100	569700	1181600	1893220	1773890
Per cent of repayment	32	54	48	67	45
Groups managing their own accounts and and/or records	0	0	0	8	20
Groups having self evolved norms	0	9	40	80	131

These 131 women groups have a cumulative capital of Rs.38,12,087/-, that on an average works out to Rs. 1633 per member.

For instance, during 1998, the women have borrowed Rs.18,20,496 and its immediate result was a saving of Rs. 4,07,917 gained through differential interest between money lender and thrift groups.

The project's efforts by providing revolving funds and encouraging thrift and loan systems helped the community to come out of the clutches of the money lenders. The situation of outside loans has considerably changed. The baseline data on the situation in 1994 is available as the intervention is planned on the basis of the same information. A study was conducted in the end of the year 1998 by covering all the households in 13 villages (baseline is available for 13 villages and for comparison purposes 7 villages are excluded from the study) to observe the status on the outside loans for heavy interest and for further exploitative marketing tie up. The data presented as table 3.

The Table shows that per household loan of Rs. 6,523 in 1994 has come down to Rs. 2,246 in 1998 that is about 66 per cent of household loan reduction. Further observation on the Table is that out of the 13 villages the outside loans have reduced in 11 villages. Moreover 5 villages [in that order are Barripeta, Konada, Kothuru (Th), Madduru and Kothuru (C)] have almost come out of the vicious circle.

Further analysis on the data was also done. The purpose wise outside loans comparison from 1994 to 1998 is presented in table 4.

TABLE 3

Comparison of outside loans from 1994 to 1998 in 13 villages

S.No.	Village Name	Loans from outside 1994	Loans from outside 1998
1.	Neela Gedda Peta	852100 (5393)*	540000** (3313)
2.	Pedduru	476500 (2941)	495500 (2881)
3.	Barripeta (C)	1846800 (6526)	1042470 (3341)
4.	Kothuru (C)	2440100 (10749)	681300 (2758)
5.	Barripeta	2407685 (15840)	257500 (1630)
6.	Thammayyapalem	92210 (2635)	87000 (1933)
7.	Puligeddapeta	93150 (1791)	125500 (2201)
8.	Kothuru (Th)	1187300 (10061)	213000 (2290)
9.	Madduru	940800 (10453)	362500 (2570)
10.	Thippalavalasa	543000 (1905)	243400 (885)
11.	Boddu Gurayya Peta	187200 (2836)	144000 (2028)
12.	Boddu Venkatesh Peta	99700 (2849)	167000 (3795)
13.	Konada	1279950 (5224)	216900 (908)
	Total	12446494 (6523)	4606070 (2246)

* The figures in the brackets are loan average per household.

** Number of households has changed from 94 to 98 and that is considered in calculation.

TABLE 4

Purpose wise outside loans in 13 villages

S. No.	Purpose	1994		1998	
		Loanees	Amount (Rs.)	Loanees	Amount (Rs.)
1.	Vessels	500	650990	97	63810
2.	Consumption	568	223506	263	148552
3.	Functions	99	114650	194	86615
4.	Business	138	100790	79	35790
5.	Health	137	94905	186	91875
6.	House repairs	42	29808	65	33965
	Total	1484	1214649	884	460607

The table clearly demonstrates a positive trend. The community, even to extent of going for outside loans, is not for productive purposes of buying of fishing vessels and businesses. This shows that : (1) the loans for fishing vessels and business involve marketing agreement and tie up for less and unfair rate hence community avoided such commitments and (2) the revolving funds are used by the community for productive purposes. Further the loanees and loan amount for consumption have also significantly come down. This is a positive trend. The outside loan situation has not improved in the case of needs such as health, function and house repairs. This, particularly health, situation is a concern and needs special attention in future by the project.

Analysis on outside loans on the basis of source from 1994 to 1998 is presented at next page in Table 5. It also shows that money lender as a source has decreased from 340 to 74 loanees and from 36 lakhs of rupees to 9 lakhs.

TABLE 5

Source wise comparison of outside loans in 13 villages from 1994 to 1998

S. No.	Source	1994		1998	
		Loanees	Amount (Rs.)	Loanees	Amount (Rs.)
1.	Neighbour	1045	739596	762	339235
2.	Land owners	26	72630	3	3990
3.	Money lenders	340	363963	74	94670
4.	Bank	69	38460	45	22812
	Total	1484	1214649	884	460607

Further analysis on the comparison of outside loans on the basis of security was also done. The data show that vessels are no more used as a security for loans in the target villages.

TABLE 6

Security wise comparison of outside loans in 13 villages from 1994 to 1998

S. No.	Security	1994		1998	
		Loanees	Amount (Rs.)	Loanees	Amount (Rs.)
1.	Faith	1313	1049474	801	400007
2.	Gold	86	84895	72	50700
3.	Vessels	69	56700	0	0
4.	House	16	23580	11	10000
	Total	1484	1214649	884	460607

Emergence of Village Development Plans

The observed outcome of the leadership trainings is :

(1) analysing and critical view on their own situation;

(2) change in thinking;

(3) understanding about leadership;

(4) clarity on the roles of members, leaders and organisation;

(5) understanding about group goal;

(6) finally, emergence of village development plans.

The emergence of development plans for all the 13 villages is the manifest and potential outcome of the trainings.

Each village in their 3 phase (spread in 6 months) training (a) analysed their situation; (b) felt the need for concerted efforts by one and all, in particular by the leaders; (c) identified the village/community needs; (d) prioritised them and (e) prepared time frame within which they may achieve the results.

The leaders took these plans into their respective groups and thoroughly discussed them and made changes wherever required. The VDS regularly meet and takes up action by divided roles and responsibilities.

The following is the list of needs, followed by number of villages planned the respective need and the result on their actions.

TABLE 7

Needs and Priorities	Villages Planned	Villages Achieved	
		Completed	In process
1. Housing (pucca)	12	4	6
2. DWCRA	13	0	6
3. Road and Culverts	11	6	2
4. Ration cards	7	0	4
5. Drinking water	13	11	1
6. Health facility	3	0	3
7. Occupation tools	13	6	7
8. Vessels regd.	11	2	6
9. Lean season incomes	7	2	4
10. Marketing	5	0	4
11. School and hostel	8	7	0
12. Community sheds	7	4	0
13. Games & cultural material	4	4	0
14. Drainage	6	1	1
15. Electrical repair	7	6	1
16. Waste lands	7	0	4
17. Latrines	2	1	0
18. Bus shelter	1	1	0
19. Cyclone shelter repairs	2	1	0
20. Panchayat	1	0	0
21. Industrial Pollution	12	0	7
22. Housing places & pattas	3	0	0
23. Adult literacy	1	1	0

Collective Actions on Local Issues

The regular meetings formed the source. The People are able to manage several issues related to their livelihood, community, health and education.

The project in the year 1996 has started working on strengthening the community with systematic approaches. It never agreed to directly tackle the issues of the community. It also never ignored the value of solving the issues in the life of marine fishing community. It has provided adequate information, arranged required resources and strengthened their hands through trainings and exposures. Thus, the community has taken up unbelievably 211 issues during the three years (1996 to 1998) out of which 186 have had results. Out of the 211, 54 are related to livelihood.

TABLE 8

	1996		1997		1998		Total	
Issue Type	I	R	I	R	I	R	I	R
Livelihood	16	13	20	12	18	10	54	35
Community	42	41	36	35	53	49	131	125
Education	7	7	5	5	7	7	19	19
Health	3	3	3	3	1	1	7	7
Total	68	64	64	55	79	67	211	186

I = issues R = Results

Collective Actions on Local Infrastructure

The strengthening of groups facilitated implementation of collective works in the villages.

The progress in this activity, for instance, for the year 1998 has been road laying, drinking water (repairs and new bore wells), sanitation, community sheds, games material, housing, fiber reinforced plastic catamarans (boats), lean season incomes, electricity repairs, new schools, latrines, bus shelters and cyclone shelter repairs. All the 19 villages have worked to achieve the basic needs and infrastructure to their respective villages. They have also mobilised sources within the village and from the government. The works are to the tune of about Rs. 88 lakhs.

Enhancement of Employment and Income

The situation analysis in 1996 revealed lack of sufficient catamarans among the families, contributing to their unemployment and poverty. Also, it was gathered that they have no access for investment. Therefore, the project provided the capital to groups as a revolving fund, for procurement of fishing equipment.

A total of Rs. 12,07,300 was provided during the 2 years and out of that amount, till date Rs. 11,19,800 was utilised for buying 138 catamarans and 78 fishing nets benefiting 745 families. The project has covered 15 villages during the 2 years.

Besides, resources were mobilised from the government for 48 FRP Boats worth of Rs. 60 lakhs during the year. The FRP boats have the advantage of fast moving, deep sea fishing and more storage facility.

The imparting of skills on improved method of drying fish covered 225 additional women with provision of drying racks and marketing of dried fish at the wholesale markets. All these three components are promoted as an integral package of this intervention.

Emergence of New Marketing System

The crucial change in marketing has come as 56 per cent of the fishermen are marketing their fish directly without any exploitative tie up with vested interests outside the community The data are presented below in table 9. The data are gathered from 13 villages for which baseline is available.

TABLE 9

Distribution of households from 1994 to 1998 on tie up with middle person for the fresh fish marketing (Reduction)

S.No	Village	1994			1998		
		House holds	Tie up with Mediator	%	House holds	Tie up with Mediator	%
1.	N.G. Peta	158	158	100	163	100	61
2.	Pedduru	162	162	100	172	58	34
3.	Barripeta C	283	283	100	312	222	71
4.	Kothuru C	227	227	100	247	141	57
5.	Barripeta	152	152	100	158	52	33
6.	Th.palem	35	35	100	45	11	24
7.	P.G.Peta	52	52	100	57	38	67
8.	Kothuru Thi	118	118	100	93	61	66
9.	Madduru	90	90	100	141	108	77
10.	Th.valasa	285	285	100	275	116	42
11.	B.G.Peta	66	66	100	71	0	0
12.	B.V.Peta	35	35	100	44	0	0
13.	Konada	245	245	100	273	0	0
	Total	1908	1908	100	2051	907	44

It is evident from the table that in 1994 100 per cent of the households are tied up with middlemen. Now on an average 56 per cent have come out of the system. The village wise analysis shows that 3 villages are totally free from the middle people and more than 50 per cent households are relieved from, in another 3 villages. Now the people are using scales instead of head counts and ice to market their catch.

By the end of 1997 they are able to mobilise 20 FRP catamarans and during 1998 they have mobilised 48 catamarans through cooperative. Further the community privately bought 96 catamarans, due to tie up with marketing centers.

Two changes have come in the marketing. Previously the community used to sell to a middleman by taking goodwill (Rs. 2000 for catamaran) and to a fixed price with an agreement to supply solely for him for 2 years. The fish is supplied by counting *i.e.*, 80 pieces as a unit. Last year a change has come in the system. The goodwill has increased abnormally to Rs. 30,000. During this year another change has come. The middlemen are giving Rs. 80,000 for buying FRP catamaran that needs to be paid without interest and in long installments. The most important thing is that he has agreed to buy for weightage using a scale and not by head counts.

Most of the people are coming out of this system but those who are in it are also gaining substantially. There are three advantages : (1) The FRP catamarans are helping to double the catch. (2) Now they are able to catch valuable fish like sharks. (3) The amount of difference from head count to weighing is about 40 per cent. Hence, even the tie up system is also helping the community.

Mother and Child Immunisation

Mother and child health care are the prime intervention in the preventive care. This intervention has begun in 1994 and continued. The mother immunisation has gone up from 15 per cent in 1994 to 80 per cent in 1998. The child immunisation has gone up from 10 per cent in 1994 to 80 per cent in 1998. And for the girl children the change is from 4 per cent to 85 per cent.

Safe Health Practices

Health education for adult women was imparted at group meetings, through a systematic schedule. The topics covered were mother and child care, personal hygiene and environmental sanitation. On the other hand, all the 15 government schools were covered with health education on care of eyes, nose, personal hygiene and environmental sanitation.

The outcome of the efforts could be noticed in the achievement of ante-natal care (2 TT, I&F from six months, monthly weight monitoring, BP, urine test) at 80 per cent and child immunisation also at 80 per cent. This is against the base line of 15 per cent and 10 per cent respectively. School health clinics were organised in all the schools and the coverage at these clinics was 88 per cent.

Increase in School Enrollment and Retention

The project has started pre-schools for the children of the age of 4 years with an objective to enroll them in government schools. During the year 1998, 19 Pre-school centers are run in 16 villages, 16 by the project and 3 by the ICDS. Their enrollment into Government schools has begun with simultaneous efforts to enroll other eligible children. The achievement is 92 per cent for overall (331 out of 360) and 100 per cent for pre-school leavers. Further, fresh batch of pre school recorded 86 per cent enrollment.

One of the objectives of the Project in education sector is to increase the levels of retention in government schools. The Project has been working with the community and teachers to achieve the levels. The table 10 below shows the year-wise retention.

TABLE 10

Year	Enroll-ment	1st standard	2nd standard	3rd standard	4th standard	5th standard
1993-94	206	122 (59%)	122 (59%)	122 (59%)	122 (59%)	110 (53%)
1994-95	205	132 (64%)	129 (63%)	128 (62%)	127 (61%)	
1995-96	317	221 (70%)	221 (70%)	220 (69%)		
1996-97	375	299 (80%)	299 (80%)			
1997-98	484	411 (85%)				

A CASE OF A VILLAGE THAT HAS WORKED FOR A SCHOOL FOR THEIR VILLAGE BY RECOGNISING THE VALUE OF EDUCATION TO CHILDREN

Kothuru is a marine fishing village with 120 households and 750 members. The village does not have a primary school. The children have to go to the neighbouring village. Last year 38 children joined in the school. The dropout rate is very high due to the location of school outside the village.

ARDAR started working in the village since 1994 and started a Pre-school in the same year. It has helped the 4 year age children to habituate to the school. ARDAR has started male and female groups and introduced leadership trainings in 1997. Village Development Plans have emerged as an outcome of the trainings. The people have identified school to the village has a priority need and decided to work for the same. They have made division of work and approached government officials.

They are able to materialise the school during this year under DPEP (District Primary Education Programme). Two teachers were also posted. Presently the school is running in cyclone relief center and in a thatched shed. The people have deposited Rs. 5000 and government has sanctioned Rs. 1,75,000 for pucca school building. The village education committee was also formed from the male group. Presently 85 children are going to the school and the regularity has improved and the learning levels also have improved.

Conclusions

The above trends in development action reveal the picture of empowerment at all the 3 levels of personal, relational and collective. The sense of self confidence and capacity among women is evident through effective management of thrift and credit; preparation and management of village development plans and management of different issues including gender and livelihood. At the relational level, the ability to influence their men and decision making in the household is evident from enrolling their children in schools; mother and child immunisation; issue management concerning to gender and changing the marketing strategy. The change is evident at the collective level, where the whole community attempted and mobilised local infrastructure; enhancement of employment opportunities and value additions to their product; collective actions on issues concerning health education and livelihood and formulation and management village development plans.

Thus, it is evident that the women and households have developed considerably during these years. The women thrift groups acted as a base for this change. However, the development is a process and the major concern is sustaining the change. The women have realised it and working towards institutionalising their efforts by forming into a Mutually Aided Cooperatives.

6

Structural and Organizational Factors in Tribal Development

—*P. Venkata Rao*

Review of Tribal Development in India

Though there is no unanimity with regard to the concept of development, it is universally considered as desirable. A national government is expected to plan for the development of the nation in all aspects. In the case of India, the Constitution laid special emphasis on the development of the weaker sections, especially the scheduled castes and scheduled tribes. For the scheduled tribes two separate schedules were incorporated in the Constitution of India, for making special provisions for areas inhabited by them. The economic backwardness of tribal areas, the negative consequences of non-tribal impact, the vulnerability of tribal to economic exploitation, the existing socio-psychological barriers resulting from centuries old isolation necessitated a special policy by the Indian government with protection and integration of tribals as its principal objective.

During the First Five Year Plan, activities taken up for tribal development can be broadly grouped under the heads of economic development, communications, education, public health and housing. The starting of Multi-purpose Project Blocks (M.P.P. Blocks) in the year 1956 (Second Five Year Plan) was the first significant step taken towards development of tribal areas. The Tribal Development Blocks which came into existence during Third Five Year Plan retained the administrative structure of the Multi-purpose Project Blocks. Though the emphasis was on agriculture, the multi-sided approach of the Block structure covering the fields of agriculture, animal husbandry, co-operation, education and rural industries continued. Along with the T.D. Blocks the Panchayat Raj bodies came into existence to supervise and monitor the functioning of the development blocks[1].

The Fifth Five Year Plan marked a significant phase in the history of tribal development in India with the application of sub-plan concept for tribal areas through Integrated Tribal Development Projects (I.T.D.P.). All the funds of the different departments and agencies are channeled through the centralized project authority, which looks after developmental activities in the different blocks in its jurisdiction. Single line approach was introduced bringing all officers under the umbrella of ITDA. The I.T.D.P. formed the unit of planning, fund disbursing and supervisory body, and the existing block organisations implementing the programmes of the sub-plan. During the VI Plan, family oriented schemes received attention when compared to earlier period. During this period the Block structure has been replaced by Mandal set up in Andhra Pradesh. The strategy of Sixth Plan continued during Seventh Five Year Plan, but for one change in extending beneficiary oriented programmes to dispersed tribal groups. Special developmental programmes for vulnerable groups living in plain areas were taken up. Programmes of providing economic assistance to raise productivity levels of tribals and to take them above the poverty line were implemented during the plan. The need for greater participation of tribal women was envisaged for the VII Plan, especially in areas relating to conservation of forests, preservation of ecology, land development and preservation of tribal culture[2].

The Development Scenario in Tribal Areas

After decades of special efforts for tribal development, large gap exists between the available potential of natural resources like land, water, and forests, and their utilisation and productivity. The resource base available for tribals is slowly shrinking with the periodical tightening of forest legislations and alienation tribal lands. Agriculture and minor forest produce of the tribals are not fetching them remunerative prices. When compared to non-tribal areas, the tribal areas lag behind with regard to various indicators like literacy, irrigated area, electrification, road length, infant mortality, etc[3]. Political unrest and extremist activity characterize tribal areas which can be considered as both cause and effect of inadequacies of the development programmes.

Several studies by anthropologists and sociologists have highlighted the social and cultural barriers existing among scheduled tribes coming in the way of successful implementation of development schemes[4]. The tradition bound, conservative tribal has been blamed for his own backwardness. Better communication techniques through extension approach have been envisaged for motivating the tribals. But, it is also important to go into the role played by the development administration which has been entrusted with the responsibility of delivering the developmental inputs. Based on the authors' field studies in the scheduled areas of Andhra Pradesh, an attempt is made here to examine the role of development personnel in the development process focusing on the structural and organizational factors affecting their functioning.

Structural and Organisational Factors

Successful implementation of development programmes in tribal areas depends on the efficiency of personnel. The grounding of delivery system cannot be an end by itself, as the administration entrusted with the responsibilities must be able to deliver the development inputs in a desirable manner. One of the most important factors in reaching the goals of tribal development is the adaptability of the development administration to the local needs and conditions. The translation of various development policies into action takes place in a particular administrative environment that has been created by the personnel system. The debate has been whether the same personnel system can deliver the goods in tribal areas and non-tribal areas[5].

The personnel connected with the implementation of development programmes play a crucial role in the success of development programmes. The functioning of the tribal developmental personnel depend on the congruence between

(1) structurally given demands (expectations and responsibilities), (2) the functionaries conception of his duties and obligations and (3) the actual performance under different circumstances. There will be demands from the organizational structure which are diverse and multiple. These are external to the personnel and have their origin in the policies, traditions of the development agencies. The demands of the organizational structures act as dominant force in shaping the approach of the individual. The works assigned, rules governing the authority — subordinate relationships, individuals place in the organization, pressures from the authorities have a role in shaping the individuals role perception. The means available, the technical and ecological facilities further influence the performance of the personnel. But, lack of proper roads and communication facilities restrict the efficiency of the development personnel as majority of tribal villages have bad roads and many have no roads. The scattered nature of the small hamlets adds to this limitation. Lack of proper amenities results in employees staying away from headquarters they were allotted to. Hard working conditions, meagre incentives, and uncooperative attitude of tribals form the perceived grievances of personnel. Under these circumstances not being able to undertake proper selection of beneficiaries and the necessary follow up action, the efforts of the personnel in charge of developmental schemes are directed towards achieving their targets only without attempting the required follow-up action.

The demands coming from the social structure also affect the functioning of development personnel. The composition of the personnel system, the social background of the persons influences its functioning. If a group unsympathetic to the people is at the helm of affairs, it may act as conservative force, wherein the expectation is that it should act as catalytic force. The socio-economic background and personality traits of the non-tribal employees make them feel superior to tribals resulting in unsympathetic attitude towards tribals. The values that are internalized by them are authoritarianism and superiority. For local tribals, they are outsiders and aliens. This is against the requirement of a human touch and down-to-earth approach that is required in tribal areas. It is the quality of interaction between personnel and the tribal beneficiaries that is crucial in the course of development process. Due to the inhospitable conditions and alien agency environment, the personnel living in villages look for the company of their own people. Some times, the indifference of the tribals towards them adds to this. The development worker from the beginning is imagined by the tribals as part of the 'other group' of officials, petty contractors, money lenders and acquires and initial handicap of distrust to be an effective instrument of social and economic development[6]. For the tribals, the personnel are outsiders and are called as *Udyogasthulu* (employees) and in the hilly areas are identified with *plainvollu* or *diguvollu* (meaning people from the plains). They establish links with non-tribal traders and money lenders. This alignment between those who are supposed to uplift the tribals and the exploiters becomes detrimental to the interests of the tribals. Hidden opposition can be expected from the non-tribals for the development and welfare of the tribals. The influences from social structure basically come from the social background of the individual, group influences, basic values, life goals, individual conception of the occupational role and internalized behaviour pattern. The other influences from the social structure include pressures from political leaders. The alignments between local tribal elite and employees results in the cornering of developments by a few and encourages misuse. For the bureaucracy the elite come handy for promoting their schemes in good time and speed and to fulfil the targets. The circle gets complete when the leaders join hands with non-tribal traders, money lenders and land grabbers. Without the connivance of the tribal leaders at village level, it is not possible for non-tribal to continue their activities in trading, usurious money lending and owning *benami* land[7].

Frequent transfers and availability of large number of vacant positions are a feature of tribal areas which affects the regular availability of services. Sending incorrigible, unwanted, inefficient and corrupt kind of officials to tribal areas under punishment postings affects the successful implementation of development programmes in tribal areas. The consequences of such postings are sabotage of programmes, escalation in the cost of inputs, poor quality of inputs, kickbacks, and scandals, manipulation of land records for the benefit of non-tribals, establishment of close links with political leaders, improper functioning of institutions[8]. On the other hand, sensitive and sincere officials are under attack from extremists, and leaders with vested interests and are transferred out of these areas. One of the important features of personnel system in the tribal areas is that the employees of the lower levels stay for a longer periods in a given area which enables them to work hand in glove with the local leaders. While the lower level staff are entrenched in the local area, establishing connections with the tribal elite, higher officials hardly stay for sufficient time to understand what had been done earlier and the outcome, especially who had actually benefited and to what extent. There is insufficient time to recapitulate form the earlier experiences from the area. This situation results in the same individuals, families, and villages taking advantage repeatedly[9]. A number of higher level staff who stay for a short duration come on deputation. It has been observed that temporary and too frequent changes of deputations is resulting in less experienced hands. The rapport between deputationists and regular employees is low and the latter have a common grievance against the deputationists as their promotional opportunities are hampered. The deputationists are under parent department which do not allow the receiving department to take action against them. The deputationists spend large amount of money without having to account for them[10]. Employees prefer regulating kind of administrative positions rather than meeting the demands of development administration. Development oriented departments like tribal welfare department need cooperation from, and coordination with regulating departments like forest and revenue departments. There are contradictions and disengagement between them[11]. Development and welfare functions need a different kind of approach and understanding, and personnel from departments not having similar approach may not perform these functions well when they come on deputation.

Clarity and consensus among all those involved is essential in an organisational situation. Differences exist between the goals set for the agency and the department and the conception of those vested with the responsibility of reaching them about their attainability. Lack of coherence between goals of the agency, and the degree of consensus about their attainability leaves the individual with greater choice in action. Ultimately under the influence of all these, the individual forms a dominant role conception which varies from the requirements and goals of the agency. Consequently what the department or agency requires may not be the same as what the individual does. Given the range of choice, the person may strive to meet the minimal requirements of the organisation with low degree of involvement. He may engage in a subversive role whenever possible. Such individuals covertly may control the organisation after gaining sufficient power. Faced with the conflicting pressures from answerability to the authorities and responsibilities to the people, good number of personnel choose a safe alternative in functioning from the point of view of the authorities in reaching the targets fixed. In this backdrop, development favours the places having communication links transport facilities. In tribal areas maximum number of development programmes are concentrated in the road point villages[12]. The reason given for favoring road point villages is, they are easily accessible facilitating close supervision. The underlying consideration is that the visiting officials and dignitaries have little or no time to visit interior and inaccessible villages. The preference for road-side villages is for their convenience and convicting them about the good work being done. On a number of occasions this sort of preference has resulted in taking up the same developed village for all new schemes. Majority of the schemes and services are located around the head quarters of I.T.D.A. and Mandals, and beneficiaries from such places are preferred. Interior and less accessible villages lag behind because of preference to road-point development, and discrimination against them in allocation of developmental benefits.

Two Grassroots Level Illustrations

The functioning of two village level functionaries illustrates the discussion carried out so far. At village level the teachers are the employees who regularly interact with tribals. The V.D.O. is the grassroots level functionary in charge of the development. Both have an important role to play in the socio-economic transformation of tribal areas.

Teachers

Majority of the teachers posted into the tribal areas are non-tribals. Absence of necessary training to work among tribal societies, lack of proper understanding of tribal conditions forms their important draw-back. It is common for the non-tribals to consider tribals as an inferior stock and to disapprove all tribal customs and practices as foolish and wasteful practices. A better appreciation of tribal systems and problems is needed to dispel this false notions of non-tribal supremacy as it affects the teachers' attitude towards tribal pupils. Several experts in this field suggested that it is essential to equip the teachers working in tribal areas with a knowledge of the working of the tribal society. Special skills for teaching disadvantaged children and first generation learners are also required from the teachers working in tribal areas.

While we see the necessity of well trained and better equipped teachers posted in tribal areas, the reality is otherwise. In general teachers are reluctant to join schools in tribal areas. Apart from climatic and geographical factors, lack of proper housing accommodation, absence of communication facilities, non-availability of modern medical services, facilities for children's education form important obstacles, which prevent non-tribal teachers to join service in tribal areas. In view of these, in organizations like Zilla Parishad posting a teacher to tribal area is considered as an act of punishment. It is normal for teachers posted to tribal villages to pay more attention get a transfer than concentrating on the job. Such teachers never feel themselves as part of the school, where they are working which ultimately affects their functioning[13].

A teacher who makes a sincere attempt at his job faces many shortages and obstacles. In tribal areas good school buildings, are very few and many schools are located under make-shift structures. The effect of these unattractive surrounds and the reluctant teachers and unenthusiastic tribal child can be easily imagined. Shortage of teaching aids like black boards, maps, etc., forms another hurdle. In fact demonstration aids are of utmost relevance in teaching children in backward and remote areas. Tribal groups which have their own dialect pose another problem to the teacher. This language barrier causes an important communication problem between teacher and tribal student in the crucial early schooling period. In multi-tribal villages the teachers have to deal with pupils speaking different languages.

The Panchayat Raj leaders use their political power to protect those teachers who are loyal to them and offer support. This leads to the dependence of teachers on Panchayati Raj leaders. Sometimes, the help of teacher is sought for writing petitions, filling in applications, maintenance of Panchayat Records, etc. This gives an edge to the teachers on local leaders which some teachers cleverly utilize. Ultimately, what matters most is the nature of relationship between teachers and leaders and not the working and sincerity of the teacher.

The V.D.O.

From the days of the Multi-purpose Projects, the strategy of tribal development underwent several changes with corresponding changes in the development administrative structure. But, the Block Organizational Frame which came into existence with the C.D. projects and N.E.S. Blocks continued to be the basic unit of programme implementation. The V.D.O. (earlier known as V.L.W.) continues to be the vital link between development administration and tribals. The V.D.O. is supposed to act as communication agent providing technical knowledge, guidance and encouragement to villagers, at the same time providing feedback to the officials. The present day V.D.O. had to adapt a different style of functioning. There is little time for extension work and follow up. Extension takes a back seat as considerable amount of time is spent on paper work, meeting, accompanying higher officials and visitors. Last minute and late allotment of funds forcing the development agencies to spend money in short time, leaves little scope for proper planning and selection of beneficiaries. This results in V.D.O. acting mostly as a disbursement agent[14]. For promoting various schemes in a short time, V.D.O. seeks the assistance of tribal elite who act as mediators between ordinary tribals and development agencies. In this process, naturally the elite, their relatives and followers corner most of the benefits.

Conclusion

The progress achieved in tribal areas with regard to all round development falls short of expectations and is not commensurate with the efforts made in the last five decades. The age old conservatism of the tradition bound tribals partly explains the reluctance on the part of tribals for actively participating in the development programmes. Faulty implementation of development programmes forms the other dimension. But the role played by the development administration under the influence of various structural and organisational factors deserves special attention in understanding the tribal development falling below expectations.

NOTES

1. For a detailed discussion on development institutions established in tribal areas and the strategies adopted by them, see P.V. Rao, *Institutional Framework for Tribal Development*, New Delhi : Inter India Publications, 1988.
2. *Report of the Working Group on Development and Welfare of Scheduled Tribes During VIIIth Five Year Plan Period*, Ministry of Welfare, Government of India.
3. For a general review of a A.P. scene, please see *Tribal Sub-Plan Draft IXth Five Year Plan 1997-2002*, Tribal Welfare Department, Government of A.P., Hyderabad, pp. 2-5, 1997.
4. For some examples see :

   Naik, T.B., 'Applied Anthropology in India' in *Survey of Research in Sociology and Social Anthropology*, Bombay : Popular Prakashan, 1972.

   Vidyarthi, L.P. and B.N. Sahay (eds.), *Applied Anthropology and Development in India*, New Delhi : National, 1980.

   Vidyarthi, L.P. (ed.), *Tribal Development and its Administration*, New Delhi : Concept, 1981.
5. Sharma, B.D., *Tribal Development : The Concept and the Frame*, New Delhi : Prachi Prakashan, p. 217, 1978.

6. See Sharma, *Environmental Context and the Personnel System and its Implications for Tribal Areas,* Occasional Papers, New Delhi : Ministry of Home Affairs, 1976.
7. In one of the early works, Haimendorf brought out the process by which the merchants who entered tribal areas became powerful by joining hands with the local leaders, see, Haimendorf, C.V.F., The Reddis of Bison Hills, London : Macmillan, 1945.
8. Punishment postings Punishment for whom ? Unpublished seminar paper of Dr. V.N.V.K. Sastry.
9. See, P.V. Rao, 'Some Aspects of Development Infrastructure in a Tribal Areas', *Adivasi,* XXXIV, 1 and 2, pp. 37-41.
10. *Report of the Committee of the House to enquire into matters related to Deficits and Misappropriations in the Girijan Cooperative Corporation,* Hyderabad : A.P. Legislative Assembly, p. 26, 1976.
11. For an illustration involving forest department and ITDA please see, P.V. Rao, *Institutional Framework for Tribal Development, op.cit.* (pp. 89-90), 1988.
12. This has been brought out in several studies. For example : Patnaik. N., Naidu. N.Y., and Pradhan, F.M., "Distance of V I W Circle from Block Headquarters as a factor of Development in Agency Areas", *Community Development and Panchayat Raj Digest,* Vol. 4(3), pp. 152-157, 1973.

    Sastry V.N.V.K., "Differential Development Among Villages of A.P : A Case Study" in Murali Manohar, Ramaiah, and Rao (ed.), *Political Economy of Tribal Development,* Warangal : I I P A Local Branch, pp. 137-140.
13. For more discussion, please see, Prasada Rao, D.L., and P. Venkata Rao, 'Problems of Teachers working in Tribal Areas', *The Educational Review,* Vol. LXXXIX, 8, 1983.
14. For a discussion on the functioning of V.D.Os in a tribal area, see P.V. Rao, *Institutional Framework for Tribal Development, op.cit,* pp. 170-180, 1988.

7

Performance of Jawahar Rozgar Yojana : An Empirical Study

—Dr. G. Sreedhar and *N. Ravindra Babu*

Introduction

Poverty and unemployment are the two basic evils affecting millions of people in developing countries. In India, nearly three-fourths of the people live in rural areas and about 40 per cent of them below the poverty line. They are afflicted by numerous deficiencies like illiteracy and social backwardness. The problem of unemployment in the rural sector is rather serious and what is more important is that the problem of under employment in the rural sector remains as intractable as that of unemployment. It is an anomaly that in many parts of the country, shortages of labour are frequently reported during the busy agricultural season, while over the greater part of the year a large proportion of agricultural labour and others engaged in allied activities are without continuous employment.

The Government of India launched several programmes since the advent of the planning era to tackle the problems of un-employmentand under-employment in rural areas. The wage employment schemes implemented up to the Fourth Five Year Plan were ad-hoc in nature and largely aimed at generating employment opportunities during lien agricultural season in some parts of the country. The Food for Work Programme was the first employment generation programme launched at the national level in 1977 and was subsequently renamed as the National Rural Employment Programme (NREP) in 1980. The Government of India launched another national level programme called Rural Landless Employment Guarantee Programme (RLEGP) in 1983.

Since the broad objectives of NREP and RLEGP were similar, these two programmes were merged into a single programme known as Jawahar Rozgar Yojana (JRY) in 1989.

The main objective of JRY is to provide gainful employment to the rural people and to create sustained employment by strengthening the rural economic infrastructure and assets in favour of the rural poor for their direct and continuing benefits. Due preference has to be given to SCs/STs and free bonded labourers in providing employment and 30 per cent of employment should be earmarked for women. Food grains should be distributed at subsidised rates @ of 1.5 Kgs. per man-day as part of wages. The JRY has two sub-schemes namely Indira Awaas Yojana (IAY) and Million Wells Scheme (MWS). The programme is implemented by the DRDA at the district level and the village panchayat at the grassroots level. The special feature of the programme is that the village panchayat are given freedom to select, plan and implement local development works based on the felt-needs of the local community within the broad framework of operating guidelines of JRY.

Review of Literature

Keeping in view the need for continuous monitoring of JRY to ensure its effective functioning, the Government of India undertook the concurrent evaluation of the programme in 1991 and 1992. The study conducted by the Programme Evaluation Organisation (PEO) of the Planning Commission in ten major states revealed that the employment generation under JRY was not to the expected extent and the coverage of women was also less than prescribed level. Another study conducted by PEO on IAY in 14 states in 1991-92 revealed that even though the coverage of SCs/STs living below the poverty line was good, the quality of construction was good only in respect of 50 per cent of the houses. The concurrent evaluation of JRY undertook by the Government of India in 1992 through 33 reputed and independent research institutions found that the village panchayats could spend only about 73 per cent of the funds available and that employment generation was much below the target laid down. The studies conducted by Bhaskar *et al.* (1994), Kripa Shankar (1994), Sudhaman

(1994), Neelakantan (1994) and Ruddar Datt (1995) also revealed that the employment generated under JRY was below the expected levels and the programme had little innovation with regard to the nature of works undertaken. Thus, the available literature reveals contradictory findings and insufficient evidence to draw valid conclusions on the performance of JRY. Hence, there is a need for comprehensive micro level studies.

Objectives and Methodology

In this paper, an attempt is made to examine the performance of JRY in the selected villages in terms of utilisation of funds, nature of works undertaken, perceptions of the beneficiaries about the programme and impact of the programme. The study was conducted in Hindupur mandal falling in the drought prone Anantapur District of Andhra Pradesh. Three villages, in which the performance of JRY may be rated as good, average and poor in terms of availability and utilisation of funds, *viz.*, Kirikera Basavanpalli, Chalivendala and Pulakunta respectively, were selected for an in-depth study. In each selected village, 30 beneficiaries were chosen on the basis of random sampling method for assessing the performance of JRY. Thus, 90 beneficiaries constitute the sample for the present study.

Socio-economic Profile of the Sample Households

The caste composition of the sample households showed that 50 per cent belonged to scheduled castes, followed by 33 per cent to backward castes and 17 per cent to forward castes. With regard to classification of the sample households by landholding size, it was found that 45 per cent were landless and 27 per cent marginal farmers (less than 2.5 acres). About 18 per cent were small farmers (2.5 to 5 acres), while 10 per cent had landholdings of more than 5 acres. Over 95 per cent of the sample households were residing in pucca or semi-pucca houses, out of which about half were government-given. The sample households were mostly wage-dependent with 75 per cent of their income coming from wage labour. As many as 96 per cent were found to be living below the poverty line. Thus, most of the sample households belonged to the weaker sections of the society in terms of social and economic status.

Utilisation of Funds under JRY

Table-1 shows the grants released and expenditure incurred under JRY in the sample villages since the inception of the programme.

TABLE 1

Grants released and expenditure incurred under JRY in the sample villages from 1989-90 to 1996-97.

S. No.	Name of the Village	Grants Released (Rs.)	Expenditure (Rs.)	Percentage
1.	Village-I	7,51,158	7,29,529	97.0
2.	Village-II	3,48,038	2,77,297	80.0
3.	Village-III	1,35,387	1,00,385	74.0
	All Villages	12,34,583	11,07,211	90.0

Note : Village I — Kirikera Basavanpalli
Village II — Chalivendala
Village III — Pulakunta

It may be seen from table — I that the percentage of expenditure incurred to total grants released was highest in village — 1 (97 per cent), followed by village — II (80 per cent) and lowest in village — III (74 per cent). In all the villages taken together, it worked out to 90 per cent. Thus, the utilisation of funds released under JRY may be termed as satisfactory.

Nature of Works taken up under JRY

The village panchayat committee headed by the president generally decides the nature of works taken up under JRY, even though it is stipulated that the decision has to be taken by the Gram Sabha. In no sample village, the Gram Sabha meeting was convened once in six months as specified in the Act. But, the works taken up and the expenditure incurred under JRY are prominently displayed on the walls of the village panchayat and school buildings.

TABLE 2

Percentage Distribution of Expenditure incurred on Different Works under JRY in the Sample Villages

S.No	Particulars	Village-I	Village-II	Village-III	Total
1.	Road laying and Construction of Culverts	36.9	44.7	55.8	40.6
2.	Construction of School Building/ Community Halls/ Buildings	31.4	19.5	32.3	28.5
3.	Sanitary Works	25.2	33.4	11.9	26.0
4.	Other Works	6.5	2.4	—	4.9
	Total	100.0	100.0	100.0	100.0

Table 2 shows the percentage distribution of expenditure incurred on different works under JRY in the sample villages. It is evident from Table-2 that the single largest work undertaken was road laying including of construction of culverts, accounting for about 41 per cent of the total expenditure in respect of all the sample villages. The expenditure on road 41 per cent of the total expenditure in respect of all the sample villages. The expenditure on road laying was highest in Pulakunta at 56 per cent, followed by Chalivendala 45 per cent and lowest in Kirikera Basavanpalli 37 per cent. The building up of community assets was the next important work accounting for about 28 per cent of the total expenditure in the sample villages, followed by the sanitary works 26 per cent and other works five per cent.

It was observed that mostly the president of the village panchayat undertook the works. Only in one village, the task of constructing the Panchayat building was entrusted to a contractor. Further, it was observed during the visits to actual work spots that the works taken up were not up to the mark in terms of quality. This could be due to the absence of training to the presidents of the village panchayats. Besides, the details regarding wage, non-wage ratio were not readily available with the village panchayats. It was reported that the former president did not hand over the measurement books to the present president. The muster rolls were also not maintained in any of the three sample panchayats. Absence of effective supervision of works by the Panchayati Raj department was found to be the main reason for all these problems. The maintenance of sanitary works was also found to be not proper, mainly due to absence of separate allocation of funds for this purpose.

Village Leadership

It is important to study the type and quality of village leaders involved in the execution of works under JRY. It was found that only in one of the three sample villages, (Kirekera Basavanapalli) the president was a graduate belonging to a forward caste. The Chalivendala panchayat was reserved for SCs in 1990 elections and at present to BCs (women); the present president is an illiterate and totally dependent on her spouse for all activities. The Pulakunta panchayat was reserved for general category (women) and the present president was the wife of the former president; even though the present president is educated up to 10th class, her spouse undertakes all activities on her behalf. Besides, the presidents are not given any training as to how to operate the funds, how to maintain the accounts properly and in other aspects needed for the effective implementation of JRY and other rural development programmes.

Perceptions about JRY

Over three-fourths of the sample respondents were aware of JRY, but their perception about JRY was right in respect of only 53 per cent respondents. Thus, a considerable proportion of the respondents (47 per cent) was having wrong perception about JRY. This could be attributed to their low levels of literacy (28 per cent). The village president (Sarpanch) was the main source of information about JRY as well as the main source of access to the programme.

The satisfaction of the respondents about JRY in terms of selection of schemes and beneficiaries is presented in table-3. It may be seen from table-3 that nearly half of the respondents expressed their dissatisfaction about the selection of schemes and 20 per cent about selection of beneficiaries under JRY. About two-thirds of them were indifferent about the selection of beneficiaries. Only 12 per cent of the respondents were fully satisfied with the selection of schemes and 14 per cent with the selection of beneficiaries under JRY.

TABLE 3

Satisfaction of the Sample Respondents about the Selection of Schemes and Beneficiaries

Sl. No.	Level of Satisfaction	No. of Respondents in villages			Total	Percentage
		I	II	III		
I.	**Selection of Schemes**					
1.	Not satisfied	12	16	16	44	49.0
2.	So, So	12	12	11	35	39.0
3.	Satisfied	6	2	3	11	12.0
	Total	30	30	30	90	100.0
II.	**Selection of Beneficiaries**					
1.	Not satisfied	5	9	4	18	20.0
2.	So, So	18	19	22	59	66.0
3.	Satisfied	7	2	4	13	14.0
	Total	30	30	30	90	100.0

Regarding the reasons for dissatisfaction of the respondents about JRY, about 43 per cent of the respondents were not satisfied because the poorer section were not covered in the programme. Another 29 per cent felt that the benefits were given to the people belonging to one faction affiliated to the political party in power. About one-fourth of the respondents felt dissatisfied because the schemes could not provide employment during the lien agricultural season.

Impact of the Programme

Table 4 shows the extent of employment generation in the sample households under JRY during the last two years. It may be noted from table 4 that about 93 members participated in the construction of school building/community hall/other building in the sample villages, followed by 79 members in sanitary works, 76 members in road laying and construction of culverts and 19 members in other works. Thus, the building up of rural community assets accounted for about 44 per cent of the employment generated, followed by sanitary works 28 per cent, road laying and construction of culverts 24 per cent and other works four per cent. In all, the JRY could provide 4,992 days of employment to the members in the sample households, enabling them to earn a sum of Rs.1,75,125 during the last two years. Employment generation per annum per household worked out to 27.7 man-days equivalent to wages to the tune of Rs. 973. Thus, the goal of providing the employment to the extent of 100 days per household was far from achieved in the sample villages.

Regarding the benefit derived by the sample households under IAY — an important subcomponent of JRY, it was found that 42 per cent were benefited under this scheme. A vast majority of 87 per cent of these households undertook the house construction on their own, while the remaining 13 per cent entrusted the work to contractors. It was found that the Million Wells Scheme, another sub-component of JRY, was not implemented in the sample villages.

The impact of JRY at the micro level could also be analysed in terms of difference in wage rate in the sample villages. Table 5 shows the impact of JRY on the wage rate per day in the sample villages according to the sample respondents. Table 5 reveals that the wage rate per day increased from Rs. 21/- to Rs. 35/- on account of JRY, recording a rise of 67 per cent in the case of males. Similarly, the wage rate per day for females increased from Rs. 12/- to Rs. 22/- on account of JRY, showing a rise of 83 per cent. Thus, the JRY appears to have had a positive impact on the wage rate in the sample villages. It was found that the actual wages paid to the labourers

TABLE 4

Employment generation under JRY in the Sample Households during the Last Two Years

S. No	Particulars	Village-I			Village-II			Village-III			Total		
		No. of members	No. of days	Wages received (in Rs.)	No. of members	No. of days	Wages received (in Rs.)	No. of members	No. of days	Wages received (in Rs.)	No. of members	No. of days	Wages received (in Rs.)
1.	Road laying and Construction Culverts	27	498	18,995	24	325	9,425	25	390	13,225	76	1,213 (24.0)	41,645 (24.0)
2.	Construction of School Building/ Community Halls/ Buildings	29	913	35,445	35	625	20,175	29	645	21,950	93	2,183 (44.0)	77,570 (44.0)
3.	Sanitary Works	30	570	20,700	22	387	2,310	27	435	15,650	79	1,392 (28.0)	48,660 (28.0)
4.	Other Works	13	154	5,250	4	40	1,200	2	10	200	19	204 (4.0)	7,250 (4.0)
	Total		2,135	80,990		1,377	33,110		1,480	51,025		4,992 (100)	1,75,125 (100)

Note : Figures in the parenthesis indicate percentages to the total.

were higher than the minium wages. But, there was difference in the wage rate for males and females, much against the guidelines of JRY. The main reason for paying higher than the minium wages appears to be the timing of undertaking the works, *i.e.*, during the busy agricultural season as against the stipulation of creating employment opportunities during the lien agricultural season.

TABLE 5

Impact of JRY on Wage Rate Per Day (in Rs.) according to the Sample Respondents

Sl. No.	Particulars	Village-I		Village-II		Village-III		Total	
		Male	Female	Male	Female	Male	Female	Male	Female
1.	Before JRY	23	15	19	11	20	10	21	12
2.	At Present	39	25	30	18	37	22	35	22
	Percentage difference	70.0	67.0	58.0	64.0	85.0	120.0	67.0	83.0

Contribution of JRY to Village Development

About 73 per cent of the sample respondents opined that JRY contributed to village development to some extent only and 22 per cent felt that the contribution of JRY to village development was to a great extent. Only five per cent felt that the programme not at all contributed to village development.

Regarding the specific ways in which JRY contributed to village development, as many as 97 per cent felt that JRY helped in the creation of rural community assets. Further, a majority of 63 per cent opined that JRY helped in providing housing facility to the weaker sections. About 52 per cent felt that JRY helped in improving road facilities including culverts in their villages. Only about 18 per cent felt that JRY generated wage employment during the lien season. Thus, it appears that one of the main objectives of JRY to generate additional employment opportunities during the lien season was not fulfilled to the desired extent.

Regarding the reasons for non-contribution or limited contribution of JRY to village development, a majority of 53 per cent of the sample respondents listed two reasons — misuse of JRY funds and non-coverage of poorer sections. Further, about 29 per cent felt that the selection of schemes under JRY was not proper, while 19 per cent opined that local resources were not utilised to the desired extent.

Conclusions

Based on the above analysis, the following broad conclusions may be drawn :

(1) The JRY could reach the poorer sections of the society in terms of social and economic status in rural areas, as indicated by caste composition and the low levels of living of households covered by the programme. But, it appears that the programme could not cover all households belonging to poorer sections.

(2) The extent of employment generated per household at the village level suggests that the JRY has to go a long way in fulfilling the objective of providing employment to the tune of 90-100 days per rural labour household in rural areas. As a consequence, the impact of JRY on income levels and quality of life of the households covered has also been limited.

(3) The JRY has been successful in creating rural infrastructure and building up of community assets to some extent, but the quality of assets created was poor in most cases.

(4) The selection of works taken up under JRY was done by village panchayat committee headed by president without the active involvement of the local community; lack of proper awareness about JRY and considerable degree of dissatisfaction about selection of schemes among the village people support this view.

(5) Besides the inadequacy of funds, the absence of proper training to the presidents of village panchayats, absence of proper planning, absence of regular monitoring and lack of proper institutional mechanism

for the distribution of food grains were the major weaknesses of the JRY.

Suggestions

Based on the findings of the study, the following suggestions are offered for the effective implementation of JRY at the grassroots level :

(1) There is a need to build up proper awareness about JRY among the rural people to enable their active participation in its implementation.

(2) Though the display of progress of JRY serves the purpose of social audit to some extent, yet there is a need to convene the Grama Sabha meetings once in six months in order to take decisions with regard to the selection of works and the timing of their execution. This would also facilitate effective utilisation of funds and creation of sustainable employment. There should also be a committee of local persons to oversee and watch the progress of the work.

(3) There is a need for giving adequate training to the presidents of village panchayats with regard to the operation of funds, maintenance of accounts, payment of minimum as well as equal wages to men and women and maintaining the wage and non wage ratio as per the JRY guidelines.

(4) Priority should be given only to those works that benefit the village most. Efforts should be made to check the usefulness, utilisation and maintenance of the assets created under JRY. Effective local participation, involvement of the Non-Governmental Development Organisations and active role of financial institutions are essential for creating economically viable infrastructure and developmental base in the villages.

(5) There is a need for developing an effective Management Information System (MIS) at the district level to properly monitor the implementation of JRY

by all the village panchayats in order to ensure the efficient utilisation of the available funds. In this context, it is important to evolve proper mechanism for fixing the responsibilities and to operate an incentive-cum-punishment system so that the presidents of village panchayats and local level officials function properly giving due recognition to the principles of transparency in administration and accountability to people.

REFERENCES

Bhaskar, G, *et al.*, "Jawahar Rozgar Yojana — New Vistas in Rural Scenario", *Kurukshetra,* Vol. XLII, No.8, May 1994, pp. 9-14.

Government of India, *Jawahar Rozgar Yojana Manual,* Ministry of Agriculture, Department Rural Development, New Delhi, 1995.

Kripa Shankar, "Jawahar Rozgar Yojana : An Assessment in Uttar Pradesh", *Economic and Political Weekly,* Vol. XXIX, No. 29, July 16, 1994, pp. 1845-1848.

Meenakshi Sundaram, S.S., "Combating Unemployment — Jawahar Rozgar Yojana", *Kurukshetra,* September 1994, pp. 32-34.

Neelakantan, M., "Jawahar Rozgar Yojana : An Assessment through concurrent evaluation", *Economic and Political Weekly,* Vol. XXIX, No. 49, December 3, 1994, pp. 3091-97.

Neela Mukherjee, "Women's participation and Jawahar Rozgar Yojana", *Yojana,* Vol. 37, No. 16, September 15, 1994, pp. 12-14.

Ruddar Datt, "Jawahar Rozgar Yojana", A Review, *Southern Economist,* Vol. 34, No. 10, September 1995, pp. 5-9.

Sudhaman, K.R., "Rozgar Yojana : Widening Yojana", *Yojana,* Vol. 38, No. 12, July 15, 1994, pp. 21-22.

SECTION 2
WOMEN EMPOWERMENT

8

Working Women in Slums : Deprived and Dehumanized

—P.V.L. Ramana and *Susan Verghese*

The economic status of women is now accepted on an indicator of society's stage of development. Ahooja-Patil (1993) in her article on 'Gender distance among countries' had identified labour force participation as one of the components of the Index of Women's Advancement (IWA). Article 23 of the Universal Declaration of Human Rights (1948) also includes Right to Work as one of the human rights. The most recent exponent of the principle of non-discrimination to work on the grounds of sex was the UN Convention of Elimination of All Forms of Discrimination Against Women (CEDAW) adopted in 1979 and ratified by over 120 countries. However, whether work is a privilege or a compulsion depends upon the socio-economic status of different categories of workers. For those living below the subsistence level like landless agricultural labourers and pavement and slum dwellers the capacity for work may not provide high claim to status (Towards Equality, 1974). This is illustrated by examining data on a sample of working women in a slum.

The slum under study is "Muslim Thatichetlapalem" of Visakhapatnam city in the state of Andhra Pradesh. It has 490 households with a total population of 2,357. The data presented here pertains to the working women of 100 households. Some of the outstanding features of the slum are the larger proportion of Muslims (50.4 per cent), higher literacy rate (72.4 per cent) males and 63.2 per cent females), higher child labour rate (31.2 per cent), low proportion of working women and small number of female-headed households (1.6 per cent). This being a Muslim dominated slum, the higher proportion of Muslims in the slum needs no special explanation. The higher literacy rate may be attributed to the fact that it has two schools within the slum, one of which is an Urdu School, specially meant for Muslims. But many of these literates can barely read and write as the majority of them have not completed even primary level education. What is incongruent is the high enrollment rate in schools along with high child labour rate. Close scrutiny of the data reveals that a good number of students enrolled in school are also engaged in child labour. This explodes the myth that stepped up enrollment in schools will automatically bring down the child labour rate. Therefore, it appears that going by enrollment rate alone can give a distorted picture of the reality. The lower proportion of working women and also lower proportion of female headed households are reflections of the Muslim predominant culture of the slum (See table 1).

The work participation rate shows that there are 46 working women in the sampled households, of whom 24 are Muslims and 22 are Hindus. The working women have been categorised according to their occupation and sector of work into six categories, namely, traditional skilled, traditional unskilled, modern skilled, modern unskilled, petty business and salaried. Table 2 shows the distribution of the sampled working women by their occupations.

Socio-Economic Characteristics of Working Women

The age distribution of the sample shows that there are 19.6 per cent child labour (below 14 years). 36.9 per cent of the sample belong to 15-29 years age group, 39.1 per cent in 30-54 years age group and 4.3 per cent in 55+ category.

Majority of the working women are illiterates (58.7 per cent), but while among Hindus 86.4 per cent are illiterate only 33.3 per cent are illiterate among Muslims. The data thus shows that the literacy levels of Muslims are superior when compared to Hindus. While 47.8 per cent are married, 32.6 per cent are unmarried. Widowed and separated constitute 19.6 per cent. It is also found that only 16.7 per cent of the sample are found to be married after attaining the permissible age for marriage (18 years), thereby indicating prevalence of child marriage both among Hindus and Muslims. Majority of the workers (65.2 per cent) are living in nuclear families. The size of household is comparatively larger for Muslims than Hindus. The main income of these workers is mere Rs. 310; 69.6 per cent have less than Rs. 250 per month, 8.7 per cent of the respondents have incomes that range from Rs. 251-500, 17.4 per cent within the range of Rs. 501 - 1000 and 4.3 per cent earn more than Rs. 1,000 per month (See Tables 3, 4, 5, 6, 7 & 8). A close observation of the occupations in comparison to literacy levels indicate that (1) illiterate women work mostly in unskilled occupation, (2) literate women other than primary level, work in skilled occupations, (3) those with primary level education are generally drop-outs and work in unskilled occupation and (4) the income levels of the literates are much lower than the illiterates, because they were unwilling to take up low status occupation such as 'coolie' which yields more income.

As such majority of the working women are engaged in traditional unskilled occupations like domestic labour and daily wage labour. Curiously, those with higher skills and higher literacy levels are found to earn lower than the illiterate and unskilled workers. As such there is no relationship between occupation, skill, literacy level and income structure in the present slum.

The data reveals that women in slum consider it more prestigious if their needs are provided for by the male members in the family rather than having to earn themselves to meet their needs. Slum culture attributes higher status to non-working women. Therefore, women perceived work as a 'curse' and the state of being 'provided for' as a blessing. In spite of this some of the women were forced to work because of the exigencies of poverty. This implies that they were working against their own will. For these women, work was a compulsion rather than a privilege and work was in no way a fulfilling experience. Added to this, the income earned is invariably appropriated by the husbands. Cases of two Muslim women who are forced to work out of sheer economic necessity, even though their culture does not encourage women to work outside home can be given as illustrations.

Shanu Begum works as a maid servant in 4 houses. Her husband has stopped working due to ill health and is now dependent on the earnings of the wife. The economic dependence on the wife does not prevent the husband from exercising control over the wife's earnings and her freedom. He follows the wife to the households where she works to ensure that she is not having any clandestine relations with other males. Further, he insists that she only works in houses where there are older men rather than younger adults. This, in addition to curtailing her freedom is also lowering her earning capacity because households of older people can afford to pay only lower wages.

Yet another example is the case of Farida Begum who is engaged in the petty business of soda-making along with her husband. She cleans the soda bottles, fills the gas and does all the operations related to soda-making. But by virtue of the fact that it is the husband who distributes the product to pan shop owners, he retains full control of the money earned, the wife being denied access to the income generated by her. Thus, work gives neither satisfaction nor rewards to these women. This brings to mind Marx's characterisation of the industrial worker who is alienated because he neither fulfills himself through work, nor receives full value of his labour.

According to the Marxist concept of 'total man', man is essentially a creature who fulfills himself through work. But if the work is merely a means to earn livelihood, work is demeaning and dehumanizing because he neither realises himself through work nor is work a satisfying experience. Further he is also denied the full value of his labour (Kon, 1967). The situation is similar to our respondents in the slum who are dehumanized by work and also deprived of their rewards.

As rightly pointed out by Blumberg (1989 : 164) one of the factors that discount the economic power of an earning wife is the ideological factor of internalized values in gender socialization. Through such socialization a woman feels ideologically bound to handover her earnings to her husband. This is an act that nibbles away the economic power compared to even a non-earning wife and explains why women in slum feel that it is better to be 'provided for' than having to 'earn themselves'. Since it is now recognized that the most important factor that influences women's overall equality is economic, it is only through increased economic leverage that her self confidence and self reliance can be enhanced. Therefore, the task here is to firstly change the perception of women about work, namely that work is a privilege rather than a curse. This can be done only by changing the reality of the current situation in which these women are placed but are these women in a position to change the realities of their situations? The obvious answer is no. They need to be empowered to take greater control of their lives. As rightly pointed out by Mies (1993), in feminist research the postulate of value neutrality and indifference towards research object needs to be replaced by identification with them so that contemplative, uninvolved and spectator knowledge is replaced by participatory action for women's empowerment. Participatory approach is a process which encourages people to identify their own needs and to take action to meet these needs. By taking a participatory approach the research process becomes a process of conscientization both for the 'researched' and the 'researcher'. Thus, we are pleading for a research committed to the emancipation of this deprived group in which firstly action will have to be taken to change the structural conditions that are making these women economically 'powerless'. This is possible by making income generating programmes accessible to them. The ability to generate income in turn will change the perceptions about work so that they will not only learn to perceive work as a privilege but will also enhance their economic leverage.

REFERENCES

Ahooja-Patel, Krishna, "Gender distance among countries", *Economic and Political Weekly*, pp. 295-305, February 13, 1993.

Blumberg, R.L., "Toward a Feminist Theory of Development" in *Feminism and Sociological Theory* (ed.), Ruth A. Wallace, Sage Publications, New Delhi, 1989.

Government of India, Towards Equality, *Report of the National Committee on the Status of Women in India*, 1974.

Kon, Igor, "The concept of Alienation in Modern Sociology", *Social Research*, Vol. 34, 1967, pp. 507-58.

Mies, Maria, "Towards a Methodology of Feminist Research" in Martin Hammersley (ed.), *Social Research : Philosophy, Politics and Practice*, Sage Publications, New Delhi, 1993.

TABLE 1

Comparative Picture of Slum Average and Muslim Thatichetalpalem

	Socio-economic features		Overall slum	Muslim Thatichetalpalem average
1.	Sex-ratio		984 (1000 males)	981 (1000 males)
2.	Percentage of female headed households		13.9	1.6
3.	Percentage of Muslim households to total households		3.6	50.4
4.	Percentage of literates (5 years and above)	All	44.5	67.5
		Male	49.3	72.4
		Female	39.7	63.2
5.	Percentage of child labour (5-15 years)	All	19.8	31.2
		Male	24.9	30.4
		Female	14.5	26.9
6.	Percentage of children not attending school (6-15 years)	All	16.7	17.8
		Male	17.0	18.2
		Female	16.3	17.4
7.	Percentage of people having own house		63.9	29.8
Civic Amenities (in Percentage)				
8.	Accessibility to drinking water		70.7	86.3
9.	Availability of open drain connection		70.9	78.6
10.	Having bathing cubicle		46.6	66.1
11.	Having soak pits		10.7	12.8
12.	Having individual lavatory		33.6	46.9
13.	Having electricity connections		64.5	78.4

Source : *Janmabhoomi Survey*, Visakhapatnam Municipal Corporation, 1997.

TABLE 2

Classification of Occupations

Occupation	Hindus	Muslims	Total
Traditional skilled	—	4 (16.7)	4 (8.7)
Traditional unskilled	20 (90.9)	12 (50.0)	32 (69.6)
Modern skilled	—	3 (12.5)	3 (6.5)
Modern unskilled	1 (4.6)	—	1 (2.2)
Petty business	1 (4.6)	2 (8.3)	3 (6.5)
Salaried	—	3 (12.5)	3 (6.5)
Total	22	24	46

TABLE 3

Age Cohorts of the Working Women

Age Group	Hindus	Muslims	Total
0-14	7 (31.8)	2 (8.3)	9 (19.6)
15-29	8 (36.4)	9 (37.5)	17 (36.9)
30-54	6 (27.3)	12 (50.0)	18 (39.1)
55+	1 (4.5)	1 (4.2)	2 (4.3)
Total	22	24	46

TABLE 4

Literacy Levels of Working Women

Literacy Levels	Hindus	Muslims	Total
Illiterate	19 (86.4)	8 (33.3)	27 (58.7)
Primary	3 (13.6)	11 (45.8)	14 (30.4)
Upper Primary	-	4 (16.7)	4 (8.7)
Secondary	-	-	-
College	-	1 (4.2)	1 (2.2)
Total	22	24	46

TABLE 5

Income Levels of Women Workers

Income Levels	Hindus	Muslims	Total
0-250	13 (59.1)	19 (79.2)	32 (69.6)
251-500	1 (4.5)	3 (12.5)	4 (8.7)
501-1000	7 (31.8)	1 (4.2)	8 (17.4)
1000+	1 (4.5)	1 (4.2)	2 (4.3)
Total	22	24	46

TABLE 6

Marital Status of Working Women

Marital Status	Hindus	Muslims	Total
Unmarried	9 (40.9)	6 (25.0)	15 (32.6)
Married	10 (45.5)	12 (50.0)	22 (47.8)
Widowed	2 (9.1)	5 (20.8)	7 (15.2)
Separated	1 (4.5)	1 (4.2)	2 (4.4)
Total	22	24	46

TABLE 7

Age at Marriage of the Working Women

Age at Marriage	Hindus	Muslims	Total
11 years and below	4 (33.3)	2 (11.1)	6 (20.0)
12-14 years	4 (33.3)	6 (33.3)	10 (33.3)
15-17 years	2 (16.6)	7 (38.9)	9 (30.0)
18 years	2 (16.6)	3 (16.7)	5 (16.7)
Total	12	18	30

TABLE 8

Type of Family and Size of Household

Type of family	Hindus	Muslims	Total	Size of household	Hindus	Muslims	Total
Nuclear	15 (68.2)	15 (62.5)	30 (65.2)	1-4 members	8 (36.4)	10 (41.7)	18 (39.1)
Extended	7 (31.8)	9 (37.5)	16 (34.8)	5-8 members	14 (63.6)	12 (50.0)	26 (56.5)
				9	—	2 (8.3)	2 (4.4)
Total	22	24	46	Total	22	24	46

9

Women and Democratic Development

—*Dr. (Ms.) B. Meena Rao* and *Dr. (Ms.) M. Vijayalakshmi*

"What is wanted for women," wrote John Stuart Mill in `The Subjection of Women' in 1869, "is equal rights, equal admission to all social privileges, not a protection apart, a sort of sentimental priesthood..". A century and a quarter later the (HDR) Human Development Report for 1995, focusing attention on the plight of women, states, "there is not a single country where women enjoy equality with men". The Humphrey Institute of Public Affairs points out "while women represent 50 per cent of the world population, they perform nearly two-thirds of all working hours, receive one-tenth of the world income and own less than one per cent of the world property". This pronounced gender inequality is a major hindrance to sustainable development.

Upholding the right to equality along with effective participation of all citizens is the hallmark of a successful democracy. While the will and the capacity of the people to participate in politics are the necessary pre-requisites of democracy, according to Mrinal Gore, "it is a woman's participation in politics that lends vitality to the democratic way of life" (Mrinal Gore : 1993 : 6). As women comprise about half of the population, this part of society cannot be ignored. It is essential to know the nature and scope of their participation without which there would not be a true picture of democratic development. The point is that competent democratic leadership by inspiring popular participation can mobilize greater involvement of women in the process of strengthening participatory democracy.

Gender inequality hampers the pace of development. Human development as Ahooja Patel put it "subsume women's development" (Ahooja-Patel : 1997). The concept of human development not only encompasses the development of the people but also as HDR 1995 states, "development for the people and development by the people", namely participatory development.

In the contemporary world human/social development has emerged as a major issue. The economic inputs as indicators of growth sometimes prove to be misleading because an economically advanced country may well have a backward society. Ensuring political and civil rights is a major development goal. Today, the bottom line is 'people centered development'. The new understanding of democratic development calls for greater participation of people. The focus is on participatory democratic development.

Development is being redefined. In the nineteenth century countries in Europe and North America experienced a tremendous progress in the field of science and technology. In contrast countries in Asia, Africa and South America did not experience such amazing growth and came to be termed as 'underdeveloped' or 'developing' countries. The terms 'developed' and 'developing' were measured in terms of economic inputs and technological development. The accent was on increasing production and development became synonymous with growth. This in turn gave rise to a narrow understanding that, per capita income, national income, gross domestic product, gross national product, rate of industrial production and consumption and of investment were the most reliable indicators of a country's success or failure in the eradication of poverty and backwardness (Sinha : 1995).

The development model followed after the Second World War, only led to greater inequalities, poverty and discrimination against some sections of people in the society. The world today is as divided as ever. Africa contains 27 of the 41 countries with the lowest per capita income and the rest belong to Asia. "Development efforts have not been able to resolve the dual realities of — plenty and famine, health and disease, unparalleled advancements in knowledge and technology and growing illiteracy and child labour". The prospects of the poor everywhere and women in particular are bleak, despite the great social struggles and resistance.

Having witnessed the failure of development in post-colonial societies policy makers were looking for an alternative to counter the hegemony of growth centric development. The (HDI) Human Development Index combines life expectancy at birth, access to sanitation, safe drinking water, health services, daily calorie intake, female-male gaps, rural-urban gap, profile of homicides, suicides, child mortality rate, illiteracy rate to mention only a few, with traditional indicators like GDP and GNP to provide a 'composite measure of human development'. The UNDP defines human development as a process of "enlarging people's choices" adding that "income is clearly only one option".

Holistic humanitarian development has become the key issue for several international conferences. For the first time, the fate of children was linked to the state of development at the World Summit for Children (1990), at the Rio Earth Summit (1992) more specifically its Agenda 21, has a number of provisions which by linking environment and development to the survival of human beings, address humanitarian issues directly. The World Conference of Human Rights (1993), the International Conference on Population and Development (1994) also addressed development issues. The World Social Development Summit (1995) asserted that attempts have to be made to "broaden women's political, economic, social, and cultural opportunities and support the empowerment of women". The process of globalization of humanitarian development in the contemporary world order is gaining importance.

Though development has a new and a broader connotation, the history of development is replete with evidence of how prosperity and well-being of some are promoted at the cost of others. Among the sections who are adversely affected and have been most vulnerable to exploitation, discrimination, instability, deprivation and violence of the worst kind are women. The issue of violence against women is an issue that transcends all borders and religion. It does not discriminate between class or economic status. According to the HDR, 1995, "Of the world's rural population 60 per cent are women, and two-thirds of the poor are women, and that half a million women die every year due to maternity related problems".

Work place harassment, like all other violence against women, "is a display of power with the intention of coercing and degrading women, with bosses or co-workers victimising the women below them in the organizational hierarchy" (Gandhi and Shah : 1992). In recent years more women in Japan have postponed marriage while some have even rejected it altogether, and stayed in the work place. This is so because they were routinely encouraged to quit their jobs when they have children. Those who choose to stay at work, or not to marry, are subjected to heavy pressure from bosses and co-workers to follow a more "normal" course. It was as recently as 1990 that a Japanese Court for the first time ruled that unequal pay for women and men doing the same work was illegal (Jordon : 1996).

In the so called developed or advanced countries like the United States of America the (CEDAW) Convention on Elimination of Discrimination against Women is yet to be ratified. The HDR 1996, states that every 18 minutes a woman is battered in America. In China female infanticide and forced abortion are still in practice.

Neither is the church a safe place for women today. In United Kingdom the priests use the church for their personal 'pleasures'. The all-male hierarchy churches are above their own preaching. They go over the line in 'comforting' women. Many women in the church are in a kind of 'abusive power relationship'. As Lala Winkley says, "The issue is not about sex, but about the male (priests) dishonourable behaviour, and how the church lets them off the hook" (Bunting : 1996).

Women in the police force face the brunt of discrimination. The protectors of the innocent are in need of some protection themselves. According to the recent edition of the Police Review, there are at least 50 cases of sexual harassment and sexual discrimination brought by women police officers in 1995. These 'cases can often take up to two years to reach tribunal level, which means a long period of humiliation and ostracism —

women cannot change posts while a complaint is going through'. Such compelling reasons make Britain's police women to turn to the press to tell their stories (O'Kane : 1996).

Nepal, a highly patriarchal society, has deep contempt for the girl child. Nepal holds the world record for "male preference". Ninety per cent of parents want male children. Woman is discriminated against not only in her daily life, but also in legal texts, of which at least 20 put them at a disadvantage. Nepal is one of three countries in the world where the life expectancy of men is higher than that of women (Langellier : 1997). In Egypt, women are used as pawns in the fight against militancy. "The deliberate degradation of women by arrest, torture and sexual abuse is intended to break the spirit of male militants" (Bhatia : 1996).

On the economic front, the HDR 1996, estimated that women perform $11 trillion worth of unpaid or invisible activity worldwide. According to the findings of a 31 country study, women work longer hours than men. On an average put in 13 per cent more time than men in developing countries and 6 per cent more than men in developed countries. Another finding is regarding the total burden of work. Women carry 53 per cent and 47 per cent in developing countries and the figures are 51 per cent and 49 per cent for developed countries. It is obvious that women contribute to more than half of the wealth of nations and yet they are denied economic and social rights and privileges.

Women's participation on the political front is also dismal. Despite a long democratic tradition, the United States, United Kingdom and France rank low in providing representation to women in legislatures. Of the 186 countries surveyed by the Inter-Parliamentary Union (IPU) in 1995, the U.S., world's highly developed democracy, ranks 43rd with the proportion of women members in the legislature being 10.9 per cent. Britain is at 49th with 9.5 per cent while France ranks 64 with 6.4 per cent. In fact it took women 156 years to become members of the French Parliament, founded in 1789 with the sterling call for "Liberty, Equality, Fraternity" (Katyal : 1997).

Records show that it took 486 years for a woman in Sweden to become a member of Parliament, which was founded in 1435. Iceland has had a Parliament in the modern sense since 1845 but is was only in 1922 that a woman gained entry into it. Switzerland, the world's "best democracy", gave women the right to vote in 1972.

At the other end of the scale are Bhutan, Comoros, Djibouti, Papua New Guinea, where the assemblies are exclusively composed of men. Kuwait and the UAE provide for equality of citizens but allow only men to become members of their legislatures (Katyal : 1997).

Other studies by policy-makers, academics and development practitioners have used (GEM) Gender Empowerment Measure to study women development. The GEM composites female share in the national parliament, as administrators and managers, as professional and technical workers and their share of earned income. No society treats its women as equals. The highest value for GEM is Norway (0.795) followed by other Nordic countries, Sweden (0.784), Denmark (0.728) and Finland (0.719), New Zealand (0.728) is ahead of Canada (0.700) and the Netherlands (0.660).

The highest participation of women in the national parliament is 40.4 per cent in Sweden. It is high in other Nordic countries, 39.4 per cent in Norway 33.5 per cent in Finland 33 per cent in Denmark and 28.4 per cent in Netherlands. New Zealand has 29.25 per cent. Women occupying the national parliament in Australia 20.5 per cent in Germany 25.5 per cent in Canada 19.3 per cent in Japan 7.7 per cent. Among the developing countries Barbados (18.4 per cent) and Trinidad and Tobago (19.4 per cent) have the highest proportion of women in the parliament.

In view of such gender inequality UN sponsored international conference regarding women's issues have been conducted.

A World Conference on Women was held in Mexico in 1975. The theme of the conference was three-fold : (1) equality, (2) development and (3) peace. Later these themes also became the issues for the 'U.N. Decade for Women (1975 1985)'. It was emphasized at this conference that "discrimination against women is an obstacle to the participation of women, on equal terms with men, in the political, social economic and cultural life of their countries (Shah 1995 : 3). Another important area it touched upon was giving opportunities to women in decision-making process. U.N. pointed out that the only way to elevate the status of women is that they should be treated as active participants in the development process. The steps taken by the Indian Government for giving the rural women this opportunity is the outcome of this conference. In 1980, a mid-decade conference was held in Copenhegen, Denmark. It may be attributed to this Second World Conference of Women the India had incorporated a special chapter on 'Women Development' in the Sixth Five Year Plan. In Nairobi, the Third World Conference on Women in 1985, these themes were incorporated in the strategies for the advancement of women. The most recent, the Fourth World Conference on Women was held at Beijing in September 1995. This became "a platform for action" concentrating on critical areas of concern, that have been identified as obstacles to the advancement of women in the world.

India a founder Member of the United Nations has ratified various International Conventions promising to secure equal rights for women, and to protect them from exploitation. The Universal Declaration of Human Rights, of the Child Convention on the Elimination of all forms of Discrimination against women (CEDAW-1079) in 1993. The Mexico Plan of Action (1975), the Nairobi Forward looking strategies (1985), the Beijing Declaration (1995) have been ratified by India for appropriate follow up.

Recognising the efforts made by the United Nations women development and empowerment, the Indian Government also is attempting in elevating the status of the women. However, fifty-one years after independence statistics show how little has been done in this regard. According to HDR 1996, "India ranks 103rd in the gender related development index. Women's earned income share is a paltry 24.8 per cent. India ranks a dismal 93 when it comes to gender empowerment measures.

A mere 2.3 per cent women are administrators and managers, 20.5 per cent professional and technical workers all of whom collectively earn 25 per cent of the shared income" (Panicker : 1996). With the liberalisation and restructuring policies on the rise women are likely to be further marginalized.

Although numerically the women in India are almost equal with men (for 1000 males 929 females in the country as a whole) they are discriminated in every walk of life. According to the World Bank Report (1991) the major axis of gender discrimination in Indian society arose from the 'inside/outside' dichotomy. The culture's very definition of the female is with the 'inside' the home. By contrast men belonging to the 'outside' where livelihoods are earned and political and economic power is wielded.

The inequalities inherent in our traditional social structure, based on caste, community and class have a very strong influence on the status of women (Towards Inequality : 1974 : 3). Women in India find themselves in a system which has failed to live up to the promises made in the Constitution. In spite of the constitutional guarantee prohibiting discrimination on the grounds of sex, the women in India are continued to be discriminated against.

During the pre-Independence period there were two major movements which brought about a drastic change in the position of women. One was the social reform movement and the other the nationalist movement. Social reform movement for the emancipation of women was set in motion by Rajaram Mohan Roy, who stood on the bridge between the old and new.

The nationalist-movement and more so the Indian National Congress in 1885 provided a political platform for the Indian women. Five years later in 1900 the first women delegates attended the Calcutta session of the Congress and spoke from a political platform. This was the dawn of the new era which saw Indian women take an increasingly active part in political activities. Mahatma Gandhi believed that if women did not join the nationalist movement, India's march to *Swaraj* would be delayed. (O'Malley:1996:25-29).

Women participated in their tens of thousands in the national struggle and took an active part in the form of imposing prohibition by picketing shops selling liquor and foreign goods. They braved the prisons along with their male counterparts. Women came out of their seclusion. Socio-political participation gained through consciousness made women shed a number of socio-religious evils from which they long suffered. Sarojini Naidu became the first Indian woman President of the Indian National Congress in 1925. Indian women had become prominent and their political awareness had begun.

Another landmark was the (AIWC) All India Women's Conference which fought for the emancipation of women. The A.I.W.C.'s main aim at the time of its inception was to safeguard the interests of Indian women. Subsequently, many other organisations and associations were founded to prepare the ground for women to promote interests through their active participation in the social, economic, cultural and political affairs (Mehta : 1978 : 31). Indian women demanded the right to vote (for which their counter parts in the West had to fight for nearly a century), which was promised and fulfilled by the Indian National Congress at its Karachi Session. An immediate result of this was the Montague-Chelmsford Reforms Act of 1919 which gave women the right to vote in elections to all the State Legislatures but not to the Covenant of State for Governor-General. Such participation had a direct impact on the attitudes of women. All these activities helped Indian women to gain self-confidence and they learned to rely on themselves.

The Quit India Movement of 1942 saw the leaders of the movement arrested and jailed and women assume leadership roles. They came from all age groups and classes, castes and religions. Their sympathy and support to the nationalist movement, including its militant activities, as epitomised by the then youngsters like Aruna Asaf Ali, Durga Bai, Sushila Devi and many others enhanced the creditability of the freedom struggle. In July 1943, in response to the clarion call of Subhash Chandra Bose, a women's regiment named 'The Rani of Jhansi Regiment' was formed in Singapore with Laxmi Sehgal as its leader (Jharta : 1996 : 60).

Women did not lag behind in the making of the Constitution for free India. The Constituent Assembly which was set-up in October 1946, a body elected legislatures, had among its members Sarojini Naidu, Durgabai Deshmukh, Renuka Ray and Hansa Mehta among others.

The initial post-independence years were a period of complacency for women, since many feminists at the time had placed their hope on an egalitarian free India and the creation of a welfare state (Desai and Krishnaraj 1987). Nevertheless subordinate place had been allotted to women in the process of development. Programmes that were financed by the Ford Foundation in the 1950s and 60s involved training women in the skills of 'family management' and 'home economics'. Ironically, the women's acceptance of subjected roles in traditional social arrangements refers to entrenched inequality that is supported by the women's conditioned acceptance of comparative deprivation (Sen : 1992 : 150).

But it is clear that a subsequent generation of women in the 1970s were shaken by the absence of a women's perspective in the overall development process and the indifference of policy-makers and planners. Feminists in the 1970s emphasized on the utter incongruity of projects meant to enable village women to become "good wife, a wise mother, a competent housewife and a responsible member of the village community" (Mary E. John : 1996). By exposing the ambivalent effects of development strategies that had been designed without regard for women, feminists demanded that policy-makers actively address the invisibility of women's contributions to the making of the nation.

The initial approach of the Government was to focus women as targets of welfare policies in the social sector. The concept of women's development in the First Five Year Plan (1951-56) was mainly 'welfare' oriented. The (CSWB) Central Social Welfare Board set up in 1953 was mainly 'welfare' oriented. The (CSWB) Central Social Welfare Board set up in 1953 has undertaken a number of welfare programmes and measures through the voluntary organisations. In the Second Five Year Plan (1956-61) women were organised into Mahila Mandals to act as focal points at the grass root levels for development of women. The Third, Fourth and other Interim Plans (1961-74) accorded high priority to the education of women.

In the Fifth Plan (1974-78) there was a shift in the approach from women's 'welfare' to women's 'development'. This was largely because of the influence of the International Women's Year (1975) and International Women's Decade (1975-85). The new approach aimed at an integration of welfare with development services.

The Sixth Five Year Plan (1980-85) was a landmark in the history of women's development. There was a separate chapter on women's development with a definite thrust on health, education and employment. It recommended quotas for women in schemes such as TRYSEM (Training of Youth for Self-employment) and DWCRA (Development for Women and Child and Rural Areas). In 1985, the then Prime Minister Rajiv Gandhi, created the ministry of human resources development and under it, the (DWCD) Department of Women and Child Development. In the next five years, human resource development became a major thrust, and women's development was seen a critical. The (NPPW) National Perspective Plan for Women (1988-2000) has recommended among other things, an exclusive credit scheme for women.

In the Seventh Five Year Plan (1985-90) the developmental programmes for women continued with the major objectives of raising their economic and social status and to bring them into the mainstream of national development. In 1990 the Parliament set up the (NCW) National Commission for women to monitor all matters related to constitutional and legal rights conferred on women.

As a signatory to the World Declaration on the Survival, Protection and development of Children the Government of India has drawn up an Action Plan for the Girl Child (1991-2000). In a recent legislation the Government has now banned sex-determination test to prevent female foeticide.

The Eighth Plan (1992-97) realised the need to develop special programmes so that the gains from development in various sectors do not bypass women. Now there is a shift from 'development' to 'empowerment' of women.

In preparation for the Ninth Five Year Plan an approach paper was developed. The approach paper focused on among other things empowerment of women, decentralisation and people's participation in planning and implementation of strategies.

Despite positive constitutional and legal provisions and various other measures adopted by the Government from time to time to transform from a male-dominated society to a 'gender-just' and 'gender equality' society was no easy task. Even a galaxy of outstanding women leaders including a Prime Minister (Mrs. Indira Gandhi) for 16 years, women have not been able to get adequate and proportionate representation in decision making bodies.

One of the main reasons for women's backwardness in the Indian society is their under representation in political decision making. Women disempowerment is hopelessly aggravated by the patriarchal system, entrenched in the society. Policy-making having become a male preserve while the requirements of women, their grievances and priorities receive the least attention. The Constitution has granted women equal rights, but these rights have no meaning because their voice is hardly given any weightage.

It was to improve this situation and "to make women to come out of the 'coma' of social bondage" (Davis : 1997) that the "policy of reservation" has been introduced. To empower is to give women the capacity to influence the decision making process by integrating them into our political system. Reserving seats for women will provide them an opportunity to raise their grievances in order to solve their social, economic and related problems in a formal manner. Reservation of seats is, thus, one of the instruments of political empowerment of women.

It must be understood that any reservation is a form of positive discrimination concurring with the democratic principles. In our country reservation for Scheduled Castes and Scheduled Tribes reflects in the reverse the political and social deprivations they suffer as communities, despite the fact that the Constitution has given rights to all citizens. Through reservation, the state intervenes to admit the imbalance in an effort to at least partially, rectify it. As Bhattacharya remarked, "an undemocratic method is used to make democracy broader and more real" (Bhattacharya : Seminar : 1997). Reservation for women in legislative bodies too, must be seen as a partial measure, not as a panacea for all evils that are perpetrated against women. There can no longer be development without their participation because there can be no decision-making without their involvement. Even if a small percentage of newly-elected women representatives raise their voice to highlight the needs, rights and demands of these classes, it will be a further step towards the democratisation of politics.

As it stands today, the proportion of women elected to the Parliament and the state legislatures is very low. The percentage of women contesting the Lok Sabha elections has been going down steadily from a healthy 51 per cent in 1962 to less than 11 per cent in 1991. The current Lok Sabha has only 36 women as compared to 44 in the previous. The fact that the political parties give a short shrift to women came to the fore in the recent assembly elections in Uttar Pradesh when not a single woman contestant was fielded though the political battle for Uttarakhand saw the active participation of women. These women showed leadership qualities and have forced the Union government to agree, in principle, to a separate state.

A glance at the two tables given below shows a picture of how the women have fared in the Parliament and the state assemblies during the last fifty years. Figures in Table 1 show on an average each of the last eleven Lok Sabhas had only 30 women MPs, a figure less than 6 per cent. Their share in the indirectly elected Rajya Sabha has been slightly better at 9 per cent. Through these years there is no definite trend towards and increase in this proportion except in the Rajya Sabha. The figures for Lok Sabha do not yield any steady trend, except for the general tendency for the proportion of women being very low.

TABLE 1

Women's Representation in Parliament

Year	Lok Sabha			Rajya Sabha		
	Seats	Women MPs	Percentage of Women MPs	Seats	Women MPs	Percentage of Women MPs
1952	499	22	4.4	219	16	7.3
1957	500	27	5.4	237	18	7.5
1962	503	34	6.8	238	18	7.6
1967	523	31	5.9	240	20	8.3
1971	521	22	4.2	243	17	7.0
1977	544	19	3.4	244	25	10.2
1980	544	28	7.9	244	24	9.8
1984	544	44	8.1	244	28	11.4
1989	517	27	5.3	245	24	9.7
1991	544	39	7.2	245	38	15.5
1996	543	39	7.7	223	20	9.0
Average	526	30	6.0	238	23	10.3

Source : Seminar, 457, September 1997.

A closer look at the ups and downs of women's representation shows that there was a sharp fall in Lok Sabha around in 1967 and then again in 1977. The average picked up in 1984-85 elections when the Congress swept the polls in the entire country.

The variation across the state assemblies as depicted in table 2 does not show any definite pattern. States like Kerala, West Bengal, Maharashtra and Tamil Nadu, with high literacy or comparatively high female literacy, fare worse than average

TABLE 2

Women Representation in State Legislatures 1952-1997
(Percentage of Women MLAs)

State	1952	1957	1960-65	1967-69	1970-75	1977-78	1979-83	1984-88	1989-92	1993-97	State average
1	2	3	4	5	6	7	8	9	10	11	12
Andhra Pradesh	2.9	3.7	3.3	3.8	9.1	3.4	4.1	3.4	3.7	2.7	4.0
Arunachal Pradesh	NA	NA	NA	NA	0	0	3.3	6.7	3.3	3.3	3.3
Assam	0.5	4.6	3.8	4.0	7.0	0.8	0.8	4.0	4.0	4.8	3.2
Bihar	3.6	9.4	7.9	2.2	3.8	4.0	3.7	4.6	2.8	3.4	4.3
Goa	NA	NA	NA	6.7	3.3	3.3	0	0	5.0	10.0	4.3
Gujarat	NA	NA	8.4	4.8	3.2	NE	2.7	8.8	2.2	1.1	4.2
Haryana	NA	NA	NA	7.4	6.2	4.4	7.8	5.6	6.7	4.4	6.2
Himachal Pradesh	0	NA	NA	0	5.9	1.5	4.74	4.4	5.9	4.4	3.6
Jammu & Kashmir	NA	NE	0	0	5.3	1.3	0	1.3	NE	2.3	1.5
Karnataka	2.0	8.7	8.7	3.2	5.1	4.0	0.9	3.6	4.5	3.1	4.5
Kerala	NA	4.8	3.9	0.8	1.5	0.7	3.2	5.7	5.7	9.3	3.6
Madhya Pradesh	2.1	10.8	4.9	3.4	5.4	3.1	5.6	9.7	3.4	3.8	5.1
Maharashtra	1.9	6.3	4.9	3.3	9.3	2.8	6.6	5.6	2.1	3.8	4.7

Contd...

1	2	3	4	5	6	7	8	9	10	11	12
Manipur	NA	NE	NE	0	0	NE	0	0	1.7	0	0.3
Meghalaya	NA	NA	NA	NA	1.7	1.7	0	3.3	NE	1.7	1.7
Mizoram	NA	NA	NA	NA	0	3.3	3.3	2.5	0	0	1.4
Nagaland	NA	NA	0	0	NE	0	0	1.7	0	0	0.5
Orissa	9.6	3.6	1.4	3.6	1.4	4.8	3.4	6.1	4.8	5.4	4.0
Punjab	2.2	5.8	5.2	1.0	5.8	2.6	5.1	3.4	5.1	6.0	4.0
Rajasthan	NA	5.1	4.5	3.3	7.1	4.0	5.0	8.0	5.5	4.5	4.8
Sikkim	NA	NA	NA	NA	NA	NA	0	0	6.3	3.1	2.3
Tamil Nadu	0.3	5.9	3.9	1.7	2.1	0.9	2.1	3.4	9.0	3.8	3.6
Tripura	NA	NE	NE	0	3.3	1.7	6.7	3.3	NE	1.7	3.0
Uttar Pradesh	1.2	5.8	4.4	2.8	5.9	2.6	5.6	7.3	3.3	4.0	4.1
West Bengal	0.8	3.6	4.8	2.9	1.6	1.4	2.4	4.4	7.1	6.8	3.4
Delhi	4.2	NA	NE	NE	7.1	7.1	7.1	NE	NE	4.3	5.9
Pondicherry	NA	NA	6.7	3.3	0	0	3.3	3.3	1.7	3.3	2.6
Period Average	1.8	6.3	4.9	2.9	4.4	2.8	3.8	5.3	4.5	4.0	4.0

Source: Seminar, 457, September 1997.

on this score. Surprisingly, Haryana and Madhya Pradesh, marked by a poor record on female literacy, have shown a better than average representation of women is evenly spread across all states. Like at the national level, the state legislatures also reveal a sharp fall in 1967 and again in 1977. It shows a definite decline in women's representation today as compared to the levels reached in the elections held between 1957 to 1965. The overall average of women MLAs across all state legislatures in the last 45 years stands at a mere 4 per cent.

Data concerning women contestants, rather than only the winners, provides a broader picture of the trends of women's participation in politics. The low representation of women is not just at the end point but at the starting point itself. The glaring reason why few women get elected is because there are few candidates in the fray. A revealing fact is that there are fewer women contestants than the proportion of women MPs and MLAs. Tables 3 and 4 show the women contestants in the Lok Sabha and the state assemblies.

In the Lok Sabha election of 1996, there was on an average almost one woman candidate for every one seat. The sheer number of women which has steadily gone up does not necessarily mean greater participation of women. This is to be understood in the context of the general increase in the number of candidates in the fray, men as well as women. If the overall view is seen it is clearly seen that in proportion to the total number of candidates the share of the women has not registered any significant increase. Another point to be noted is that the success ratio of women contestants has steadily fallen through out this period.

At the level of the state assembly elections, however, the proportion of women contestants is less than 0.5 per cent. But this does indicate a rise when compared to the past. This increase in the number and the proportion of women contestants has not resulted in an increase in their presence in the legislatures.

This is because as in the case of the Lok Sabha the success ratio of women contestants has steadily fallen. It is an indication that the success ratio of women candidates may

TABLE 3

Women Contestants in Lok Sabha 1952-1996

Year	Contestants per Seat	Share among Contestants (Percentage)	Success Ratio (Percentage)
1952	0.01	2.7	43.1
1957	0.14	4.4	38.6
1962	0.14	3.4	50.0
1967	0.13	2.8	47.0
1971	0.17	3.1	25.6
1977	0.13	2.9	27,1
1980	0.26	3.1	19.1
1984	0.29	2.9	27.7
1989	0.37	3.1	14.3
1991	0.06	3.7	12.0
1996	0.09	3.4	7.9
Average	0.30	3.2	28.8

Source : Seminar, 457, September 1997.

fall further. The logic of free competition in other words is likely to work to the disadvantage of women.

Even though the government is encouraging the democratic process and is providing the necessary conditions for greater participation of women in all spheres of human endeavour, the sad reality is that women's participation in decision-making at all levels is still low. In order to be successful, democracy and development, need maximum involvement of people not only at the national and state level but also at the grass-root level. Panchayati Raj (local self-government) is an important political instrument and a vital conduit for popular participation. Women's participation in democratic development in these institutions, therefore, assumes vital significance. Participation, initiative and leadership in rural political institutions can be of

TABLE 4

Women Contestants in State Assembly Elections (1952-97)

Year	Contestants Per Seat	Share among Contestants (%)	Success Ratio (%)
1952	0	2.7	43.1
1952	0.06	1.2	31.4
1957	0.11	3.1	58.0
1960-65	0.1	2.4	48.8
1967-69	0.08	1.6	35.3
1970-75	0.12	2.5	36.1
1977-78	0.15	2.4	18.5
1979-83	0.16	2.5	23.6
1984-88	0.26	3.1	20.3
1989-92	0.38	3.2	11.8
1993-97	0.47	3.8	8.7
Average	0.19	2.8	21.0

Source : Seminar, 457, September 1997.

immense help to the women living in rural areas not merely for their own empowerment but also in bringing a feminine perspective to the processes of planning, policy formulation and execution of rural development.

Regarded as the first step to reorganise and recreate the Panchayati Raj institutions in modern India, the Balwantrai Mehta Committee was set up on January 7, 1957. This committee recommended a three tier system of local self government, *viz.* : Gram Panchayats, Panchayat Samitis and Zilla Parishads. One of the salient features of the Balwantrai Mehta Committee report was the provision to co-opt or nominate two women in all three tiers after the elections have been held. The committee also specified that the action of these two women should be based on the interest they took in activities they took in the welfare of women and children.

Though not as elected members, this was the first occasion women were given a role in the Panchayati Raj system. It may be underlined here that those who were co-opted invariably happened to be the kith and kin of the rural elite. The empowerment of these Panchayats themselves being uncertain, the few women who were co-opted in these institutions were virtually kept away from the exercise of political power.

Article 40 of the Indian Constitution provides for the establishment of panchayats in the country. Since it is part of the Directive Principles of State Policy, it was not legally enforceable. It was in 1974 that a committee on the "status of women in India" suggested the establishment of statutory women's Panchayats at village level. The purpose of these bodies, in the committee's view, was to look after development and welfare programmes for women and children with resources of their own. The objectives was to ensure that the social and cultural inhibitions that prevented women from taking part in and contesting the Gram Panchayat elections get diluted through these exclusively women's bodies.

It was the 73rd and 74th Amendments to the Constitution, in 1992 which made the establishment of the Panchayat Raj Institution compulsory and legal and the participation by women in local politics the law of the land. By giving this opportunity it was felt that the elected council could become a platform of action, where the rural women interact among themselves regarding the problems. It can also become a training ground for the rural women in the art of polity. As a result of this constitutional amendment, the Draft paper for the Beijing World Conference on Women noted, "around 8,00,000 rural Indian women will be entering public offices in rural areas alone". Introduction of 9 lakhs women (33.3 per cent of the total seats) in the local bodies is a strong and definite step towards empowerment.

The general perception then was that the reserved seats in Panchayats would remain vacant because women by their very nature were not 'political activists'. The intervening years have proven this wrong. Today there are an estimated 10 lakh women in Gram Panchayats at the village level, the block

Panchayats at the intermediate level and the Zilla Parishads in the districts.

Of course this participation is very mixed phenomenon. While a state like Karnataka has a percentage of female representation as high as 46.4 per cent, a so called developed state as Punjab trails behind the rest with a representation of 29.7 per cent, which is even below Haryana, with 33.19 per cent. West Bengal, initiated the measure much before Central legislation and Benoy Chowdhury, the former land reforms minister of West Bengal, is justly proud of the fact. According to him, "more than 35 per cent of West Bengal's Panchayat bodies are women". The former West Bengal relief minister Chaya Bera, adds : "Today no development in rural West Bengal is possible without accounting for woman's views" (*Indian Express*, September 20, 1996).

A survey of women — led local bodies revealed that their priorities are domestic needs — water supply, school, firewood and ration shops. Quite a change from liquor shops, roads and Panchayat ghars (Jain : 1996). The women who entered local self-government has shown that they know what power and politics is all about. However illiterate, however managed by husband or sons and however ignorant of governance they may be.

The 73rd and 74th Constitutional Amendments may be regarded as the crowing achievements of the current decade which guarantees one-third representation to women in all local bodies both in the rural and urban areas and also reserve in one single stroke, one-third of all posts of chairpersons for women. This process of public participation which is a good beginning will take the Indian women into the 21st century.

As Madhu Dandavate says, women have moved from a 'footnote' to an 'objective'. This gives the development process a `women's face (Ahooja-Patel 1998). While this is indeed an achievement, a lot more is required to ensure woman of her rightful place in the society. The more we accept women as individuals, the more egalitarian would be the general climate. The more egalitarian the climate, the more likely would women be participating in all walks of life. Affirmative action, wherever necessary, can provide an opportunity for women's personality and career development. It can certainly contribute to economic and human development of 'mankind' in general and women in particular. But to achieve this, they have to participate more actively in the planning and policy making process than before. As was already mentioned the reasons for low participation may be attributed to the nexus between traditional factors such as caste, religion, family status and feudal economic dependency. As a result, women are generally marginalised in the political process. Bringing women into the mainstream political process is easier said than done.

In the final analysis, women will need to work persistently and consistently at the national, state, district and village levels to understand the policy process and make themselves heard in the relevant bodies and monitor the implementation of plans and policies. The concept of empowerment of women will remain something only on paper, until and unless the women can break from the above mentioned shackles.

REFERENCES

Bhatia Shyam, *Women Tortured in War on Islamists, Guardian Weekly*, 6, October, 1996.

Bhattacharya Malini, *Democracy and Reservation,* Seminar, 457, 1997.

Bunting Madeleine, *Women and the Priesthood, Guardian Weekly*, 29, September, 1996.

Davis Karoline, *Through Reservation and Panchayats,* Women's Link, Vol. 3, No. 3, April-June, 1997.

Desai Neera and Maithreyi Krishnaraj, *Women and Society in India,* Ajanta Publications, Delhi, 1987.

Gore Mrinal, *Women in the Political Process : What Does it Mean* ? in Kaushik Susheela (ed.), *Women's Participation in Politics*, New Delhi, Vikas, 1993.

Jain Devaki, *The 33 per cent Solution : Women in Power — The idea is to change power Equations,* September 22, Times of India, 1996.

Jharta Bhavana, *Women and Politics in India : Impact of Family and Education on Women Political Activists,* D & D, New Delhi, 1996.

Jordan Mary, *Japanese Bank Lose Sex Bias Trial, Guardian Weekly,* 1996.

Katyal Anita, *Leaders Become Learners When It Comes To Women's Participation, Times of India,* February 12, 1997.

Krishna Ahooja Patel, *Merging Gender Inequalities in Asia and Pacific*, RGICS, Paper No. 40, New Delhi, Rajiv Gandhi Foundation, 1997.

Krishna Ahooja Patel, *Development Has A Women's Face : A Paradigm Shift*, Mainstream, April 11, 1998.

Langellier Jean Pierre, *Nepalese Girls Caught Up In Sexual Slavery*, August 28, *Guardian Weekly*, 1997.

Mary E. John, Gender and Development in India, 1970-1990, *Economic and Political Weekly*, November 23, 1996.

Mehta Usha, *Indian Women and their Participation in Politics, Social Change*, September, Vol. 8, No. 3, 1978.

Nandita Gandhi and Nandita Shah, "The issues at stake, Theory and Practice in Contemporary Women's Movement in India", Kali for Women, Delhi, 1992.

O' Kane Maggie, WPC Blues, September 1, 1996.

O' Malley L.S.S., *India's Social Heritage*, Delhi, 1996.

Panicker Lalita, *Rights of Passage, Women in Political Equations, Times of India*, September 20, 1996.

Raghuram Shobha and Manorama Rulli, *Fourth World Conference on Women Gendering Development Issues and Politics, Economic and Political Weekly*, September 2, 1995.

Sen Amartya, *Inequality Re-examined*, Oxford University Press, 1992.

Shah Vidyaben, *Beijing conference towards an equitable society, Social Welfare*, Vol. 42, No. 7, October, 1995.

Sinha Dipanker, *Summit led humanitarianism-towards fourth world women's conference*, EPW, August 26, 1995.

Sushma T.N., Rural Women's March to Beijing, Kurukshetra, Vol. XLIII, No. II, August, 1995.

Towards Equality, Report of the Committee on the Status of Women in India, New Delhi, Ministry of Education and Social Welfare, Government of India, 1974.

UNDP, Human Development Report, Oxford University Press, 1995.

UNDP, Human Development Report, Oxford University Press, 1996.

10

Human Values, Feminism and Social Change

—*K. Ranga Rao* and *P.V.L. Ramana*

Gender, caste and communal prejudices are the bane of contemporary Indian society. Whether or not these have moorings in the tradition and history and if it is so, to what extent and at what stage in history they have become important is not easy to trace the origins authentically. While caste is peculiar to Indian society, gender prejudices are almost universal and in some societies race or ethnicity take the place of caste. As put succinctly by Leela Dube "Caste is not dead; Gender is a live issue. The principles of caste inform the specific nature of sexual asymmetry in Hindu society; the boundaries and hierarchies of caste are articulated by gender" (Leela Dube, 1996 : 21). Unlike others class prejudices are fluid; along with the change in the status of a person in the class hierarchy, his attitudes also undergo change and hence class-based prejudices are not that permanent as are the prejudices based on caste, race, religion and gender. In India today, there is a near revolution in the character of literature produced by different kinds of groups and at any rate in Andhra, feminist literature and Dalit literature have taken new shape since 1980 and 1990 respectively. Recent literature is a product of the writings of those who hailed from the affected categories. Women have been eloquent in expressing and writing about their own problems and the Dalits themselves have come out depicting their own life-situations vividly and this is what we call the 'insiders' view of the social problems. From sociological and anthropological angles these 'insiders' views are bound to have a powerful impact on the attempts for enhancement of the status of the affected groups and the values connected with the process. This calls for an enquiry into the nature of the so-called core values of Indian society *vis-a-vis* the changes expected by the feminists and the Dalits in their respective areas of social interaction, behaviour and social action. In what follows, an analysis of the human and social values in the Indian society, the feministic philosophy and the likely impact of these on the nature of family structure is attempted.

II

Values refer to selective orientations of men and women in a society. They are found in the large and diverse universe of selective behaviour. They are conceptions of the desirable as against the undesirable, influencing the mores or what we call the moral behaviour of individuals and groups (See Williams 1972 : 283). Values are the "higher normative needs of humanity which individuals experience as inner moral or aesthetic imperatives or goal seeking" (Bhajanananda, 1996 : 18-19). While the peripheral values may undergo some change subject to changes in population, technology, economic production and so on, the core moral or human values may remain more or less constant, guiding human social behaviour as also controlling the limits of change in the peripheral values. As pointed out by Williams, "Sociological thought generally attributes strategic importance to moral values in processes of institutionalization and social control" (Williams, 1972 : 286). In the words of Parsons "Moral standards constitute, as the focus of the evaluative aspects of the common culture, the core of the stabilizing mechanisms of the system of social interaction" (Parsons, 1964 : 22).

Dr. Shankar Dayal Sharma, who is an authority on Indian Philosophy, says 'equality, justice, compassion, service, truth, non-violence, concern for the well-being of all, mutual respect for each other's point of view, the spirit of cooperation, friendship and sharing, the yearning to relieve the sufferings of all living things and the aspiration to build true peace are all the core values and ideals of the great religions and philosophies that have flourished in India and all these positive aspects go into the making of India's national identity, national psyche and the personal identity of all of us as citizens of this great country' (*The Hindu*, 15th August, 1996). These qualities, according to him, are responsible for a national as well as global movement for the emancipation of the subjugated, the oppressed and the downtrodden all over the world. Once we accept the above said ones as the core values, it is difficult to explain the aberrations in our social polity over time and in the contemporary society. There were times in history when the aberrations were justified as values and all kinds of actions which we term today as vices or injustices based on gender, caste and religion were supported as desirable ones. This resulted in divergent precepts and practices and a clash in values of different kinds and at different levels. In a given context, however, for the sake of establishing an order, just or unjust, the peripheral values or values of second or third order should be assessed against the moral or first order values known as 'virtues' such as truthfulness, kindness and equality and respect to others and the moral or core values or virtues should be regarded as 'ends in themselves'.

Why is such a culturally great society such as India rocked by prejudices of all kinds ? Swami Bhajanananda offers an explanation to this. According to him 'the explanation lies in the peculiar ethos of Indian people'. Here the word 'ethos' refers to the 'moral temper of a race, or nation, or a community' and the way the people react to various problems and situations in life (Bhajanananda, 1996 : 30). Elucidating the point he writes "the Indian ethos favours the cultivation of certain values such as renunciation, charity, chastity, filial duties and spiritual disciplines. People in this country can be more easily prompted to pursue these values. But the ethos has not been so favourable to the pursuit of some other values such as justice, equality, scientific objectivity, dignity of labour, and collective responsibility. The inadequacy of the ethos of this land is the main cause of this nation's loss of political power, loss of economic prosperity, loss of intellectual vigour and moral stamina, and dismal performance in international sports and games. Social tyranny, and corruption at all levels of administration still persist in modern India mainly because of the supportive nature of the ethos of the people" (Bhajanananda, 1996 : 30-31).

III

Broadly speaking, feminism is commonly used to refer to "all that which seeks, no matter on what grounds to end women's subordination" (Jaggar, 1983 : 5). It first arose in 17th century and recent resurgence occurred in 1960s in the U.S.A. and other places. In India, it became popular since 1980s, though the struggle for Independence under Gandhiji brought women to the fore and recognised the importance of emancipation of women. Starting with a stress on rights and equalities, today feminism talks of women's oppression and liberation. Feminists try to demonstrate the place of gender in social life and how social life is structured, among others, by gender. In the 18th century liberal philosophy emerged with the growth of capitalism and women of upper classes began to claim authority for themselves in social relations or in other words rebelled against traditional male authority. Women pleaded for egalitarianism and individual freedom irrespective of sex, class or creed. The logic put forth by them was that the observed psychological differences between man and woman are not innate and that these are the result of sex-role conditioning. Hence, liberal feminism was for disappearance of gendered psychological and social differences. The liberals listed a number of areas of social, economic and political life in which women were formally and informally discriminated against. They brought to the surface the fact of worse treatment of women at home and at work and the play of double standards of behaviour based on gender discrimination and pleaded for unbiased laws for justice for women and removal of restrictions on the use of contraceptives or right to abortion, etc.

Marxian feminism draws its inspiration from Marxian philosophy. In many respects it is different from the perspective of liberal feminism. Marxism essentially believes that the nature of individuals is determined by the mode of production and their place within class system and the dominant ideology of a society is that of a dominant class. To them, only in a developed socialistic society men and women would be in a position to utilise their mental and physical capacities properly. It is the social being of female or male that determines her or his consciousness. The human consciousness and the social organisation do change along with the transformation of the mode of production. As such, the status of women and the division of labour between sexes will be different in a socialistic society from that of a capitalistic society. In a capitalistic society the nature of upper classes will be different from that of working class. In fact, this means gender-relations are conditioned by class-relations and gender has no independent identity of its own. Borrowing from Engels, Marxists argue that with agricultural surplus, mother right or mother authority was substituted by father right or patriarchy. It is only the end of capitalism that would bring the end of male supremacy. One of the criticisms of Marxist feminism is that Marxist categories are sex-blind and they do not really explain different forms of discrimination against oppression of women in contemporary society. On its part, Marxism rejects the liberal view of freedom as guaranteed by civil rights or considers it as totally inadequate. Within the Marxist framework, the liberalistic values of justice and equality do not have any clearly identifiable place apart from class and mode of production. Marxists believe that the sex-specific form of oppression is rooted in the specific sexual division of labour of capitalism. The dependency of women on men is a function of the economic dependence of wife on husband and the domination of men — is expressed both inside and outside marriage and includes the constraints imposed on women's sexuality resulting in wife-battering, etc. Marxists plead that one way of liberating woman from household harassment is to bring the whole feminine sex back into public industry and make her struggle together with man. Marxists characterise male-female antagonism as friendly antagonism and, therefore, do not see the necessity of gender conflict independent of class.

Radical feminism is the latest strand of feminism. It perceives and interprets the world in terms of gender and assets that the distinctions of gender structure the whole life of men and women. In line with the general social thought radical feminists stress not only that women are made rather than born, but go beyond this and critically analyse the nature of women's oppression in different walks of life. More than any other group, radical feminists vividly bring out the nature of women's oppression in the so-called private life in general and the family in particular and plead for determined efforts to end such oppression. These feminists claim that women's subordination is the root of many other social problems and that women constitute a class and in a patriarchal society men form the ruling class and the removal of male dominance could be accomplished only through a fight by separate and autonomous women's organisations. They are not serious about legal reforms. The issues taken up by them in the U.S.A. and Britain included campaign against anti-abortion laws, better position for battered wives, changes in the law on rape, improvement in child-care facilities, etc. Thus, radical feminists feel the need for struggle against men and this perspective clearly seems anti-male in nature. The slogan "the personal is political" is popular among the radical feminists. It is the view of radical feminists that there is no distinction between the political and personal and every aspect of life is a sphere of sexual politics. It reveals how male power is exercised and reinforced through `personal' institutions such as child-rearing, house work, love, marriage and all kinds of sexual practices from rape through prostitution to sexual intercourse itself. The assumption that these institutions and practices are natural or are of purely individual concern is presented by them as an ideological curtain that conceals the reality of women's systematic oppression. On the whole it expresses strong opposition to patriarchy or women's suppression in all forms. They see sex as a form of oppression independent of social class and to some of them any talk of socialism for removal of oppression is irrelevant. One popular American radical feminist, by name Firestone, based women's oppression in the very fact of reproduction itself and pleaded for artificial child-bearing and for breaking the tie between the woman and the reproduction. To her, the relations of procreation rather than reproduction constitute the base of society. She claims that "beneath economics, reality is psycho-sexual" (See Jaggar, 1983 : 90) and concludes that primary class division is between men and women and this is what is called the materialistic view of history based on sex. The goal of radical feminism is to bring about a change in consciousness and to redescribe reality. The radical feminists use poetry and metaphor to present their view points. Quite a number of feminists in Andhra have echoed these feelings in different poems written by them. The immediate change needed according to their view is that woman should resign control over her body by escaping from forced motherhood and sexual slavery by building a woman culture and separating as much as possible of their lives from those of men. They even plead for escape from marriage and hetero-sexuality (See Jaggar, 1983 : 271). Going further, the radical feminists attack the traditional sex roles within marriage and family, the so-called romantic love and the position of wife as unpaid domestic labourer. The advocacy of the ideal of celibacy and the open advocacy of lesbianism as a final symbol of sisterhood are really radical in character (Banks, 1986 : 230). The radical feminists today attack beauty contests and oppose the presentation of women as a sex object in any form. All these protests are a kind of reflection of opposition to the norms existing in a male dominated society.

Socialist feminism is a synthesis of radical feminism and Marxist feminism and has become popular since 1970. It analyses capitalistic patriarchy using historical-materialistic method and recognises the importance of both class and gender. Together with radical feminism it analyses the power relations and male dominance in the so-called private areas of sexual activity, child-bearing and child-rearing. It views women essentially as a product of social relations and its ideal is full development of women's potentialities irrespective of sex. It subscribes to the idea that in the patriarchal family woman suffers from a special from of alienation from her body. Feminine narcissism is explained as an example of alienation of women from herself and her own potentialities. The goal of socialist feminism is to abolish capitalism as also patriarchy which creates workers and women who are subordinated. To them, sexuality and procreation are a part of the economic foundation of the society. Socialists also subscribe to the slogan 'the personal is political'. It pleads for a total transformation of the social and economic structure including the norms relating to sexuality, parenting educational process, etc. Today woman is seen as nothing more than a sum of her body parts, that is nothing more than a sex object and this view is in line with that of radical feminism, and considers women as alienated as a mother in child-birth as well as in child-rearing. Basing on such notions relating to women's exploitation, socialist feminists want to accord reproductive freedom to women in all its forms and would like to transform the patriarchal society into one which eliminates the gender-structured social behaviour by making child-rearing the job of both men and women and abolition of sex-segregated job market by providing freedom of mate selection and sexuality. Socialist feminists plead for a strategy for change which involves change in material conditions as also change in the existing thinking. As Jaggar says, socialist feminism is firmly in 20th century tradition and pleads for an effective revolutionary strategy which includes techniques for demystifying the prevailing male-dominant capitalist ideology and for developing alternative forms of consciousness, that is, for alternative ways of perceiving reality and alternative attitudes towards it (1983 : 333). Together with radical feminists, socialist feminists plead for women's culture and for encouraging their political organisation by incorporating values of equality, cooperation, sharing, political commitment, freedom from sexual stereotypes and freedom from personal possessiveness. In a way, they are strongly in favour of an alternative to the present-day form of family structure and living by providing a base for men and women to be 'equal nurturers of children' and to each other as well as equally autonomous (Jaggar, 1983 :337).

IV

Thus, from what has been said above it is clear that the entire effort of the feminists is directed towards realisation of selfhood of women in full measure by fighting injustice of any kind and any form she is subjected to in the patriarchal society today. Undoubtedly, this is in accordance with the human values of social justice, which all of us cherish.

All over the world the movement for women's liberation is gaining momentum and the member countries of the U.N.O. are moving towards implementation of the Beijing Resolution on Women, India is no exception to this. The efforts for women's welfare and development in India have roots in the Independence movement. Advocating an implementation programme for the 21st century for fulfilling the basic needs of women Neoleen Heyzer, Director of UNIFEM, pointed out that the recent report on women's progress which was brought out by the UNDF for women has suggested that the world has been witnessing a new phenomenon, the 'feminization of poverty', with 70 per cent of the poorest being women. She identified political and economic empowerment of women as the two immediate steps to be taken for development of women. She also emphasized that empowerment does not simply mean getting elected to public offices; it would essentially have to be empowerment of women at the family level so that women are bale to take their lives in their own hands and take decisions pertaining to families (*The Hindu*, 29th August 1996). Empowerment of women is now recognised as one that includes the right to hold and dispose of property, right to education and political participation. Bina Agarwal, who is doing work on the problems of women in rural areas in SAARC countries comes to the conclusion that absolute right to property including land is an essential part of empowerment of women along with political participation and education (See Eenadu, 25th August 1996 and Bapuji, 1996) though Lowie after reviewing various field work based studies among tribes did not find a positive correlation between property rights and political power even among matriarchal societies (Lowie, 1929 : 1986). The same situation does largely hold good even today.

The problem of gender inequality and the status of women has to be analysed at two different levels — one is, her status in public, and second is, her private — family life which involves intimate personal relations. By and large, the need for granting political, economic and educational rights to women is accepted and governments are taking all legal and administrative measures in this direction. Woman is now placed in all positions in the political set-up and is provided with opportunities for educational advancement in all areas. The Indian Government is proposing 33 per cent reservation to women in all legislative bodies. In all these areas she is tolerated by man as his boss and/or his equal. But the real problem arises in the treatment meted out to her in private life and in the family (See Ramana and Ranga Rao, 1996). The treatment meted out to woman and the liberty she is given in the fields of economic and political activity and in education are no doubt important indicators of her status, but respect to her individuality at the family level is the real test of her 'selfhood' and 'selfworth'. The radical feminists and the socialist feminists, more than the liberal and Marxists are concerned with this aspect of women's status. Writing about the changing status of Indian women, M.N. Srinivas says that "paradoxically as it may seem, as a married couple got older ...... the relationship between the husband and wife became increasingly egalitarian. In fact, if anything, the balance was tilted in favour of the women, but this was concealed more or less effectively by symbols of wifely deference, and expressions of devotion to the lord and master" (Srinivas, 1978 : 19). But we have to note that this happens at the old age and that in cases where the husband appears considerate beyond a point, he is even dubbed as hen-pecked!

Mrs. Amarjeet Kaur is of the opinion that women's movements in India differed from those in the West at fundamental levels. Indian women desired full partnership at every level of activity including decision-making without compromising on the family, which is the fundamental unit of society. In contrast, according to her, the women's liberation movements of the West have assumed that the family was an impediment to the freedom of women (*The Hindu*, 16th August 1996). Suma Chitnis is of the opinion that the perceptions of normal Indian women are different from those of the Western influenced feminists. She identifies three points : the first is, the average Indian women's disapproval of feminist anger, the second is, confused reactions to the feminist emphasis on patriarchy, and the third is, their relative inability to tune in to the demands for equality and personal freedom (Chitnis, 1993 : 319). She asserts that the ideological position of Indian women is so, in spite of the fact that the conditions of Indian women are worse than those of women in America and Europe. The feminist anger in the West is attributed to the "hypocrisy of a culture that accords centrality to the values of equality and individual freedom but nevertheless denies equality to women" (Chitnis, 1993 : 319). She argues that in a hierarchical society like that of India, women cultivated the philosophy of self-denial and she is happy that in India after Independence the Constitution granted equal status to women with that of men and those who pleaded for women equality and women welfare in India were men under the leadership of Gandhiji and others. By implication this would mean that the more the participation of men in women's liberation movements or more the support of men for women's liberation movement less would be women's anger against men and this is what is happening in India.

Referring to the values and their hold on women in India, Suma Chitnis says that the greatest obstacle to change in the direction of gender equality in India is the value system by which women abide. Contrasting the Indian situation with that of the West she says in the West "there is a compulsion to a logical resolution of conflict to confrontation and categorical choice" and in contrast, the Indian culture places a greater value of compromise on the capacity to live with contradictions and to balance conflicting alternatives and this capacity to compromise' could and should be carefully employed to co-opt men in the movement for advancement of the status of women in India. If this is skillfully done, she feels, the women's movement could be lifted "from its current status as a feminist issue to the status of a much larger issue of human rights, which is what is essence it is" (Chitnis, 1993 : 331).

Nivedita R. Bhide says that in the Indian social system the unit of society is not an individual but a family. She says the principle which predominantly ruled in the family was dharma, a word which defies definition in English and 'family' does not mean a group of people related to each other by law or blood or living together; it is a social unit with a definite purpose, namely man making and nurturing of society (Bhide, 1996 : 62-63). These notions exhort self-effacement of not only woman but also of man and this may be taken as expecting man to be considerate to woman and respect her. As put by Nivedita "self effacement at its maximum by each at his or her level, lends sweetness to the family. The more everyone becomes individualistic, the more will be the fragmentation of not only the family but, ultimately, of even the minds and personalities of the family members. That is why in America, when 66.0 per cent of children are now of single parent, crime is on the rise" (Bhide, 1996 : 66).

Apparently the implementation of Nivedita's statement is that for a family to be stable and to be able to perform all its expected traditional functions man and woman should practice self-effacement. It would mean that in a family if both man and woman observe self control and self effacement and avoid confrontation it would lead to diminishment of male egoism and male dominance and enhancement of woman's selfhood, thus leading to harmony between wife and husband and maintenance of family stability. Obviously this strategy of change based on self-denial is different from the one being proposed by the feminists, particularly the radical and socialist feminists, today.

Reviewing the growth of feminist movement in India, Radha Kumar says in 1979 certain women groups launched a campaign against dowry murders and it is felt that it was for the first time that the private sphere of family was invaded. The right wing of Hindu groups were not very much for this kind of agitation (Radha Kumar, 1989 : 22). In fact, a number of women groups put forth arguments against the feminists by accusing them of as "westernized, upper class and urbanised and, therefore, ignorant of, and unsympathetic to traditional 'Indian' society (Radha Kumar, 1989 : 27). A small fringe took this argument saying that the modern views of the feminists were drawn from the capitalistic Western society and were thus incapable of appreciating the nobility of traditional philosophies, especially Hindu. At any rate, it does appear that in India tirade against patriarchy or male dominance could not become that powerful as it could in the West among certain feminist groups and the present Indian ethos does seem to be mainly responsible for this kind of situation. Whether or not the Indian ethos (in the sense used by Bhajanananda) could strongly move in a direction of adopting a positive orientation under the influence of feministic thought, particularly that of radical and socialistic feminism, one would advocate assertion of self and discardment of the philosophy of self-denial, and would yet protect the stability of family is a matter for us to watch and observe the developments as they take place as a part of broad social change. Meanwhile, however, there is a definite need for feminist movements in order to rouse the conscientiousness of the Indian population in general and that of the men in particular in favour of human rights and human worth. After all, there is no gainsaying the fact that for social change to take place, it should be preceded by a strong social movement supported by effective implementation of social legislation.

REFERENCES

Banks, Olive, *Faces of Feminism*, New York, Oxford University, 1986.

Bapuji, B.R., 'Engels and Women's Property Rights', *Economic and Political Weekly*, Vol. XXXI, No. 52, pp. 3400, 1996.

Bhajanananda, Swami, 'Values, Yoga and Reality' in *Values*, Madras, Sri Rama Krishna Math, 1996.

Bhide, R. Nivedita, 'Values in Family' in *Values*, Madras, Sri Rama Krishna Math, 1996.

Chitnis, Suma, 'Feminism : Indian Ethos and Indian Convictions' in Yogesh Atal (ed.), *Understanding Indian Society*, New Delhi, Har-Anand Publications, 1993.

Eenadu, *Telugu Daily*, 25th August 1996.

Jaggar, M. Alison, *Feminist Politics and Human Nature*, Sussex, Harvester Press, 1983.

Leela Dube, 'Caste and Women', in Srinivas M.N. (ed.), *Caste : Its Twentieth Century Avatar*, New Delhi, Viking, Penguin India, 1996.

Lowie, H. Robert, *Primitive Society*, London, Routledge and Kegan Paul Ltd., 1929

Parsons, Talcott, Social Structure and Personality, New York, Press (As quoted in 'International Encyclopedia of the Social Sciences', *Values,* Vols. 15, 16 & 17, 1964.

Radha Kumar, 'Contemporary Indian Feminism', *Feminist Review,* 33 : 20-29, 1989.

Ramana, P.V.L., and Ranga Rao, K., 'Changing forms of gender discrimination and oppression', Forthcoming in *Gender and Society in India,* New Delhi, Manak, 1996.

Srinivas, M.N., *The Changing Position of Indian Women,* Delhi : Oxford University Press, 1978.

The Hindu, 'President's call to safeguard national interests', 16th August 1996.

The Hindu, 'Democratic families', 16th August, 1996.

The Hindu, 'Gender-equality : Progress Report every two years', 29th August, 1996.

Williams, Jr. M. Robin, (Reprint Edition) *Values,* 'International Encyclopedia of the Social Sciences', Vols. 15, 16, and 17, Index complete and unabridged, 1972.

SECTION 3
DEVELOPMENT THROUGH IRRIGATION AND WATER CONSERVATION

11

Sociology of Major Irrigation in India — Some Dimensions

—M. Venkata Reddy

Irrigation in India is an age-old system. However, major irrigation[1] is essentially a post-independence phenomenon. The development of major irrigation has been considered as one of the strategies for fostering much needed rural development. Therefore, heavy investments have been made in the successive five year plans to build a number of projects in different parts of the country. By the end of the Sixth Five Year Plan (1980-85), the cumulative investment on major and medium irrigation projects has been of the order of Rs. 1,50,260 million[2] which constitutes about 78 per cent of the total investment in irrigation. In spite of the large investments made in the irrigation sector and the phenomenal growth of irrigation during the past 30 years, the returns from the investment both in terms of yield as well as finance are very disappointing (Sixth Five Year Plan, 1980-85). The failure of major irrigation projects in yielding intended results in terms of attaining higher yields of crops and social justice has made the planners, technocrats, bureaucrats and also social scientists think about the possibilities of increasing cost-effective benefits.

The objectives and goals of an irrigation project are visualised and expressed by the policy-makers, technocrats and bureaucrats keeping in view the best interests of individuals, communities and society at large. However, many a time these goals and objectives do not converge with the interests of farmers and local resource endowments. This tendency may, in the long run adversely affect social relations. In a country of continental dimensions, endowed with diverse natural resources and human ethos, it is very important to know how the dynamics of society and bureaucracy operate in accomplishing the target outputs estimated by irrigation planners. Thus, an attempt is made in this paper to reflect upon some of the social realities, the cognisance of which is very crucial for the successful implementation of irrigation programmes.

The sociological problems, supposedly being induced by major irrigation projects, have been discussed and analysed in this paper under the following four broad categories :

(a) Problems arising out of a mis-match, if any, between apparently well-conceived theoretical assumptions and estimates and practical field and social realities;
(b) the dominant caste phenomenon as a determining factor in sharing irrigation benefits;
(c) politico-administrative dynamics of the irrigation-bureaucracy in ensuring efficiency and equity of irrigation water availability and
(d) clientele perceptions about irrigation benefits.

Empirical data (if and where available), field instances, and reflections of the author based on his experience, interviews and discussions with farmers and irrigation officials have been cited to illustrate and analyse the problems.

The development of major irrigation could broadly be treated under two distinct, but interrelated phases. The first phase is the construction of dam and the conveyance system, an exclusive domain of engineers, and the second is the utilisation of water where interaction between the bureaucracy and the farmer begins and lasts as long as irrigation supply lasts. Irrigation has hitherto been considered synonymous with the construction of dams and canals and releasing water in the canals. Water distribution, utilization and management, an important phase of irrigation development, seem to have been considered an automatic consequence of the construction phase and has thus received much less attention. In recent years it is being realised that this simplistic view on the utilization phase of irrigation has led to conflicts between irrigation users (farmers) and irrigation owners (state).

These conflicts, it is believed, tend to start at the outlet, the last point in the water conveyance systems (see chart I), and may ultimately lead to a kind of inter-farmer and farmer-bureaucrat polarization. It is necessary to combat the tendency of such events to develop through appropriate and realistic policy interventions in the areas of distribution and delivery of water.

Let us now look at how some of the processes of the development of the irrigation system influence the social structure in the countryside. In doing so we begin, in sequence, with the first category of problems as mentioned earlier. Several socio-logical problems seem to originate from presumably realistic theoretical plans. For instance, the estimation of water-duty[3] (called 'delta' in irrigation parlance), a crucial factor for fixing the extent of Culturable Command Area (CCA)[4], is based on certain macro-level parameters like localization pattern[5], agro-climatic conditions and conveyance and distribution losses of water. The duty thus assumed is expected to be realistic and conform with actual field conditions. Water use and distribution plans are prepared and administered on the basis of this assumption.

The process of operating an irrigation system starts with the notification, season-wise and farmer-wise, of the area for irrigation. This sort of notification provides an unwritten, but implicit, kind of social right to a farmer on the use of water for irrigation. The design of the structural components of irrigation system has, however, certain assumptions built into the framework, such as farmers are normally disciplined, responsible enough to observe a designed cropping pattern and use water economically as per the duty. These assumptions most frequently have to do with the management of the system

CHART 1

WATER DISTRIBUTION SYSTEM

Reservoir

Main Canal

Branch Canal

Distributory

Sub distributory

Minor

Direct Control of Irrigation Department

———————— Outlet ————————

Supervision	Field irrigation channel	Zone of Social Conflicts
	Farm gate	
	FARM	

or the operational policies guiding its use. The management methods are not generally specified and not based on cultural precedents and known or predictable behaviour patterns (Early, 1981). Unaware of the emerging limitations of a theoretically conceived operational plan, farmers enthusiastically prepare lands for irrigation, investing heavily in land leveling and other on-farm developments. It is but natural that a farmer having invested in land preparation will be eager to irrigate all of his area. He tries to maximise returns to investment through a market-economy oriented cropping pattern. This is believed to have led to such hazards of irrigation, as scarcity of water for tail-end farmers and the consequent social tensions in the society.

Bureaucratic Soft-peddling

Before we go into the details of violations by the farmers of the cropping pattern, it is important to know whether irrigation planners are realistic enough in assuming that a particular cropping pattern or localization pattern could be enforced in a given project. In a democratic country, where land is privately owned and skewed towards large holders, is it really possible to enforce a cropping pattern? Mere provision of penal clauses in Irrigation Acts may have much less significance, provided there is a strong political will to implement it. Power conscious politicians are always hesitant about taking hard decisions, which they believe adversely affect their political prospects. In such circumstances the bureaucracy resorts to soft-peddling in administering penal clauses and allow the problems to perpetuate.

It is equally important to know why farmers violate the so called localization pattern. The immediate and apparent reason one could think of its market economy. This apart, it is possible that seemingly effective technical underpins in irrigation design camouflage the practical problems or realities and make the system inoperative. In either case farmers tend to violate the cropping pattern and the problems of inequitable water distribution arise. An illustrative analysis of social dimensions arising out of inequitable water distribution is presented in what follows.

For instance, in some of the major irrigation projects in Karnataka, namely, Malaprabha and Ghataprabha, with a view to extend irrigation facilities to a large number of farmers and a wide area, the localization pattern is based on 40 : 20 : 40 ratio. That means, out of the total culturable command area (CCA), 40 per cent should be earmarked for kharif crops, 20 per cent for two seasonal crops like cotton, chillies, etc., the crop period of which stretches into two seasons, and 40 per cent for rabi crops. From the view point of social justice it appears to be a good design. Because it enables a large number of farmers to share the benefits of irrigation. But a social reality, namely, subdivision and fragmentation of holdings, was given much less importance by the planners when they visualized and put forward an apparently welfare-oriented localization pattern. Of course, consolidation of holdings is one of the objectives of command area development programmes. It has, however, not been possible to achieve consolidation of holding due to a variety of social constraints like deep-rooted attachment to one's own piece of ancestral land. On the other hand, the designers seem to have failed to visualize the need for separate distributaries for kharif, rabi and two-seasonal crops, which would hopefully have facilitated the implementation of the envisaged ratio. Instead, they assumed that farmers follow the ratio on their own, which appears rather unrealistic.

Dichotomy Among Irrigation Water Users

The head-reach and other influential farmers always tend to take advantage of a less realistically planned water distribution system to match with the theoretically conceived localization pattern. This automatically leads to the much talked about tail-enders' problems. The advantageously located once enjoy more than a fair share in the available water supply, leaving little or some times no water to the tail-enders and other weaker sections. This situation seems to have led to a kind of dichotomy among irrigation water users. It is important to know the consequences of such a dichotomous situation.

The survey data from Malaprabha Command Area in Karnataka State have been used to examine and analyse the problems and consequences of inequitable distribution of irrigation water. A priori conclusion that one tends to draw is that it widens income inequalities among farmers. Let us look at the substantive evidence for such a conclusion. Irrigation engineers strictly go by project design and release water accordingly. Minor deviations from the design may be possible temporarily, but certainly not major deviations. Thus, it becomes more difficult to release additional quantity of water, if and when available, to compensate for more than a fair share used by top-end farmers. In such circumstances tail-end farmers are forced to be content with available water.

The irrigation-bureaucracy has not been successful enough to ensure equitable supply of water across space and between farmers because of the less realistic localization pattern. The survey data prove this point in clear terms. This shows that farmers in the head-reaches of canals could use about 26 acre inches[6] of water per cropped acre of a commercial crop (hybrid cotton), followed by about 22 acre-inches by the middle reaches and only about 16 acre-inches by the tail-end farmers. On the other hand, for foodgrain crops water used per crops water

TABLE 1

Area Under Crops by Location

Sl. No.	Crop	Percentage of Area Allowed for Crops		
		Head-end	Middle	Tail-end
1.	Hybrid Cotton	34.0	34.2	8.6
2.	Local Cotton	0.9	—	1.2
3.	Maize	9.4	7.9	5.3
4.	Hybrid Jowar	2.9	4.1	2.9
5.	Local Jowar	8.7	9.2	19.3
6.	Hybrid Wheat	19.7	20.6	9.9
7.	Local Wheat	13.5	10.0	27.2
8.	Others	10.9	13.9	25.6
	Total Area (in acres)	1225	875	2237

Note : One acre=0.4047 hectares.

used per cropped acre has been 11 inches, 10 inches and seven inches in head-reaches, middle reaches and tail-end areas respectively. These variations in water use have resulted in conclusively differential output rate. Less than adequate water made available to tail-end farmers had led to lower yields of crops and thus lesser income. On an average, farmers in the head and middle-reaches of canals have obtained a net output[7] of about Rs. 1,600 per hectare as against only about Rs. 600 per hectare by the tail-end farmers. These inequalities observed in output give a fairly good idea about the possible income inequalities in irrigated regions. We will come to the question of corrective measures a little later.

As a logical sequence, it is also important to examine the cropping pattern which explains the different output. The following table gives the crop pattern at different locations.

It is observed from the table that high-value commercial crops like hybrid cotton are grown predominantly by the farmers belonging to head- and middle-reaches of a canal, whereas the tail-end farmers could hardly grow these crops. Hybrid cotton is grown in only about eight per cent of the tail-end areas, as against 34 per cent each in head- and middle-reaches. Had there been equitable supply of water tail-end farmers could also, on par with others, have grown profitable crops like cotton. In the absence of equity they are left with no option but to grow low-value traditional crops like local varieties of jowar and wheat. This is how the process of income inequalities sets in where the social gulf between the rich and the poor with its attendant problems tend to increase.

The gross value of output per cropped hectare has been worked out from the survey data to understand the process of inequality in substantively clear terms. The value of hybrid cotton output per hectare works out to about Rs. 8,000 as against about Rs. 2,000 each of maize and hybrid jowar, Rs. 1,000 each of local jowar and local wheat and about Rs. 2,500 of hybrid wheat. It shows that locationally advantageous farmers (head- and middle-reaches) could get more income because a higher percentage of their cropped area was being allocated for high-value commercial crops. Others are compelled to grow only traditional low-value crops and get lower income. This illustration makes it manifestly clear that problems of social inequalities emanate from less efficiently managed irrigation systems. In the long run it is likely that the project irrigates income inequalities defeating the very purpose of irrigation. That is why Bagchi (1973), taking a long term perspective, held the view that the canals assisted in the creation of structures within the rural sector which were exploitative and obstructive to efforts to promote growth.

The discussion so far makes one point clear, that theoretically conceived plans for efficient water utilization could not be operationalized, the consequences of which have been analysed. The main contributing factors for operationally less efficient irrigation systems appear to be lack of well articulated rules, demonstrated scientific water-use practices and above all an appropriate legal framework to enforce equitable distribution of water. It was deemed sufficient if a predetermined quantity of water was allowed at the outlet point leaving the distribution of it to the farmers. But in reality, we have seen what has happened.

Introduce Water Rationing Systems

Therefore, how to ensure equity in water distribution is a thousand million dollar question before irrigation planners and administrators. It could perhaps be partly tackled if some structural changes were effected in water distribution policies. For instance, the current system of notifying area for irrigation could be substituted by a relatively more realistic approach. Since government is the owner of irrigation waters in major irrigation projects, it may be easier to exercise control on water delivery, than trying to enforce a cropping pattern on privately owned lands. When, how and how much water a particular farmer uses is difficult to monitor under the existing rules and conditions. That is why, it may be more appropriate and meaningful to introduce water rationing systems, which would indirectly tend to control the cropping pattern also. Water may be allocated with the hour as a unit of measurement or water-hour, we could call it, in proportion to land owned by a farmer. For example, a farmer with one acre of land in the command area may be supplied with water for two hours (two water hours) once in a week, or once in 15 days as the case may be, with a given flow of water in the channel, instead of the present practice where it is said a farmer will get water for one acre to grow a particular type of crop. The former is free to grow crops of his choice and irrigate within allotted water-hours. By experience he could easily decide the kind of crops to be grown with the water at his disposal. This shift from area notification to water-hours may hopefully solve the problem of inequality to a great extent. Of course, this is loud thinking open for a debate. The Warabandi system, if implemented properly would be good enough to solve the problems of inequality, provided the practice of notifying area is dispensed with.

Some of the sociological problems in major irrigation projects could be associated with the dominant caste phenomenon. It is generally held that in India the dominant caste tends to exert significant influence on sharing benefits, either directly or indirectly, from every programme intended for rural development, of which irrigation is no exception. A dominant caste has been defined by Srinivas (1984) as one which enjoys strength of numbers in relation to other local castes, owns a good quantity of the locally available arable land, has a tradition of agriculture, and also of violence..

A majority of the problems related to water distribution in major irrigation projects seem to originate from the traditionally established caste tangles. Deep-rooted traditions get established, the impact of which is reflected in day-to-day actions. Normally, an individual or a family belonging to a dominant caste, with political and bureaucratic affiliations either by lineage or by deliberate action, always takes the lead in deciding matters relating to community work and participation.

Inherent Class Conflicts

Farmers belonging to the dominant caste, I was told, always express a big brotherly attitude in using irrigation waters. This has been corroborated by farmers as well as grassroots irrigation executives. The Scheduled Caste and other backward caste farmers are not generally given a free hand to use water like the dominant ones. Sometimes, they may have to wait till the dominant caste farmers' fields are irrigated. Many a time they are forced to take water during night as they cannot afford to compete with others for day-irrigation. One may argue here, from the view point of getting water to the fields, how does it matter whether a farmer irrigates during night or day and after or before the other. But the intensity of humiliation such disadvantage farmers undergo is beyond measurement by any yardstick. This apart they generally fail to get adequate and timely supply of water, which ultimately leads to lower productivity and hence less income. Less affluent farmers among the dominant castes also seem to be facing the same situation, not necessarily the farmers belonging to weaker sections. Therefore, one should take into account the inherent class conflicts in the country-side while planning for efficient irrigation system.

The findings of an empirical study (Venkata Reddy, 1986) in one of the major irrigation projects, namely Ghataprabha Command Area, have been used here as an illustration. In the Command Area under reference the Lingayat caste is the dominant one. In order to examine the relative efficiency of different caste groups in terms of crop output, which indirectly reflects their accessibility to water, the per hectare value of output has been worked out. It is interesting to note that the per hectare output of farmers belonging to the Lingayat caste has almost been double that of the others. It is about Rs. 4,000 per hectare in the case of dominant caste farmers, whereas it varies between Rs. 1,000 to Rs. 2,000 in the case of those belonging to non-dominant castes like Scheduled Castes and others. Higher output per hectare has been possible for dominant caste farmers essentially for two reasons : (a) They have violated the cropping pattern envisaged in the project plan and grown more high-value commercial crops like sugarcane and cotton and (b) they were able to give reasonably, if not fully, adequate water to the crops they have grown. By virtue of their dominant position in the society they could manage to get a higher proportion in the available water and obtain higher yields. It is commonly held that a farmer, when hopeful of getting adequate water, goes for largest doses of yield-enhancing inputs like chemical fertilizers, hybrid varieties of seeds and other related managerial inputs. Higher crop output among dominant caste farmers could partly be attributed to their use of output augmenting technology. It is a question of farmer's confidence to get, by hook or by crook, water for the crops they intend to grow. Non-dominant caste farmers, not confident of getting adequate water, continue to grow traditional low-value groups. In their case it is a kind of vicious circle : Less inputs — low yields — low income (where low inputs results in low yields and low income).

Increased Litigation

There seems to be other social dimensions of these caste tangles. For instance, many farmers have opined that irrigation has led to increase in water-related conflicts. According to them, lack of socially relevant water distribution policies, coupled with the exploitative attitude of influential farmers, has increased litigations among farmers. For example, major irrigation systems in India are designed for continuous flow, with the expectation that farmers go for night irrigation as well. But, in practice, night irrigation is more an exception than a rule, especially in the irrigation systems of Southern India. Given the option, all the farmers want to irrigate their fields only during the day. Thus, there is competition to use the available water during the day, allowing the night flows to go waste (Chambers, 1986). This situation has led, apart from the wastage of scarce resource (water), to social tensions. While the non-dominant farmers compromise to a great extent with the situation, the competition sometimes appears to be more between the affluent and less affluent among dominant groups. Sometimes it leads even to murders.

To illustrate the point, a field incident may not be out of place here. Once a relatively less affluent farmer had challenged a more affluent farmer of the same caste by not allowing water to his fields during day time. He had diverted the water flow from the field of the affluent farmer to his own. After diverting the water he sat near the turn-gate with a sharp sickle in his hand ready to attack the affluent farmer if he attempted to stop the flow of water to his field. This was reported to the concerned engineer at the division level. When this news came to the engineer, I happened to be in his office discussing about the research study that was under progress. Initially he was reluctant to go there and defuse the situation. Finally, he obliged as I was curious enough to go and witness the scene. By the time we reached the trouble spot, there was already some commotion and the rival farmers were getting ready for a fight. When we asked the less affluent farmer, why he resorted to violence, he pleaded that his crop had completely dried up and thus he had been left with no choice. When we went and saw the crop we found he was speaking the truth. The crop had withered. The affluent farmer never allowed water the others' fields, as the water flowing in the canal was just enough to irrigate his own fields. Irrigation supervisors found it difficult to blame the farmer because he had irrigated the area for which he was entitled. He was legally correct. His not allowing the fellow farmers to take advantage of available water as well as a moral issue which could be considered irrelevant of the situation. But for the timely intervention of the engineer there would have been major violence resulting in loss of life. Several such instances take place because of improper water distribution and lead to social disharmony in the countryside. Thus, Srinivas (1984) has rightly stated that 'caste, class and factional ties and antagonisms become relevant in the delivery of any goods or services to the community. It is essential to underscore this point for irrigation systems tend to be viewed as complete in all respects when the channels reach the fields. In a very important sense, this only marks the beginning of the problem and not its end.

Farmers' Committees for Water Management

It is important to identify the kind of organisational interventions that could have avoided or minimized the caste- and class-based exploitation in irrigation water-use and the consequent tension, litigations, etc. Farmers' participation in irrigation water-management is the talk of the day. Had there been management strategies in the form of farmers' committees at various levels, right from the outlet point and above, the magnitude of the problems could have been reduced to a great extent. Collective or community resistance is always more effective than individual resistance. In this context let us go back to an earlier point where it has been mentioned that water-hour as a unit of distribution may be preferred to notification of area. When a farmer's entitlements for water is fixed in terms of hours in a particular day of a week or a month it automatically creates a sense of ownership. It forms a basis to question everybody who encroaches on one's scheduled time. This arrangement, supported by well-planned and organized farmers' committees at different locations, would certainly reduce if not totally eliminate exploitation by the so-called dominant or influential farmers. Under the current *laissez-faire* kind of water-use system no farmer can question another farmer's right to use water. Water flows in canals and might is the only right to use it, the way an individual wants.

Let us have a look at the third, in sequence, category of irrigation-related social problems : The behavioural pattern of the irrigation staff. It may be interesting to know how irrigation officials are subjected to various pressures and their responses. Irrigation executives work in an organizational frame, with sets of rules and regulations governing different cadres, whereas farmers, whom they have to serve, are free from all such rules. In a way these two groups live in two different social locations and yet move towards a common goal. Here the common goal is to maximize the benefits from scarcely available water resources. In their forward march to reach the common goal, irrigation officials' prime concern is to ensure equity and efficiency and that of the farmer is to maximize profits with little concern for equity. In such a situation the farmers tend to exert pressures on the officials for more water. Irrigation officials are expected to resist such pressers and ensure equity and discipline in using irrigation water. Is it possible for the officials to do so? If not, what are the constraints they face? These are the two important questions that need to be tackled.

Let us start with a promise that in a democratic polity the bureaucracy is highly sensitive to political, social and economic dynamics of the society. They are subjected to political influences, some times facing threats of transfers and other humiliations for non-compliance with pressures from influential people. Caste and class affiliations often influence their behaviour. Sometimes they tend to fall prey to unfair means to augment their own financial resources, with the result that many a time their behaviour takes twists and turns.

Need for Motivation Among Bureaucrats

There are several instances of irrigation officials showing courage and resisting pressures and managing to ensure equity in water distribution. For example, in one of the major irrigation projects of Andhra Pradesh, namely, Tungabhadra High Level Canal Stage I, some villages under distributary seven of Tadpatri Branch Canal[8] have not received adequate water for 11 years though the area was notified for irrigation. The influential farmers at the top-end, I was told during informal discussions, have been cultivating paddy unauthorisedly and never allowed water for tail-end farmers. All the efforts of the irrigation department to prevent unauthorised cultivation seem to have failed due to the nexus the top-enders had with politicians and bureaucrats. Therefore, farmers of the tail-end villages had not been in a position to draw water and were content with rainfed cultivation. However, a committed bureaucrat, as the administrator of the project in the early 1980s, could successfully prevent unauthorised cultivation by farmers at the head-reaches and allow water to tail-end villagers. He managed to get encouragement and support from the district collector and police officials. In spite of that, some of the irrigation engineers associated with the task have been beaten up by the influential farmers. The tribe of such committed bureaucrats is fast dwindling due to too much interference by politicians. In such circumstances, how many officers will be prepared to take the risk of ensuring water supply equitably. Therefore, irrigation engineers fail to perform their tasks and conform to local dynamics by adopting safety-first principles. On the other hand, the engineer responsible for taking water to the tail-end village against all odds, risking his life, was regarded in high esteem by the farmers and was considered a messiah. Farmers volunteered even to construct some of the irrigation structures, and supervise water distribution. If there is necessary motivation in the form of incentives and protection from political interference, irrigation officials hope to prove certainly better.

Sometimes engineers working in their native regions play a different role. For example, in one of the major irrigation projects of Karnataka, there had been scarcity of water for tail-end farmers in a particular sub-division. The concerned Assistant Executive Engineer who hails from the same region solved the problem of scarcity in a different way. He could successfully persuade all the farmers coming under the distributory, where there was acute scarcity of water, to cultivate only 50 per cent of their notified areas, so that all the farmers, irrespective of the location of their lands, could get the minimum quantity of water. This officer being a local man knew the dynamics of the village and prepared an action plan accordingly. But one cannot rule out the possibilities of more problems when a local man is posted. The success however, depends upon the individual's outlook and ability to integrate local skills with resources available.

Difficult Role for Grassroots Executives

The grassroots executives in the irrigation administration have a difficult role to perform. They have no say in the policy formulation nor are their views sought, or given any cognisance if offered voluntarily. Thus, they become cautious about expressing their views on hierarchy-oriented rules and at the same time become answerable to both their clientele and bosses in the department, when they fail to accomplish presumably realistic programmes.

Let us see how sensitive the grassroots executive are to certain irrigation offences of farmers. In one of my periodic visits to some distributaries in Ghataprabha Command Area in Karnataka where an action research on water distribution was in progress in the 1985-86 agricultural year. I happened to come across an interesting incident. The Executive Engineer (Head of an irrigation division) and some of his staff members accompanied me to visit a distributary at about 7 p.m. On our way, at one place a group of four or five farmers were found tampering with the distributary bund to draw water. The officer was very upset about the farmers making a breach in the canal. This was perhaps particularly because a person who did not belong to his department (that is me) had witnessed the incident and might form a poor opinion about his irrigation administration. The engineer shouted at the farmers for breaching the canal and told them that they were liable for prosecution. The farmers maintained their cool and pleaded with the engineer that the field irrigation channel provided by the department to draw water for their fields is defective. In spite of their bringing it to the notice of concerned officer several times the problem had remained unsolved. That is why finally they resorted to breaching the canal and take water. Then the engineer asked the concerned Patkari[9] and supervisor whey they had failed to prevent the breaching of the bund or bring the matter to his notice. They pretended as if they too had come across it for the first time and asked the farmers not to take water from that point. The farmers, however, adamant about taking water from that point, only to save their withering crop. The Executive Engineer ordered a memo to be issued to the Patkari and the supervisor for their neglect of their duty.

Between Two Fires

The next morning I met the concerned Patkari and the supervisor separately and asked them why they had failed to prevent unauthorised use of the irrigation system. Then they came out with the truth. They did bring the farmers' complaint against the defective channel to the notice of their bosses, but were snubbed by them. They were aware that farmers excavated a separate channel to take water. They also knew, I was told, that the alignment of the channel provided by the department is really not correct. But they were afraid to point this out to the officer. Professionally, a supervisor is not competent to question the wisdom of the superior officers who have designed the canal network. On the other hand, if the grassroots executives complain against the misdeeds of farmers to superior officers, they will have to face the wrath of the farmers. Because the officers have often to move alone during night to supervise and monitor the flow of water they feel insecure and find that lives are in danger. Because of such fears they have not reported the breach of the canal by the farmers. That apart, the Patkaris who are mainly responsible for the distribution of water at the field level, mostly belong to non-dominant inferior castes of the same village. Therefore, they find it difficult to act against the wishes of the local farmers. At the same time, they are answerable to the officers. Given our bureaucratic ethos, the staff is not responsible to the farmers, who are the users of the irrigation service but to the bureaucracy (and may be influentials in the command area, including politicians) (Patil, 1988). This kind of a situation often results in different twists and turns in their performance.

The politicians espouse egalitarian objectives while formulating the project plans. In reality they contribute to the maintenance of the essentially inegalitarian local situation. For example, once an MLA encouraged the farmers during a crop season to use water to which they were not eligible. When the concerned engineer took action against those farmers who unauthorisedly used water, he was gheraoed by them at the instance of the MLA. It is unfortunate that this is happening in a democratic polity committed to an egalitarian normative structure. Thus, the bureaucrats, in order to avoid conflict with politicians, compromise with the local situation. The politico-administrative dynamics converge with local dynamics to strengthen the clientele linkages to sustain individual interests. This is believed to have resulted in the disarray of developmental programmes, giving rise to several social problems.

Inter-disciplinary Approach Necessary

After considering some of the field incidents cited as illustrative examples, one question that arises is how best could be performance of the professions and disciplines involved be improved to tackle the problems. One should not take a light view of the situation and regard these as people's problems and, therefore, bound to exist. There seems to be a strong case for an interdisciplinary approach to solve these problems. Engineers should be trained in social sciences to enable them learn skills necessary to solve their day-to-day problems in irrigation administration. Similarly, social scientists and agronomists, associated with the irrigation development, should be trained in engineering aspects of water use, distribution and management. They together should think in terms of the management of people and of the political economy, of who gains and who loses (Chambers, 1980). One common complaint from the irrigation officials, especially from grassroots executives, is the lack of adequate judicial powers for them to punish the farmers who violate the cropping pattern, go for unauthorised cultivation and tamper with the irrigation structures. All these ultimately depend upon the political will, which is well beyond the purview of researchers and administrators.

So far, we have given an account of the problems associated with the limitations of theoretical assumptions in irrigation planning, the dichotomy of irrigation users (farmers) and the behaviour of irrigation officials. Now in this section we hope to give an overview of the views of the beneficiaries about irrigation and its impact.

The introduction of irrigation in a traditionally dry region gives rise to certain hopes and aspirations among the clientele (people benefited by a given project). They visualize some changes in the socio-economic set-up in the light of the anticipated higher yields of crops under irrigated conditions and the consequent higher incomes. It is important to find out to what extent these changes visualize by them have been realised.

People (it includes agricultural labourers and other service classes and not necessarily the farmers) are almost unanimous about the positive impact of irrigation on overall levels of their living. But a majority of them feel that it has heightened the income inequalities in rural areas. This viewpoint confirms the empirical findings we have presented earlier. However, there is a feeling among the traditionally dominant groups that though irrigation has helped consolidate their economic position, it has generated a threat to their authoritarian leadership at the grassroots. Irrigation has provided some kind of insurance against the total failure of crops. This has minimised the economic dependence of the non-dominant and socially oppressed classes on the dominant and rich farmers. Assured output, even if it be little, under irrigated farming creates confidence among the economically backward farmers and gradually makes them resist the authoritarian attitude of dominant groups. Some of these challenges emerging at the village level appear to be causing concern to the caste-based or lineage based leadership. Because of these fears the dominant groups try to sabotage the plans aimed at an egalitarian distribution of water. For example, some of the progressive measures like 'Warabandi'[10] system of irrigation have failed to make any dent, especially in Southern India.

Increasing Addiction to Alcohol

The increase in income levels, as reported by a majority of farmers is reflected in the conspicuous expenditure on luxury items. It is true that Engel's law operates more effectively in less developed countries. But what is disturbing, according to local people, is the increasing addiction to liquor many people in the village after the introduction of irrigation. Hitherto, consumption of liquor had attracted a social stigma in the countryside. That is why if some people, especially those belonging to the upper social strata, wanted to drink occasionally, they used to do so stealthily without attracting any attention. But the affluence brought about by irrigation has changed the outlook of the people. Now, drinking is considered a necessity by many and no more attached to a social stigma.

Radical changes seem to have taken place in food habits too. The shift from inferior cereals like jowar, ragi (millets) to superior cereals like rice and wheat is conspicuous in the irrigated villages. As reported by some farmers, they are even able to come out of certain religious rigidities regarding food habits. For instance, eating non-vegetarian food is prohibited among certain caste groups. But after the introduction of irrigation, rural-urban linkages have increased. Frequency of visits to the neighbouring towns and market centres by the farmers has increased because of the necessity for more purchases of inputs like hybrid seeds, fertilizers and pesticides. The farmers are now exposed to new varieties of food, especially non-vegetarian. When they go to restaurants in the town along with friends they prefer to take food of their liking which is not possible in the village because of rigid customs and also non-availability. Of late, this tendency has even reached the village. If cooking such food is not allowed at home, a small group of people get together and cook at some other place. Once I was staying in a village in Dharwad district of Karnataka, where the majority of the population are Lingayats (Lingayats are one of the dominant castes in Northern Karnataka and are strict vegetarians). I was invited by the Village Level Worker (VLW), now known as Gram Sevak (GS), who was a Lingayat, and some other farmers in the village belonging to the same caste, I was under the impression that the dinner would be in the house of one of the farmers and vegetarian. But to my surprise I was taken to a lonely house and non-vegetarian food was served. I was surprised, because on an earlier occasion, when conducting a benchmark study in the same village, in the pre-irrigation days, we asked a person, who was running a small hotel to prepare egg curry. He refused, saying that it was not possible to prepare non-vegetarian food. But in the same village, after a lapse of just eight years, chicken curry was prepared and served. I was told that many people had started eating non-vegetarian food. This change in outlook they attribute partly to affluence and more to urban linkages, after irrigation.

Changes in Marriage Customs and Relations

Marriage is an occasion when one wants to exhibit one's affluence through social extravaganza. Apart from lavishly spending money on marriages, the outlook on kinship and other related issues too seem to have changed in the post-irrigation days. The prosperity brought by irrigation has motivated people to go beyond the traditional local kinship ties for matrimonial relations. The shift from known nearby kinship circles to far off urban centres is perceptible. Improved income levels following irrigation have made farmers think of matrimonial relations with the urban-oriented service class. In the past they used to confine matrimonial relations only to traditional agricultural families.

Yet another interesting effect of major irrigation is in-migration of land-poor agricultural labourers and land-rich farmers. These two types of in-migrants have both positive and negative effects on the local peasantry and socio-cultural values. Several empirical studies confirm that irrigation, accompanied by the cultivation of high value commercial crops like hybrid cotton, sugarcane, paddy, etc., increases employment opportunities. This creates more demand for seasonal labour. Non-availability of adequate labour to meet the demands of newly introduced crops in irrigated tracts, makes farmers look out for immigrant labourers to supplement the locally available labour-force. It is here that a kind of polarization starts emerging between local and migrant labourers. Local labourers always consider the migrants a threat. Because, had they not come, the locals feel, their bargaining capacity for higher wages would have been more. Breman (1985)[11] says that in-migration can contribute to the immiserization of the local landless labour, as in the case of the Halpatis in South Gujarat, who have to compete with a stream of migrants and 'find themselves cntrapped in a process of acute pauperization' in an area enjoying accelerated economic growth from irrigation.

Farmers welcome in-migrants as they help meet labour requirements for timely sowing and harvesting without depending too much on local labour. Otherwise, they had to resort to forward trading in order to ensure availability of labour in the peak seasons. Forward trading here means lending money or food grains to labourers to bind them to an agreement to come for work during the peak season. This agreement is based on an understanding that the ruling wage rate at the time of harvesting will be paid. Many farmers are reluctant to employ permanent labourers (called zetas in some Southern states), a practice prevalent for several decades, because of the fear of political overtones to such an institution as a form of bonded labour. Therefore, they look out for temporary labourers.

Recruitment of Labour From Other Areas

In the process of drawing surplus labour from dry regions to irrigated regions, an intermediary class, a sort of commission agents appears to be emerging for supplying migrant labourers to meet local farmers' needs. These agents, I was told, go to areas of dry land cultivation and recruit labourers and bring them in groups to the villages where there is a demand. They take care of the initial needs of these labourers of food and shelter and fix up their wages. In the bargain they get commission from both the parties — the labourers as well as the farmers. Sometimes the farmers themselves go to distant places, negotiate with the agents and bring back groups of labourers. The local labourers ignore their own caste differences, about which they are otherwise very particular, and unite to dissuade the migrant labourers through indirect means. They do not accept even migrants of the same caste and treat them with contempt. This shows how social interactions change at times of threat perceptions with regard to livelihood.

The in-migration of labour is generally highest during the harvesting season. The interesting part is that certain village systems are well adjusted to accommodate both local as well as migrant labourers during peak seasons. For instance, weekly marketing is an important factor in rural areas. These are held in most of the big villages. Locally known as Shandis, these markets are normally start at about 10 a.m. and go up to 5 or 6 p.m. But during the harvesting season the market timings are adjusted to the convenience of the labourers. Once I was staying in a village in the Malaprabha Command Area, in Karnataka, in connection with a research study, I observed that the market started at about 3 p.m. and went up to 10 p.m. I was somewhat surprised. On enquiry I was told that the market timings had been adjusted to suit labourers who leave for work in the morning and come back by evening. Even the food grains and other materials are made available according to food habits of the migrant labourers. This is another illustration of how social systems adjust to local needs.

In-migration of land-rich farmers to major irrigation projects adds another dimension to the local social fabric. Though land-poor labourers and land-rich farmers migrate to irrigated tracts with a common purpose, namely, earning more income and stable livelihood, the interest of the former is temporary and that of the latter a permanent one. When farmers migrate to a new socio-cultural set-up with a view to settle down permanently, they try to understand the social behaviour and cultural norms of the region and adjust to it in the initial years, until they are able to find a strong base. After a few years, the local farmers feel that the migrants are showing their true colours, which some times come in conflict with the locals and create problems. The details of such problems should be treated in a historical perspective, which is not within the scope of this paper.

The positive impact of migrant farmers on irrigated farming may be worth looking at. They often come from both dry as well as irrigated regions. Farmers migrating from irrigated regions bring along with them irrigated-agricultural technology which is most important for a traditionally dry-cultivated region. These migrants at times serve as agricultural extension agents. For instance, most of the migrants to the Tungabhadra Command Area in Karnataka are from the traditionally irrigated coastal districts of Andhra Pradesh. They have a rich experience of paddy, sugarcane and cotton cultivation. When they migrated to the Tungabhadra area, they had no problem in adopting the technology which they were quite familiar with. Therefore, their crop yields were quite high, when compared to the yields of the local farmers. Local farmers are divided in their opinion about migrants getting higher yields and their consequent prosperity. Some are of the view that the migrants work day and night like devils to get more production. The locals are contemptuous of them. But some others have taken up the challenge of an equal if not a higher yield than the migrants, by following their farm practices and application of input. They visit the migrant farms, discuss with them and learn the irrigated-agricultural technology. This is the positive aspect of the demonstration effect of the migrants on the locals. This kind of healthy competition is praiseworthy and should be encouraged. Therefore, in-migration seems to have left a mixed impact on the socio-cultural scene of an irrigated project.

Failure to Appreciate Social Reality

Irrigation has, no doubt, improved the economic conditions of the farmers. However, an egalitarian distribution of these benefits has not been possible due to a variety of technical and social problems. The planners, technocrats and bureaucrats have not succeeded in appreciating the social realities and integrating them with the apparently welfare-oriented technical designs of an irrigation project. This has resulted in a skewed distribution of benefits from irrigation, widening the already existing social gulf between the rich and the poor.

Traditionally established caste-based local dynamics has played a determining role in using available water in canal common areas. The absence of well-articulated rules regarding water-use and distribution has helped dominant groups to appropriate more water to grow high value crops and obtain higher incomes. While politicians converge with local dynamics to consolidate their power-base, so essential in a democratic polity, the bureaucrats have remained sensitive to local dynamics and cautious in their actions. In the process influential groups in the society have appropriated the maximum benefits from irrigation.

The prosperity brought by irrigation has changed the outlook of the people in terms of food habits, cultural norms and matrimonial relations. Water-related conflicts have increased over a period of time. There is an imperative need to study the social realities before a project is formulated and to integrate them into the project design. This would help avoid social conflicts and attain socially desirable and economically viable benefits for all from irrigation. The in-migration of land-poor agricultural labourers and land-rich farmers had had a mixed impact on the local social fabric.

A closer look at the labour requirements in irrigated tracts is necessary. The strategies required to meet the increased demand for labour should be worked out and integrated in the project plan. When in-migration of labour is inevitable or in a way good from the view point of providing employment opportunities, necessary steps should be taken to reduce their exploitation by middlemen. Some kind of labour camps with facilities for stay could be organised at important places or clusters of villages. This might even help to reduce the possible tensions between local and migrant labourers.

NOTES

The author wishes to thank Dr. M.V. Nadkarni, Institute for Social and Economic Change, Bangalore, for his useful comments on an earlier draft of this paper.

(An earlier version of this paper had been presented at the Seventh World Congress for Rural Sociology, held at Bologna, Italy, 26 June-2 July 1998).

1. According to the revised classification made in April 1978, projects having Culturable Command Areas (CCA) of more than 10 thousand hectares each are classified as major projects, those having a CCA of between two thousand hectares and 10 thousand hectares as medium schemes, and those

having a CCA of two thousand hectares or less each are classified as minor irrigation schemes.

2. Computed from the data taken from The Seventh Five Year document, 1985-90, p. 73.
3. Area to be irrigated per unit of water is called water-duty.
4. The total area that could be irrigated with a given storage capacity of a reservoir is known as Culturable Command Area (CCA).
5. Demarcation of area to different crops under a given irrigation project is called localisation pattern. This is mostly confined to irrigation projects in Southern India.
6. Since water is not supplied on a volumetric basis, it is difficult to measure the quantity of water used by the farmers. However, the number of irrigation given by each farmer, selected for the study, to the crops they have grown has been taken as a proxy. Depending upon the time taken to irrigate a plot with a given flow of water in the canal, the quantity of water in terms of acre-inches has been estimated. For example, if a farmer has allowed one cusec of water for one hour for an acre of cropped area it is considered one acre-inch.
7. Net output has been arrived at on the basis of cost 'C' concept used in farm management studies.
8. The author personally visited the Command Area. Observations made here are based on discussions with irrigation officials and farmers.
9. A person, who looks after water distribution and management at the field level, is the lowest cadre in the irrigation department.
10. Supply of water by rotation on a predetermined day and period of time, on the pro-rata basis of land owned by a farmer is known as Warabandi system of water distribution. This system, if implemented properly cuts into the freedom of farmers to use water the way they like. That is why big farmers are generally not inclined to its implementation.
11. This has been quoted by Robert Chambers (1988) in his article, 'Irrigation Against Rural Poverty', published in J.S. Kanwar (ed.), Water Management — The Key to Developing Agriculture, Agricole Publishing Academy, New Delhi.

REFERENCES

Bagchi A.K., "Foreign Capital and Economic Development in India, A Schematic View", in Gough K. and Sharma H.P., (eds.), *Imperialism and Revolution in South Asia* (New York), 1973.

Chambers Robert, "In Search of Water Revolution : Questions for Managing Canal Irrigation in the 1980s", *Report of a Planning Workshop on Irrigation Water Management*, International Rice Research Institute, Phillippines, 1980.

Chambers Robert, "Canal Irrigation at Night", *Irrigation and Drainage Systems,* Vol. 1, No. 1, 1986.

Chambers Robert, "Irrigation Against Rural Poverty" in Kanwar J.S. (ed), *The Key to Developing Agriculture*, Agricole Publishing Academy, New Delhi, 1988.

Early, E. Alan, "Irrigation System Management and Improvement Methodologies Developed in the Phillippines, Discussions paper for the Workshop on Methodologies for improved Irrigation Systems'', Management Research, Coimbatore, India, September 21-26, 1981.

Government of India, Planning Commission, Sixth Five Year Plan, 1980-85.

Patil R.K., "A Neglected Phase of Benefit Cost Analysis in Irrigation Development" in Kanwar J.S. (ed.), *The Key to Developing Agriculture*, Agricole Publishing Academy, New Delhi, 1988.

Srinivas M.N., "Inaugural Address at the International Conference on 'Community Responses to Irrigation in South Asia'', held at Bangalore, India, 4-6 January, *WAMANA*, Vol. 4, No. 4, October 1984.

Thavaraj S.H., (1976), "The Importance of Integrating Non- engineering Aspects in Irrigation Systems Design, in Taylor Donald C and Wickham Thomas H. (eds.), *Irrigation Policy and the Management of Irrigation Systems in South-East Asia*, The Agriculture Development Council, IAC, Bangkok, 1979.

Tungabhadra Project Command Area Development Authority (Anantapur, A.P.), Final Report of Integrated Water Management in 7th Distributary of Tadpatri Branch of Canal of HLC Stage-1, 1980.

Venkata Reddy, M., "Water Use Efficiency in Ghataprabha Command Area — Preliminary Report, Institute for Social and Economic Change, Bangalore, India, 1986.

12

Irrigation Management Transfer — Farmers' Participation and the Role of Social Action Research and Diffusion Process : A Conceptual Framework

—D. Sundaram and *A. Thandeeswaran*

Introduction

The use of water for irrigation has a management dimension wherein self-management, participatory management and administration transfer are the concepts that are being used. Irrigation Management Transfer (IMT) is a concept over which the social scientists have directed their enquiries. It is a social process to cause social change through farmers' participation and voluntary social action. As a key strategy of social change, it seeks to involve the total participation of the farmers for equality in the control and maintenance of water as a natural resource use. That the irrigation management in our society has been becoming an increased state-craft and shaping itself with a monolithic character, is the issue. De-emphasising and replacing that situation with farmers' participation has certain conceptual issues and action principles that require theoretical orientation and clarification.

Farmer, Social System, And Participation

Conceptually, the farmer is bound by the features of the social system. The way in which the farmer behaves when he is between the two ends of the resource utilisation continuum, namely, resource allocation to him and resource control by him, hence, has to be understood in the light of his socio-economic outfit. Relating his behaviour to his socio-economic outfit, along with a critical analysis of his dependency on the resource distribution structure, *i.e.*, both the irrigation bureaucracy and the village power structure, is a challenge to the participatory social action researcher, who, if not a behavioural scientist, will find it difficult to have a grip over the issue. Very often, the change agents, without the behavioural science knowledge of the community dynamics, become a victim or captive of the structure they wish to change.

Farmers in India, today, are stripped of their collective involvement. The traditional village institutions, in the process of change, have divorced themselves from the philosophy of "each one according to his ability, to each one according to his need" and have developed fragmented collectivism and exhibit fragile individualism. The forms and structures of the spirit of farmers' participation in the traditional irrigation management (we call it non-institutionalised and non-professionalised one) have to be recaptured after a critical evaluation and made use of in the contemporary, institutionalised irrigation management.

The need is, now to combine appropriately the traditional and the contemporary frameworks. In this context, the ordinary farmer might be educated in such social skills of traditional participatory process and the invasion of the institutionalised and professionalised irrigation services may have to be minimised accordingly. The spirit of voluntarism has to be revived through a process called organised voluntary effort by which the farmers would feel the need to get something done which needs doing when that is not attended by anybody else or when that is attended by some body which does not have any sense of farmers' traditional participatory process. This conscious and organised participation becomes a new social process in the irrigation management exercise. The existing institutions of irrigation should, therefore, enrich themselves with the spirit of farmers traditional voluntary participation and the practice of farmers new conscious and organised participation.

Dimensions of Farmers New Participation

The farmers' participation should be able to convert the

deficiencies and should be an instrument in achieving the desired object. What are the dimensions of the new participation? Borrowing from behavioural sciences, participation as an ideal-ladder-type ideology may be looked into as an action framework for farmers participatory process as follows :

Farmers' Control

8————————————8

Delegation of Power

7————————————7

Partnership

6————————————6

Placation

5————————————5

Consultation

4————————————4

Information

3————————————3

Therapy

2————————————2

Manipulation

1————————————1

In the above framework, as given in the form of ascending steps of ladder, there are specific action strategies. The farmers who remain apathetic are to be manipulated and injected into them with a sense of involvement (therapy). The exercise is to be integrated with three other strategies, namely, information, consultation and placation by which the involvement of the farmers will be established. These three strategies are to be further consolidated by institutionalising the farmers as partners and delegating an extent of power to them and ultimately enabling them to have control over the resources management process.

Conditions For New Participation

Perception of attitudes of the farmers and the perception

of responses of the farmers should be the two conditions for farmers' participation. The situations in which the contemporary farmers get themselves entangled have to be considered. The conflicts generated by individual and group interests of farmers in today's society lead the farmer to take opposite camps on the problems and priorities of the issues in water use, particularly, in water distribution and conservation. So, those who develop the essence of participatory process should have the ability to perceive the attitudes of the farmers in the sense of their origination. The capacity to see things 'as is where is' (what is the meaning of this phrase?) is a fundamental necessity for those who develop the participatory process. Not only that the perception on the part of social action researcher in irrigation is an essential condition, but also developing a positive response from the farmer is a necessary condition which will transform the sufficient elements of farmers' participation into efficient elements.

A Framework of Knowledge and Action

Theoretically, a discussion of Action and Institution framework, contribute the basis of how human social interaction is organised. The knowledge on this aspect may be briefly explained that the human individuals, be they the farmers or anybody else, have several things within their conscious knowledge in an unconscious level and that every one of their actions with the knowledge base provides capabilities as taken for granted. The agents or outsiders as experts do put in more efforts to define what the knowledge is and what the capability is. At the same time the clients have no understanding of what the agents do propose as a consciously significant one. The 'unconscious conscious substance' among the clients, *i.e.*, farmers in the context of irrigation, is a framework to be pondered.

To clarify our standpoint, let us borrow from Anthony Giddens' definition of 'action,' as he cites the illuminating of Erwing Goffman. According to Giddens, 'action' refers of two components of human conduct, which he calls, 'capability' and 'knowledgeability'. 'Capability' implies the possibility that the actor 'could have acted otherwise' or that he is 'capable of a range of potential alternatives of conduct'. 'Knowledgeability' implies that the members of a society know a great deal about the workings of that society, and must do so if that society is recognisably a 'human society'. Knowledgeability is not to be equated with what is known 'consciously' or 'held in mind' in a conscious way. The knowledgeable character of human conduct is displayed above all in the vast variety of tacit modes of awareness and competence which actors chronically employ in the course of daily life. The vast bulk of day-to-day social activity is predicated upon 'capability' and 'knowledgeability' of the social actors. Giddens calls this 'practical consciousness'. Goffman's writings, notes Giddens, display a strong awareness of each of these features of human action. Goffman treats human beings as capable and knowledgeable agents, who employ such capability and knowledgeability routinely in the production and reproduction of social encounters. The subjects Goffman portrays for the most part know what they are doing and why they are doing it : but much of this knowledge does not operate at an immediately conscious level. He shows us many of this knowledge does not operate at an immediately conscious level. He shows us many of the things we 'know' about social conventions, and other aspects of society, but which we 'know' in a tacit rather than an explicit sense. They become clear to us only when Goffman points them out, but nevertheless we do already know them : and very dazzling and complex these forms of tacit knowledge turn out to be, however much we ordinarily take them for granted as members of any given society. Of course, this is not to say that Goffman is only concerned with tacit knowledge or practical consciousness; rather he shows how the tacit and explicit are interwoven in the texture of every day social activity (Giddens 1981).

This theoretical standpoint on the convergence of knowledge and social action highlights how farmers as social actors are to be reckoned with by the agents of social action programmes for IMT. Although it may appear that capability and knowledgeability of the farmers in a given social context are more subtle than explicit, the real situation is such that this conceptual understanding is a basic requirement by social action agents. In a sense, social action process is an educational programme, although not a formalised one. It is a pedagogy intended for mobilising the community in realising the 'unconscious consciousness' to a plane of action and using it for institution building. It is, hence, a participatory educational process.

Social Action Research as a Participatory Educational Process

Although the social action research is demystifying, appropriate and useful one for community action, it should have the component of educational approach to develop problem-solving orientation among the participants. That creates an ideological interaction among the participants of the resource use, through which everyone learns critical corporate self-consciousness and develops himself.

The participatory concept in social action is well elucidated by educational researchers, particularly, by those like Paulo Friero. His insistence on participatory education has forced a re-examination of the relationship between education and its clients. According to him, human beings all through the history exhibit a fatalistic outlook that the ordinary persons need no choice and are vulnerable to being crushed by the strong as a legitimacy. They accept the imposed change passively without understanding its implications. It is all the more true in the existence of farmers of different social classes in the given tank or canal system and, therefore, the exploitation and oppression occurs. To such a situation, Friero, in his 'Pedagogy of the Oppressed', has outlined a methodology of social action. It underlines the sociological dimensions of oppressive structures and suggests to transform the perspectives of the participants. The encodings of critical consciousness and defining their own solution are the ultimate outcome of Friero's participatory component of social action, particularly, through education.

Social Science Research and Participatory Social Action

Participatory social action research was a result of the endeavours to suggest an alternative to the over-simplified, alienating, and ill-efficient survey research. Responding to the call of Friero, Budd Hall of Canafa and Francisco Vio Grossi of Chile formulated the need for participatory research for social action the context of social sciences development, and as a response to the myth of objectivity in social sciences research. While Hall listed the short comings of survey research, Grossi realised that the established notion of scientism model of social science as diagnosing trends of change in society tended to know more and more of less and less. These responses led to the development of the 'critic' position of social science of 1970s, as a recognition of the divergence between the elite notion of theoretical and methodological discussions and the realities of socio-economic problems of the less privileged. Participatory social action is nothing but the action of the communities themselves to investigate their reality to transform it. The community should become research oriented in the sense that the social scientist must anchor his objectives and methods in the base of the community in which he works. Hence, it is a step forward as it is both a research for the masses and a research produced by the masses.

To sum up, the emergence of participatory social action as a process for social change is a due to the recognition that the social science should have a quest for precise efforts in solving critical social situation. Its advocates codified that it is only research but also an educational and social mobilisation process.

In the context of the increased and precise effort in solving problems through social action, social science is said to have a demonstrable feasibility. At the same time, there is a dichotomy between the feasibility of social science and the credibility of social science. The much talked about techniques of research sophistication, though enable the feasibility, do not reflect the understanding of reality, and thus, the credibility of the social science is in crisis. It is all the more true in developing countries, where the feasibility-credibility gap is evident between social science research and its end-use. This gap may much be attributed to the several short-comings of the survey-research approach and to the changing concepts of development. An effort may be envisaged in closing the gap by combining the community participation in decision making. This refers to the efforts in developing research approaches which involve those persons who are 'expected beneficiaries' of the social action. It is said to focus on involvement of those who are traditionally the researched in formulation, collection and interpretation of information.

In brief, the participatory social action research —

- — provides immediate and direct benefit to the community;
- — involves the community or population in the entire research project from the formulation of the problems to the discussion on seeking solution and the interpretation of findings;
- — remains as a total educative experience which serves to establish community needs and awareness, and commitments within the community;
- — acts as a dialectic process — a dialogue over time and not as a static picture from one point in time;
- — liberates human creative potential;
- — mobilises human resources for the solution of social problems and
- — implicates ideological contest also.

The Tanzanian example of the application of participatory research process responding to a local concern about spoilage of food after an abundant harvest is an excellent example of the relevance of participatory social action process in the field of innovation in the community. The participatory social action, thus, concentrates on the process of knowledge consciousness among persons, as both individuals and groups, in sustaining behaviour by knowledge and explanatory theories on the conditions under which people are willing to behave consistently with the best interest of better resource use. The place of formal education in creating and accumulating knowledge is only a foundation that has to be expanded by a continuing-education process.

Village Dialogue is an approach that puts villagers' perception of the problem; aimed not to impose an alien analysis of the problem on the villagers but to work from the basis of their perceived and understood reality. Mass participation in decision making and the use of adult education is a vehicle for liberation (Hall 1975, Norgi 1976, Mounda 1976). 'Discussion-groups' provides the possibility for engaging in the social act of 'naming the world' (Freiro 1971), through which individuals' awareness of their reality increases and they develop a confidence that they themselves can improve their situation. When discussion-groups are also 'action-implementation-groups, the balance between reflection and action is achieved and it is possible to mobilise human energies on a vast scale. Here, the convergence of non-formal education with formal education for obtaining, ultimately, the water conscious society has to be highlighted. The need for learning rather than teaching (simply, the transmission of information) is most important towards sustainable water use and management.

Interest-Groups and Motivation

Farmers as groups and the changing nature of Interest-groups in general and irrigation in particular, for instance, women as interest-groups, need to be analysed and integrated into the participatory social action in irrigation. The existing knowledge of women in development and women and development has certain convergence of sociological issues, namely the integration of 'domesticity' into 'externality'. Herein, the dominance of ideological consciousness about women as a secondary human resource confined with the roles of domesticity needs to be confronted and the rural women are to be converted into interest-groups in the Turnover System in irrigation management. The examination of the size of women-groups as interest-groups and their impact on the policy making process are the needs of the hour. The farming system is not devoid of the involvement of women as a human resource, as they are currently involved in weeding, watering, harvesting and post-harvesting works in the field, and processing and storage of grains, besides the routine domestic chores. The sociological issue, here, is to explode the conventional myth that men alone are interest group in Irrigation Development scheme and to integrate women also within the interest group mechanism in irrigation. Thus, the farmers' association and water users' association in irrigation must be analysed within the framework of interest-groups for participatory social action.

Related to the interest group concept, a closely analogous idea is the motivation of farmers by organising themselves in the management transfer programme. The actual problem, here, is not in the creation of awareness of the programme in the farmers. The problem is, if the farmers do not perceive it to be in their interest, the motivation for participation will be minimum or peripheral. The motivation process and interest structure among the farmers do not go together automatically. As it is said in the AID document of 1982, "it should be the actual motivation of that particular group of farmers and not what someone imagined would be the motivation if he were the member of that group". The Handbook further clarified that the source of motivation may be different for different groups. For example, if one group is motivated by the desire for increased power and prestige, another group may desire to follow opinion leaders and so on.

Social Action and Diffusion

Social action for irrigation management transfer and the diffusion and adoption of IMT, go beyond institution-building and structural change. Besides giving lectures through social action to popularise the irrigation management transfer, the question of diffusion for adoption of IMT in a given spatial system is a dimension in farmers' participation process in irrigation management. It is often said that the diffusion for adoption will be a possibility when the perception of farmers is reinforced by the fact that the on-farm development benefits to them are obvious. If the social action research does not concentrate is making these benefits obvious, the diffusion of the practice will not be effective. Thus, the social action agencies are supposed to convince every farmer about the obvious benefits rather than just making them aware in broad terms of the new system of farmers participatory process. To meet this, the social action research in an area has to establish co-ordination among all the agricultural development agencies.

Further, the development of the diffusion process in the

social action research cannot ignore the power-structure of the farmers, as the power structure of water use is distinctly different. Water as a natural resource has the characteristics of common property. Also, water for irrigation by farmer is not a consumption product, not an input, but it is increasingly getting commoditised first and then becomes a consumption product/input. The nexus between this fact and the existing farmers' power-structure has to be reckoned with by the social action researchers, to motivate the farmers in a given spatial area through various development agencies. In this process, the power of the opinion leaders of the farming community happens to be the main source of information about the management transfer process. The link with these opinion leaders can be made a possibility by working with the interest groups and rural voluntary agencies. Thus, the communication of the ideas about IMT becomes a component in the diffusion process leading to the adoption is conditioned not only by the power of the opinion leaders but also by both the workings of the interest groups and the special knowledge on IMT. This special knowledge increases its adoption when the farmers, in a changed structural condition of the village, realise that the transfer process is within their reach. These and other ingredients of the diffusion process leading to the adoption of the transfer of management are to be reckoned with by the social action researchers.

The social action research in an area need not be extended to every tank and river system. Instead, the diffusion process has to be encouraged. The diffusion of innovated or spread-effects is thus a crucial issue in participatory social action, wherein the inter-sectoral and interdisciplinary approaches are to be resorted to. Here, the role of the opinion leaders, in the except position, is to act as spread-agents or extension-workers. But, care should be taken that interest of the opinion leaders should be in conformity with aims and objectives of the participatory social action. The inclination that the diffusion will take place automatically has to be exploded and there should be a planned effort towards diffusion.

Conclusion

The work relating to sociology of irrigation thus far,

particularly, turnover of irrigation management, may be briefly summarised as follows :

Unlike other social sciences, sociology is heavily biased against the understanding of elucidation of bureaucratic factors. So, sociologists look into mono-determinism, *i.e.*, sociological determinism and ignore multiple determinism. The success and failure stories of turnover of irrigation management cannot be constructed without the knowledge on multi-determinism.

In this context, the mechanism of institution building, such as farmers' association or water-users' associations, need to be analysed as a policy measure by sociologists within the following framework :

Contextualising the existing tested models of participatory social for farmers in irrigation in Indian cultural contexts exhibits certain amount of prismatism. Besides this, there is an academic utopia among social action and participatory research that it is enough to institutionalise the action for participatory groups in irrigation management. Rather, it is a challenge before the social scientists toward irrigation development, because there is a need to identify the detrimental human behaviour and to take efforts to appeal to farmers' values and effect new preferences by drawing upon public re-education campaign and community leaders.

The management and technical solutions without understanding the farmers/water-users within the above framework are only utopian and partial. The conceptual issues of social science for social action, in nature, are plenty in IMT. A review of the existing literature will be a lesson for learning.

REFERENCES

Aid Handbook, 3rd Appendix, 3f Social Journal Analysis, September 1982.

Arenstiem, Sherry R., "A Ladder of Citizen — Participation in USA", *Journal of the American Institute of Planners,* 1969.

Athena, Theodre, "Social change and Voluntary action", in D.H. Smith *et al.* (eds.), Voluntary Action Research, Lexicon Books, London, 1972.

Cain, B.J., "Participatory Research", Working paper No. 3., International Council for Higher Education, Toronto, 1977.

Friero, Paulo, "Pedagogy of the Oppressed".

Giddens, Anthony, "Agency, institution and time-space analysis", in K. Knorr-Cetina and A.V. Cicourel (eds.), "Advances in Social Theory and Methodology", Routledge and Kegan Paul, Boston, 1981.

Hall, Budd L., "Participatory research : an approach for change", Convergence, VIII, 2, 1975.

Hall, Budd L., "Research methods, participation and Development", Occasional Papers, International Council for Adult Education.

Horowitz, I.L., "Social Science and Public Policy", in *Foundations of Political Sociology*, Harper new publications, 1972.

Rayant, Joseph C., "Strategies for Change", *Canadian Conference of Social Welfare*, Mimeo, 1972.

Sanjeevi, K.S., "Health Care for the Rural Poor", *The Hindu*, 1977.

Sundaram, D., "A Pedagogy of Ecological Responsibility : Conceptual Issues in Environmental Planning and Water Management".

13

Urban Water Crisis and the need for Rainwater Harvesting : The Case of Hyderabad

—*C. Ramachandraiah* and *B. Janaki*

Introduction

"All people, whatever their stage of development and their social and economic conditions, have the right to have access to drinking water in quantities and of a quality equal to their basic needs" was the commonly agreed premise at the United Nations Water Conference in 1977. Despite significant progress achieved in the provision of safe drinking water, one in three people in the developing countries are estimated to lack this basic requirement for human health and dignity. Provision of adequate water supplies also depends, to a large extent, on the protection of freshwater resources taking into account the functioning of aquatic ecosystems and the perenniality of the resource.

The freshwater that is readily available for human consumption is estimated to constitute only 0.007 per cent of water on the planet. Many of the freshwater resources like rivers, lakes, ponds, etc., have suffered a decline in quality and quantity due to disposals into them of untreated urban sewage, industrial effluents, soil erosion, agricultural run off etc., in the catchment areas. Expanding urban centres have consumed water bodies and agricultural lands on a large scale throughout the world. Rivers passing through the cities practically became drains carrying sewage and effluents. Consequently, drinking water had to be transported from long distances making huge investments in the process. This has given rise to conflicts between different states, regions, and sectors for water. As a result, debates are going on regarding pricing of water to meet the costs and treat it as an economic good, as opposed to water as a basic need to be taken care by the society.

The coverage of protected water supply in urban centres in India differs among regions, urban centres, and among different localities and sections of people within individual cities. The position of bigger cities is better off in this regard, so also is the position of well-off sections of people. The surface water sources especially rivers are getting highly polluted in India. Most of the urban centres do not have adequate treatment facilities for sewage which is let into water bodies. Similar is the case with industrial effluents. The most polluting industries of our rivers are identified as those of sugar, fertiliser, cement, fermentation and distillery, aluminium, petrochemicals, thermal power, caustic soda, oil refineries, tanneries, copper smelters, zinc smelters, iron and steel, pulp and paper, dye and dye intermediators, pesticides and pharmaceuticals. About 1629 industrial units are estimated to be in these most polluting categories, as per the Ministry of Environment and Forests.[1]

Many urban centres are depending on groundwater to a larger extent to meet non-potable demands. The share of surface water is estimated at 73 per cent in class I cities as against 23 per cent by groundwater. The corresponding figures are 50 and 43 for class II centres.[2] Besides depletion and lowering of water table, contamination of groundwater has also become a serious problem. Intrusion of saline water into freshwater aquifers in coastal cities is making them dependent on surface water sources only. Water business (of supplying through tankers) has become a flourishing activity in many cities during February-June of every year. High density of concrete structures in urban areas, tar roads, encroachment of water bodies, absence of open spaces etc., have resulted into a situation in which rainwater is not allowed to percolate down to recharge groundwater. The urban centres are going to face serious difficulties if the extraction of groundwater is continued recklessly without sufficient recharge of the aquifers.

Consequences of Excessive Groundwater Extraction : International Experience

Several factors like growing urban and industrial activity and demand, and the increasing use of water-consuming domestic appliances, such as washing machines and dish washers, as a result of increasing material living standards etc., lead to higher per capita consumption of water.[3] This as the wealth of the citizens increases, per capita consumption of water also tends to go up. To meet such growing needs, there is heavy dependence on groundwater. Continuous extraction of groundwater, without compensatory recharge of the aquifers, has led to land subsidence in several cities in the world like Houston, Beijing and Osaka apart from those mentioned in table 1.

TABLE 1

Examples of Land Subsidence in Cities due to Groundwater Extraction

Locality	Maximum Subsidence (mts.)	Area Affected (sq. km.)
Tokyo	4.60	2400
Venice	0.14	400
London	0.35	450
Mexico City	8.70	225

Source : Simmons, I.G., *Changing the Face of the Earth, Culture, Environment, History*, Oxford, Basil Blackwell, 1989, as cited in Graham Haughton and Colin Hunter, *Sustainable Cities*, Jessica Kingsley, London, 1994, p. 170.

The compacting of underlying soils in Bangkok, due to overdrawing of groundwater, has causes land subsidence ranging from 5 cm to more than 10 cm per year in the main aquifer regions 23. In the central area of Mexico City, during 1935-85, the elevation has fallen by more than 7 metres from above 2240 to 2233 metres above mean sea level causing extensive damage to the city's infrastructure, building foundations and sewer systems. This is because of excessive withdrawal of groundwater from its main aquifer that underlines the metropolitan area. Given the city's location at a high altitude, water importation is an expensive alternatives.[4] Some of the drinking water to Mexico City now has to be pumped up by 1000 metres over the mountains thus spending large amounts of energy.[5] Coastal cities in the world are facing the common threat of salt water intrusion into aquifers. Where saline and fresh aquifers lie in close proximity, man-induced hydrologic changes can alter the pressure systems underground thus causing the barriers separating the aquifers to become more porous. Intrusion of saline water to the extent of as little as 2 per cent can render an aquifer unusable; and once such intrusion starts, it can persist for years.[6]

It is in this context that rainwater harvesting measures assume tremendous significance for future groundwater resources in urban areas. Rainwater harvesting is widely practiced in several parts of the world including developed countries like Germany, Japan, and Singapore, and developing countries like Israel, Thailand, Sri Lanka etc. It is practiced in diversified areas like urban, rural, arid, semi-arid, humid, hilly, and high rainfall areas. In Tamil Nadu, the Chennai city authorities have made it mandatory, under the building regulations, for all new recharge of groundwater aquifers. Rainwater harvesting involves capturing run-off from rooftops and local catchments, capturing seasonal flood-waters from local streams, and conserving water through watershed management. In urban areas, such measures help in the provision of drinking water, increase of groundwater recharge, reduction of stormwater discharge and overloading of sewage treatment plants, and reduction of urban flooding.[7]

Hyderabad : A Fast Growing Metropolis

Hyderabad is one of the fastest growing state capitals in the country. The city has recorded 43 per cent and 67 per cent growth during seventies and eighties respectively, and is spread over Hyderabad, Rangareddy and Medak districts. Its present population is estimated to be more than 56 lakhs (which includes the twin cities of Hyderabad-Secunderabad, nine surrounding municipalities, and a few additional areas). The core city has a density of more than 14,000 persons per square kilometre. The culture of multi-storeyed apartments had picked up in Hyderabad from late 1970s onwards. Despite dubious advertisements like "flats in the midst of greenery" by the builders, neither there is any thought of planting trees nor any space is left for it around the apartments. Multi-storeyed buildings have contributed to the rapid decline of groundwater reserves. A remote sensing study on Hyderabad has revealed that the built-up area of the city has increased from 245 sq. km. in 1973 to 355 sq. km. in 1983, 522 sq. km. in 1991 and to 587 sq. km. in 1996, that is, an increase of 139 per cent during 1973-96. During this period, agricultural land to the extent of 128 sq. km. was converted into residential, commercial, institutional and industrial purposes.[8]

Loss of Greenery and Water Bodies

The present-day 'baghs' of Hyderabad like Kundenbagh, Jorbagh, Basheerbagh, Bagh Lingampally etc., (which are busy localities) were once lush green natural vegetation zones. It is known that the present Nizam College buildings in the heart of the city were once forest guest houses for those who go for hunting in that area. The outskirts of earlier Hyderabad have now become its interior areas. The story would be more or less similar in the case of many other cities also. It is estimated that the city has at present less than 0.5 acres of actual public open space and greenery per 1000 people whereas the international standard recommended is 4 acres per 1000 people[9].

Historically, Hyderabad was full of lakes like Hussain Sagar, Meer Jumla Tank, Meer Alam Tank, Ibrahimpatnam Tank, Jalpally Tank, Masab Tank, etc., built during 1567 to 1724 A.D. In course of time several small tanks were constructed. With the presence of these water bodies, a lot of greenery thrived in and around the city. They played a key role in storing rainwater and help in recharge of groundwater. In course of time, a number of lakes and tanks have disappeared due to encroachments. In 1995 the Andhra Pradesh High Court had issued directions to the state government, MCH and HUDA to take necessary steps to protect 170 lakes and water bodies in and around the city. It was feared that 30 of these lakes had already disappeared and about 40 were on the verge of extinction[10]. The above mentioned remote sensing study also had found that there were 932 tanks in 1973 which came down to 834 in 1996. The area under water bodies got reduced from 117.98 to 110.08 sq. km. and about 80 tanks of below 10 hectare size and 18 larger tanks were lost during that period.[11]

Drinking Water Supply

The city is located in a semi-arid region of the Deccan Plateau and receives an average rainfall of about 800 mm. It is also deficit in groundwater reserves. The drinking water requirements of Hyderabad are met by four main storage reservoirs as given in table 2.

TABLE 2

Main Water Supply Sources to Hyderabad

Sl. No.	Source	Year	River*	Name of the scheme	Distance (Km.)
1.	Osman Sagar	1922	Musi	Osman Sagar	15
2.	Himayat Sagar	1927	Esi	Himayat Sagar	8.6
3.	Manjira Phase I	1965	Manjira	Manjira Barrage	59
4.	Manjira Phase II	1981	Manjira	Manjira Barrage	59
5.	Manjira Phase III	1991	Manjira	Singur Dam	80
6.	Manjira Phase IV	1994	Manjira	Singur Dam	80

*Esi is a tributary of Musi which in turn is a tributary of Krishna river. Manjira is a tributary of Godavari river.

Note : In effect, Sl. Nos. 3 and 4 represent one reservoir, and 5 and 6 represent another.

Source : Hyderabad Metropolitan Water Supply and Sewerage Board (HMWSSB), Sixth Annual Report, 1995.

It may be noticed from the table 2 that as the years pass by, the distance of the sources of supply is increasing to meet growing demands for water. After the city was hit by devastating floods of Musi in 1908, Osman Sagar and Himayat Sagar were planned with the advice of the famous engineer Mokshagundam Visweswaraiah. As the population grew rapidly (after the formation of Andhra Pradesh in 1956), especially in sixties and seventies, new sources had to be located for water. Located on a ridge, Hyderabad and its environs fall into the river basins of both Krishna and Godavari. All the above sources of supply are gravity systems. With the increase in distance of the source, the cost of bringing water as well as distribution and transmission losses have increased[12]. About 130-145 mgd (million gallons a day) of water is supplied currently in the city. The water loss is estimated between 20-25 per cent of the net demand.

Even in good rainfall years, though the water is full up to FRL (full reservoir level), what is lost sight of is the reduction in their water storage capacity because of siltation of their beds. It is estimated that the gross storage capacity of Osman Sagar has declined by 12 per cent, and that of Himayat Sagar by 20 per cent, during 1973-88[13]. The water supply is now on alternate days, with occasional daily supply for short periods. The perennial water problem of the city has become a contentious issue for political parties. When water supply was restricted for only two hours a day on alternate days in January 1986, it became a major issue in elections to the Municipal Corporation of Hyderabad in February 1986.

The city depends on groundwater as the major source to meet its requirements. Groundwater table has either dried up or is going down every year in several parts of the city. Digging of bore well up to a depth of 600 feet is not uncommon these days in multi-storey complexes. As a consequence, bore wells of individual houses in the vicinity are drying up. Selling water by private tankers has become a lucrative business in the city. As per some studies, the quality of groundwater is also declining due to seepage of contaminants into aquifers. The well waters near solid waste dumping sites at Amberpet and Golconda are found to be not suitable for drinking, as the sodium, chloride, and iron contents are higher than normal limits. Their levels decrease with distance from these landfill sites.[14] It is imperative that the landfill sites are lined properly both at the bottom and sides to prevent seepage of contaminants into groundwater. Since solid waste is going to be a continuous and increasing problem in future, the dumping sites may pose serious threat to groundwater quality in urban areas. Similarly, polluted water are threatening groundwater quality. Within one kilometre radius of the Hussain Sagar lake, groundwater samples revealed consistently higher levels of toxic metals like lead, cadmium, nickel, and zinc etc., due to percolation of effluents into the water table.[15]

Demand for Krishna Water

For the past several years, there have been persistent demands from virtually all political parties for bringing Krishna water from the Nagarjuna Sagar (NS) reservoir to the twin cities. With the ever-ready-to-lend World Bank at hand, the political leadership has no hesitation in borrowing heavily and push the state into the morass of indebtedness. Since there will be a lot of money at stake for vested interests, hardly any criticism is heard on such large scale projects from these sections. All the elite sections have stakes in Hyderabad, irrespective of region, caste or party. They would like the state to borrow and invest heavily in the capital city while the small and medium towns starve for funds even to provide minimum level of amenities.

Though the present Krishna water project is expected to be completed in five years, one can presume with certainty that it may take at least a decade or so. By which time, the cost of the project will have escalated phenomenally. The planned supply of additional 90 or 135 mgd (million gallons a day) may not mean much by then in view of the growth of population and the enormous investment made. Over the years, the vested interests have launched a propaganda blitz that Hyderabadis would starve of water in future if the Krishna waters are not brought at any cost.

The Nagarjuna Sagar is located at about 130 km. from the twin cities. What is important is the difference in elevation between these two places — NS at about 500 ft. and Hyderabad at about 1750 ft. above mean sea level. Which means that a huge quantity of water has to be pumped to a height of about 1250 ft. over this distance which requires a lot of power. This at a time when the unit cost of power is likely to rise with many private parties eager to enter this sector. The consumers would also be forced to pay heavily for procuring water in such a manner. The unit cost of water has gone up by two to three times in the World Bank — financed water supply projects in several countries. While it costs 4-5 paise per kiloliter of water to be brought from Gandipet (a lake located a few km. away) to the city, it costs about Rs. 4 per kiloliter from Singur. If Krishna water is to be brought from Nagarjuna Sagar, it is likely to cost about Rs.20 per kilolitre.[16] Water rates may be steeply revised to meet such high costs. The poor and lower middle class people may suffer heavily in obtaining (purchasing) water in future.

Need for Rainwater Harvesting

The State Groundwater Department has estimated the groundwater potential in Hyderabad Metropolitan Development Area (HMDA) as 36 mld (million liters a day) within the city, 80 mld within 9 municipalities area, and 215 mld within 15 km. radius outside the 9 municipalities area. These estimates may not hold true for long with increasing extraction of groundwater by high rise structures in the city. Time has come to design rainwater harvesting methods in urban areas. Check dams across streams may be feasible around the urban centres. Most of the cities have a number of institutions (like universities, colleges, research organisations), government office complexes, and parks/recreation sites etc., which contain large areas[17]. Uncontaminated rainwater flows in these areas during monsoon seasons. High density residential buildings are located around many of these places. A number of institutions are located along the old Bombay Highway between Mehdipatnam and Lingampally. It is necessary to construct a number of groundwater recharge of groundwater so that the water table does not go down rapidly. Large multi-storey residential complexes must also be encouraged, if need be imposed through legislative means, to construct even small scale percolation pits or trenches within their compounds. In addition to these, office complexes and individual houses, built on plot sizes of more than 300 and 1000 sq. yards etc., must be made to construct recharge pits within their compounds. Through this process groundwater levels would rise considerably over a period of time.

Conclusion

The government of Andhra Pradesh has taken interest officially and is playing an important role in propagation of the techniques for rainwater harvesting. As a starting point, a state level conference was held on "Rainwater Harvesting and Water Recycling Implementation Programme" at Hyderabad on August 10, 1998. The participants were government officials, commissioners of municipalities, engineers, university officials, college and school managements, NGO, corporate sector executives, opinion leaders, and important public figures. A curious aspect in this programme is the active involvement of builders' associations. They have probably realised that without assured water supplies, the real estate business may not progress well. The groundwater department has calculated that, with an average rainfall of about 800 mm in Hyderabad, the total volume of rainfall recharge in a plot of 100 sq. metres would be 55 cubic metres which is equal to 55,000 liters of water. This would meet the requirement of a five-member family for about 100 days. A few apartment complexes and individual houses have constructed such percolation pits. Hyderabad Metropolitan Water Supply and Sewerage Board (HMWSSB) has constructed some pits in some localities for demonstration purposes. Though these methods have generated a lot of interest, the public, especially the middle class, is still very slow in adopting them. The public must be made to realise that these simple measures would be lot more beneficial to them than the costly schemes which may be difficult to sustain in the long run.

With increasing pollution of water bodies, nature cannot be expected to provide unlimited quantities of water continuously. Unless existing water resources are protected, not only do they get polluted or dried up, the groundwater also get contaminated. The laws must be strictly implemented to protect at least the existing lakes and other water bodies. It should be made mandatory for new townships and colonies to construct recharge structures and promote greenery. Reckless paving of open areas should be discouraged so that more open spaces are available for seepage. Most of our urban centres do not have proper storm water drainage system. Because of which rainwater flows over roads, damaging them in the process, into low-lying areas. Wherever possible, storm water drains should be provided and rainwater should be collected and stored at some locations outside the city limits. Structures should be constructed for such storage. This water can be used for recharge by constructing special filter beds, and also for irrigation wherever possible.

In this process, awareness would also raise regarding conservation and rational utilisation of resources among people. Simultaneously, steps must be taken to desilt the main storage reservoirs and treat their catchment areas (to prevent soil erosion). These measures can be implemented with a much lower investment than the Krishna water scheme. A number of polluting industries which are releasing effluents into these reservoirs, especially Manjira, must be either shifted elsewhere or forced to treat their effluents fully before discharging. Without taking these measures with a holistic view, taking up of large scale projects will not yield the desired results always.

REFERENCES

1. Ummareddy Venkateswarlu, *Urbanisation in India : Problems and Prospects*, New Age International, New Delhi, 1998, p. 88
2. D.P. Martin, "River Pollution in India : An Overview", *Employment News*, Vol. 22, No. 52, 1998, pp. 1-2.
3. World Resources Institute, *World Resources 1996-97*, New York, pp. 64-65.
4. *Ibid*.
5. Ronald Steven Parker, "Vulnerability and Resiliency : Environmental Degradation in Major Metropolitan Areas of Developing Countries", in Alcira Kreimer and Mohan Munasinghe (eds.), *Environmental Management and Urban Vulnerability*, World Bank Discussion Papers, 168, 1992, p. 111
6. World Resources Institute, *op. cit.*, pp. 64-65.
7. From the Draft Statement of the *National Conference on Water Harvesting : Traditions, Policies and Social Mobilisation*, New Delhi : October 3-5, 1998 by the Centre for Science and Environment, New Delhi. One of the outcomes of the Conference is the formation of a National Water Harvestors Network.
8. *The Hindu*, "Concern Over the Haphazard Growth of the City", January 25, 1997, Hyderabad.
9. SPEQL, *Hyderabad Bachao — Save Hyderabad*, A Bi-monthly Publication, Society for Preservation of Environment and Quality of Life, Hyderabad, Vol. 1, No. 5, 1995, pp. 6-7.

10. *Ibid.*
11. The Hindu, *op. cit.*
12. R. Maria Saleth and Ariel Dinar, *Satisfying Urban Thirst* (Water Supply Augmentation and Pricing Policy in Hyderabad City, India), World Bank Technical Paper No. 395, The World Bank, Washington D.C., 1997, p. 4
13. Hyderabad Metropolitan Water Supply and Sewerage Board (HMWSSB), *Sixth Annual Report*, 1994-95.
14. K. Jeevan Rao and M.V. Shantaram, "Groundwater Pollution from Refuse Dumps at Hyderabad", *Indian Journal of Environmental Health*, 37(3), pp. 197-204
15. EPTRI, *State of Environment for Hyderabad Urban Agglomeration*, Environment Protection, Training, and Research Institute, 1996, Hyderabad.
16. The Chief Minister, Mr. N. Chandrababu Naidu, in his address at the State Level Conference on Rainwater Harvesting and Water Recycling Implementation Programme at Hyderabad on August 10, 1998, which appeared in the press the next day.
17. Some of these are Survey of India, National Geophysical Research Institute (NGRI), National Institute of Nutrition (NIN), Central Institute of English and Foreign Languages (CIEFL), Indian Institute of Chemical Technology (IICT), National Remote Sensing Agency (NRSA), Osmania University, Cantonment, P.G. College, Nizam College, Centre for Economic and Social Studies (CESS), Institute of Genetics, Administrative Staff College of India (ASCI), College of Nursing, Hyderabad Public School, Indian Institute of Health Studies, Chest Hospital, Unani and Ayurvedic Hospital, NISIET, Institute of Administration (IOA), Jawaharlal Nehru Technological University (JNTU), Dr. B.R. Ambedkar Open University, A.P. Agricultural University, Sardar Patel Academy, Film Studios, Hindustan Aeronautics Limited (HAL), Electronic Corporation of India Limited (ECIL), Indian Drugs and Pharmaceuticals Limited (IDPL), Nuclear Fuel Complex (NFC), Zoological Park and a number of industrial units.

SECTION 4
PEOPLE'S PARTICIPATION — KEY FOR SUSTAINABLE DEVELOPMENT

14

Rural Development and People's Participation

—D. Sunder Raj

Introduction

"People's Participation" has become a standard rhetoric in India today. Different actors interpret it differently. One view is that participation means getting people to agree to and go along with a project which has already been designed for them, or to get support of a few leaders. This has been the approach in many development schemes that did not work. People did not identify themselves with the assets created such as the hand pump or trees planted, nor did they undertake the responsibility of maintenance of assets. "I manage, you participate", was the dominant underlying principle behind such projects. These tended to try to make people aware of their responsibility without giving them any authority to spend funds or to manage assets. People's participation was then expressed not in a manner that would establish their rights over assets, land or its produce (Saxena, N.C., 1998).

Rural development and People's Participation should go

together and both these components are highly essential for the integrity and the unity of the Nation. In order to keep people united and feel responsible involving indigenous people in developmental programme framed for their own development is very much necessary. This not only helps to accelerate economic growth of nation, but also to achieve balanced regional development, which alternatively checks the drift of rural population to cities, in search of employment, to a large extent.

It is universally acknowledged that the goals of our socio-economic development are not achievable unless the citizens actively involve themselves in the preparation, implementation and follow-up of the developmental plans and programmes. Though this basic philosophy is highly accepted right from the days of planning, till today, the spirit of participation has not been realised. During the last two decades several new approaches like 'top-down planning', 'planning from below', 'bottom-up planning', 'micro-level planning', 'resource-based planning' and 'multi-level planning' have been thought of in the context of involving the people in every phase of development. Participation in decision-making has also received increased attention. So the idea of maximum participation of the citizen which forms the central idea of democracy has been constitutionally activated in *73rd Amendment*. It aims at reducing the political and bureaucratic interference in rural development programmes (Behera, Santosh, 1998).

Importance of Rural Development

India is predominantly an agrarian society. As per the 1991 Census, out of its total population 74 per cent are inhabiting in around 5.67 lakh villages which are more or less categorised with high levels of illiteracy, ignorance, low level of quality of life and so on. Therefore, it is essential to concentrate more on rural development.

According to Lahiry, Amitabh (1995), if we compare the development of the nations which achieved independence around or after the year 1947, some of the nations, for example Israel, are far ahead of us in terms of socio-economic development. Rural development helps to liberate the energies of the rural people, especially the poor, so that they can realise their full potential and thus improve their capacity as well as commitments to development, organise and govern themselves towards the attainment of a higher quality of life for the individual and for the entire community. The twin major objectives of rural development programme are accelerated economic growth with wider participation and most equitable distribution of its gains.

Indian Government in Rural Development

History tells us the concept of rural development is not a new one. Several dynasties concentrated on this aspect and achieved substantial growth. Independent India too recognised the need for rural development and it is worth while to recall Mahatma Gandhi's words : "Our cities are not India. India lives in her seven and a half lakh of villages, and the cities live upon the villages.... It is my belief based on experience that India is daily growing poorer.... And if one do not take care, she will collapse altogether" (1947). The Government of India was committed to formulate various plans on rural development, and did so during the plan periods by formulating strategies for future plans and allocating substantial amount to attain faster rural development. This particular concept was given due importance in each and every Five Year Plan. During Eighth Five Year Plan (1992-97) this plan emphasis was on building up of rural infrastructure. Priority for all weather roads, particularly in tribal, hill and desert areas, minor irrigation works and water harvesting structure schemes for soil conservation and social forestry. Participation of people in programmes through Panchayati Raj institution, co-operatives and other self-managed institution, provision of short-term employment through IRDP and JRY.

Ninth Five Year Plan attempts to make a serious effort to raise the level of agricultural and rural incomes, the ultimate objective is to improve the living conditions of the poor and the various disadvantaged sections of the society. Priority to agriculture and rural development with a view to generating adequate productive employment and eradication of poverty.

Ensuring food and nutritional security for all, particularly the vulnerable sections of society. Ensuring environmental sustainability of the development process through social mobilisation and participation of people at all levels. Empowerment of women and socially disadvantaged groups such as scheduled castes, scheduled Tribes and other backward classes and minorities as agents of socio-economic change and development. Promoting and developing people's participatory institutions like Panchayati Raj Institutions, cooperatives and self-help groups.

Planning and development policies for the eradication of poverty in rural India have started since the inception of the Five Year Plans. Though, importance of rural development was recognised in the earlier plans, it was only from the Sixth Plan onwards the due emphasis was laid on rural development. And over a period more and more emphasis was laid in building rural India as real India. For the first time, need of people's participation at the grassroot level was felt essential in the Seventh Five Year Plan, from there it went on to people's self-managed institutions in Eighth Five Year Plan, with greater voice and choice.

Basing on the Five Year Plan the government framed and implemented various rural development programmes in our country from time to time to achieve balanced development. The following are the different kinds of programmes :

1. Community Development Programme (1952)
2. Intensive Agriculture District Programme (1960)
3. Intensive Agriculture Area Programme (1964)
4. High Yielding Variety Programme (1966)
5. Small Farmers Development Agency (1971)
6. Marginal Farmers and Agricultural Labour (1971)
7. Rural Works Programme (1970), renamed as Drought Prone Area Programme (1973)
8. Accelerated Rural Water Supply Programme (1972)
9. Desert Development Programme (1977)
10. Command Area Development Programme (1974)

11. Tribal Area Programme (1972)
12. Hill Area Programme (1975)
13. Integrated Rural Development Programme (1980)
14. Training of Rural youth for Self-Employment Programme (1979)
15. Crash Programme for Rural Employment
16. Pilot Intensive Rural Employment Programme (1972)
17. Food for Work Programme (1977)
18. National Rural Employment Programme (1980)
19. Minimum Needs Programme (1972)
20. 20-Point Programme
21. Western Ghats Developmental Programme
22. Special Programme for the North-Eastern Region
23. Special Incentive Programme for the Industrially Backward Areas
24. Rural Labour Employment Guarantee Programme (1983)
25. Development of Women and Children in Rural Areas (1982)
26. Wage Employment Programme
27. Jawahar Rozgar Yojana (1989)
28. Employment Assurance Schemes (1993)
29. Supply of Improved Tool Kits to Rural Artisan
30. Indira Awaas Yojana (1985)
31. Million Wells Scheme (1988)
32. Members of Parliament Local Area Development Scheme (1993)
33. Ganga Kalyan Yojana (1997)
34. Whole Village Development Programme (1978)

Many of the above said target based developmental programmes were started at different times during the 70's and 80's. Some of the programmes were discontinued either because they have been replaced by other programmes or have been merged into new ones.

However, it is remarkable to note that most of these target based developmental programme performed poorly to achieve desired results, and increased the burden on nation's exchequer. Different developmental programmes are designed and targeted to eradicate poverty, inequality, low socio-economic growth, regional imbalance, illiteracy and unemployment and to gain rural development, yet repeatedly failed to involve wider participation from people.

There are several reasons for either failure of the programmes or poor results. Lack of Awareness, Accessibility, Availability and Adaptability are observed to be the main root causes for the poor performance.

(a) *Awareness* : To be specific, rural people are not aware of the developmental programmes. Many beneficiaries expressed their unawareness of the programmes under which they are assisted.

As an illustration, while interviewing a young beneficiary in Siddipet Mandal of Medak district who was assisted for xerox machine under Andhra Pradesh Scheduled Castes Co-operative Finance Corporation Limited, another friend of the beneficiary lamented that "Sir, I have failed S.S.C. Ours is poor family I do not know about this kind of schemes. Even my friend kept it as secret. Please do something for me or give me your address, I will come to Hyderabad and pursue the matter". This is the case with rural people and many do not know that there is no need to come to Hyderabad for getting a scheme for self-employment. Moreover, a beneficiary who has taken assistance does not give the details of the scheme to the fellow villagers.

Similarly a section of villagers at Undabanda, Vidapankel Mandal in Ananthapur district expressed their unawareness of the large subsidies available for seeds, fertilizers, and other specific schemes.

(b) *Accessibility* : Being aware of the schemes and activities is one level and its accessibility is another. Villagers have to visit three to four weeks for just submitting an application. Misguidance by middle men and lower level staff is further narrowing the path of accessibility.

An instance at Veesampalli village, Maripeda Mandal in Warangal district reveals that only a few villagers who are considered as favourable to village elders are receiving schemes, irrespective of their eligibility and selection.

(c) *Availability* : More often the availability of the choicest has been a major problem, since villagers do not possess skills to pursue any activity. For example a beneficiary of Ranjole village, Zahirabad Mandal, in Medak district, was given financial assistance for Kirana Shop under Andhra Pradesh Scheduled Castes Co-operative Finance Corporation Limited, but was not pursuing the activity as he is poor in counting rupees and can't do little addition and subtractions. When asked the reasons for opting Kirana Shop activity he says, "Sir, I have asked for Milch Animal but, our village elders and officials told that only Kirana Shop activity is available. With a fear that I may loose benefit, I have taken it".

(d) *Adaptability* : Adaptability is another important part of the successful pursuance of the activity. Most often negligence has resulted in less interest or no interest at all in adopting an activity. People's lack of or poor knowledge to identify suitable which developmental activity and pursue the same with interest coupled with undue delay between selection of beneficiary and distribution of scheme are found to be the contributing factors.

Apart from the above reasons, illiteracy, communal disparities, exploitation and suppression are major hindrances, which are keeping people away from developmental programmes. Hence, people's direct participation at grassroot level is the effective remedial measure.

Need of People's Participation in Rural Development

It has been long argued that people's participation is essential for the success of rural development programmes. People's participation should be encouraged owing to the fact that people in villages know their needs better than government officials working at block, district and state levels. Non-involvement of people in the development programmes is also a great concern and challenge to rural development. No programme can be a success without the involvement of the people (Dhillon D.S., and B.S. Hansare, 1995).

Participation is not some process of involving every one and reducing all to a common denominator. Rather, it consists in evolving institutional structures from which diverse individuals with a sense of dignity and self-respect, as being that are to determine their own destinies. This 'people's participation perspective', *inter alia* in its operational-design will imply that most plan options, for the urban section and as well as the rural section be complimentary, supportive and reinforcing in character (Seth S.C., 1988).

According to Behra, Santosh, (1998) participation broadly is of three types. First; spontaneous : where-people come forward on their own to participate without any external support and force. Second; sponsored : where people participate because of some mandate and official endorsements. And third; compulsory : where people participate because it has been made compulsory and its violation may invite coercion. In a democratic country like ours, compulsory participation is not desirable. Between spontaneous and sponsored, the former is most suitable. This will sustain for longer period as well as establish the ideal cooperative and participatory situation.

In connection with the people's participation for community and rural development, Mr. N. Chandra Babu Naidu (Chief Minister of Andhra Pradesh) efforts are note worthy, where he has brought notable awareness among people about the people's participation for rural development, with the programme called Janmabhoomi; (motherland) which intends to motivate and involves local people in all village developmental activities, such as laying of connecting roads, construction of school buildings, community halls, digging of drainage, canals and planting trees along the road etc., to keep villages green and clean.

Janmabhoomi was launched in Andhra Pradesh on January 1st, 1997. It is a people centered development programme aimed at achieving overall growth of the entire state and improving the quality of life of every man, woman, and child in the entire state. People centered development process means, (i) people to identify and priorities their felt needs in the Gram Sabha, (ii) people to share partly the cost of community works through materials or labour or cash or a combination of any one of them, (iii) people to execute community works through their self help groups without any intermediaries, (iv) people to review and audit their own expenditure and (v) people to own the community assets thus created and manage their own institutions.

So far seven rounds of Janmabhoomi programmes have been conducted within a span of 20 months and with wider people's participation. The programme has made remarkable achievements.

(a) 66,662 different community works have been grounded, of which 54,164 works have been completed. The completed works are valued at Rs. 650 crores out of which government's share is Rs. 446 crores, *i.e.* 69 per cent.

(b) In Sixth round 11,577 community works grounded are valued at Rs. 139 crores, of which government's share is Rs. 104 crores, *i.e.* 75 per cent.

(c) Altogether 80,610 non-financial community needs have been redressed out of total 98,411.

(d) Out of total 14,54,000 individual family needs received, 11,43,000 have been redressed leaving a balance of 3,11,000 (Deccan Chronicle).

It needs to be highlighted here, that without Janmabhoomi Programme, the above mentioned achievements could not have been achieved with the normal government programmes and course of actions; and that too within a short span of period.

Hence, it is more or less empirically proved that, people's participation in rural development is an effective tool to meet targeted goals and to achieve desired healthy results.

Suggestions for securing People's Participation

As Passmore said : "Society as much as nature, resists men's plans; it is not wax at the hands of the scientist, the planner, the legislature." Securing people's participation is not an easy task. Participation cannot be imposed on from above, but it should be voluntary and based on the will of the people. To increase the acceptability and utilisation of resources and make the programmes realistic and effective, it is necessary to secure people's participation in rural development programmes.

The following are few suggestions aimed at securing people's participation :

1. The rural development programmes should be based on the felt needs of the people in order to achieve greater people's participation and sustainability in the development.

2. Motivate people to participate in rural development programmes, by making them aware about the benefits they receive from these programmes.

3. People should be made aware of the importance of rural development in eradicating rural poverty and rural illiteracy.

4. Invite people for small focus group discussion prior to planning and implementation, in order to consider their felt needs.

5. Consult different community leaders within the village, to gain their confidence.

6. Identify problems faced by the people and give importance to eliminate them, keeping in view their seriousness.

7. Greater amount of patience is required for the officers and field staff while dealing with people of different cultures, social environments like illiterates, tribals, etc.

8. Officers and field staff in connection with people's participation, should be technically sound and competent.

9. Do not leave the development programmes half way through, but pursue to the end, by providing necessary technical and financial guidance.

10. Involve existing local voluntary organisations/NGO's in securing people's participation for rural development, since they are more experienced and exposed to rural minds.

11. Greater effort should be made by involving media such as radio, television and newspapers by using local language.

12. Empower people to have a greater say and role in their own affairs at the grassroot level.

13. Encourage participation of people in decision-making, planning, formulating strategy, implementation, follow up, sharing the benefits of development and evaluation.

14. Extension Workers should be given incentives, for motivating people to take part in rural development programmes with as certificates, trophies and cash prizes etc.

Conclusion

Half-hearted measures towards people's participation have only resulted in wastage of funds with no substantial returns. It must be, therefore, understood as a process by which the people are able to organise themselves and through their own organisations able to identify their own needs, and share in the design, implementation and evaluation of the participatory action. Various elements of participation are decision-making at various stages, control and management of funds and resources, share in final produce, and of benefits. In other words, participation should not only stop at information sharing or consultation but decision-making and initiating actions as they are important and essential components of participation.

The Human Development Report (1993) also notes that despite the accumulating forces for greater participation, large number of people continue to be excluded from the benefits of developments, especially, the poorest segments of the society and people in the rural areas. Hence, decentralised planning for the socio-economic and comprehensive development of the people is done at the local level, *viz.*, at the district, mandal and village level.

One of the characteristics of participation is that it cannot be turned on and off like a tap, *i.e.*, 'now you participate, now you don't'. Participation is an evolutionary process that gathers momentum and defies breakdown into neat, self-contained categories, except for analytical purposes. Establishing participation is particularly important in the early stage, because expecting responsible behaviour in the later stages is not only misguided but may result in ineffective projects. Participation should include the notions of contributing, influencing, sharing, or redistributing POWER and of control, RESOURCES, benefits, knowledge, and skills to be gained through beneficiary involvement in decision making. The essence of participation is exercising voice and choice, and developing the human, organisational and management capacity to solve problems as they arise in order to sustain the improvements (Saxena, N.C., *op. cit.*).

All will finally depend upon the quality of leadership at the grassroot level. With the spread of awareness, people will perhaps participate in rural development. Till then, sincere encouragement, close relation and effective monitoring is necessary to cease the leakages in the development pipe line purported to reach the rural poor, (Lahiry, Amitabh, 1985).

However, planning in this way and executing is not enough since the rural people are particularly illiterate who are not aware of the provision. Because of their low socio-economic standard they do not think of it. Hence, it is important to bring them closer and to create high level of awareness among them. To make them feel sufficiently concerned to participate, a sense of belongingness and sharing should be created among the rural people. Unless the people come forward to participate, all the noble purposes of plans and policies will remain merely on paper.

REFERENCES

Behera, Santosh, 1998, "Community Participation for Education Development in Tribal Areas", *Kurukshetra,* Volume 46, No. 11, August.

Dhillon, D.S. and B.S. Hangra, 1995, "People's Participation in Rural Development Programmes", *Kurukshetra,* Volume XLIII, No. 4, January.

Gandhi, M.K., 1997, "India of my Dreams", Navajivan Publishing House, Ahmedabad.

Lahiry, Amitabh, 1995, "The Concept of Rural Development — An Overview", *Kurukshetra,* Vol. XLIII, No. 4, January.

Ramanujam, K.N., 1995, "The Philosophy of Rural Development", Kurukshetra, Volume XLIII, No. 4, January.

Saxena, N.C., 1998 "What is meant by People's Participation?", *Journal of Rural Development,* Volume 17, No. 1, NIRD, Hyderabad.

Ibid., p. 12, NIRD, Hyderabad.

Seth, S.C., 1988, "Managing Rural Features : A Conceptual Cybernetic Developmental Frame-work", Paper presented in a Seminar on Future for Rural Development, NIRD, Hyderabad.

Singh, S.K. and Yogesh Upadhyay, 1998, "Rural Industrialisation : Perspectives and Prospects", *Kurukshetra,* Volume 46, No. 11, August.

UNDP, 1993, "The Human Development Report, Oxford University Press, New York.

Deccan Chronicle, 1998, *Janmabhoomi,* September, 28.

SUGGESTED READINGS

Atal, Yogesh Else Oyen, 1997, "Poverty and Participation i Civil Society", Abhinav and UNESCO Publishing, New Delhi.

Banerjee, N.N., 1987, "Industry, Agriculture and Rural Development", B.R. Publishing, New Delhi.

Chaturvedi, H.R., and S.K. Mitra, 1982, "Citizen Participation in Rural Development," Oxford and IBH, New Delhi.

Gupta, Jiya Lal and J.P. Yadav, 1994, "People's Participation in Social Forestry — A Felt Need in Inida", *Kurukshetra,* Vol. XLIII, No. 3, December.

Gurumurthy, K.G., 1998, "Rural Development and Factional Politics", Reliance Publishing, New Delhi.

Mukherjee, Amitava, 1995, "Participatory Rural Appraisal : Methods and Applications in Rural Planning'', Vikas Publishing, New Delhi.

Prodhani, M.A., 1995, "Poverty Eradication Programmes and Rural India", *Kurukshetra,* Vol. XLIII, No. 4, January.

15

Development and People's Participation — Role of Literacy

—*P.S. Dixit, B.S. Vasudeva Rao* and *Dr. S.D.A. Joga Rao*

'In the rapidly charging world of today, one thing is certain; yesterday's educational system will not meet today's and even less so, the need of tomorrow' (Kothari, D.S. 1960). With the dawn of the Independence the national leaders decided to launch the process of nation building within the framework of a democratic society. Free India inherited from the British rule the most important obstacles particularly, the problem of illiteracy, ignorance, inertia, poverty, ill health and over population. The basic cause for all the problems confronted by the young Independent India was the problem of illiteracy among 70 per cent of the Indian population. For the effective implementation of any programme which aims at nation building, people participation is vital. The citizens should not remain as silent spectators for the vast changes that are taking place in the society but they should participate effectively in all the phases of planning and development. There should be development communication, dialogue and debate in order to educate the people regarding the benefits of developmental plans and their responsibilities in the process.

For one reason or the other the Government of India ignored the problem of illiteracy and ignorance confronted by the majority of the people consequently the much desired people's participation in developmental programmes could not be achieved. Further, women illiteracy contributed for the growth of major problems like, environmental pollution, pollution explosion, low status of women, infant mortality, communicable diseases and so on. Government of India after realising the reality that the people are not showing interest in their own developmental activities mainly due to illiteracy, has recognised that education for all is a must. Accordingly a national programme was launched in the year 1977-1978 for the removal of illiteracy. This programme was further strengthened with the constitution of National Literacy Mission in the year 1985-1986.

This effort gave the needed boost to make literacy a national movement. Presently all out efforts are being made to wipe out this national stigma.

Literacy and Development

Education is a process which dispels ignorance and promotes rational thinking. Education is the only instrument for bringing social change. When the society is changing at a rapid speed in the areas of Science and Technology the attitude of the people should also change to suit to the changing situation. When the people do not have faith in the programmes and fails to understand the purpose and requirements of such development oriented plans, people's participation cannot be achieved. Due to ignorance the people cannot come out freely from the age old customs, blind beliefs, prejudices which hamper rational thinking. The social and economic institutions of the yester-years do dominate the lives of the people. Thereby making people lethargic, less motivated and silent spectators. 'Education should become an instrument of social change and it should encourage the people to participate in setting up goals and in their implementation' (Kothari, D.S. 1971). They must be made aware of the progress that is being achieved in all aspects. They must be made to understand the spirit of self-help and the need to participate in their own developmental programmes. Fulfillment of these aims will ensure sound democracy.

Present Situation

In the entire country 100 districts have been identified to make literacy as cent per cent movement. In the rest of the country many organisations both public and voluntary are actively participating in this movement. Already the Kerala State has wiped-out illiteracy. In certain other pockets of the country

100 per cent literacy was achieved. The recent Census 1991 indicates that 52 per cent of the entire population are literate. Even though the literacy movement has been initiated with all the necessary pre-planning, the results are not up to the expectations of the planners of the movement.

The following factors are observed about the programme :

(1) Had the Government of India realised the illiteracy as a major obstacle in democratic planning in the beginning days of Independence this problem could have been wiped out by this time.

(2) Even though the Constitution emphasises universal primary education nothing substantial has been achieved in this regard.

(3) The efforts made are very little when compared to the magnitude and size of the problem.

(4) Mass attack on a mass problem should be the principle and all the educated should involve in the programme to remove the problem. Necessary efforts may be made for motivating these persons properly.

(5) It is observed that men are not showing interest in the learning process. On the other hand, women are participating in larger number. Hence, only 50 per cent of the illiterate population can be covered.

(6) It is a welcome trend that the people belonging to weaker sections are evincing keen interest in the programme.

(7) The illiterate adults in fact realised the values of education and expressing their strong desire to educate their children.

(8) The drop out rate in the primary schools is getting rapidly reduced because of the impact of awareness programmes on literacy undertaken by various agencies.

(9) It is also suggested that the success of the programme depends more on the effective functioning of non-formal education centres.

(10) The main lacuna observed in the entire movement is that the people's participation is less. The political parties, trade unions which have cadres right from the national level to the village level are not showing keen interest in the literacy movement. There must be a political will to do the programme.

(11) Compulsory element may be introduced to make the programme more effective.

(12) The success of the programme mainly depends on the spirit of voluntarism, among the functionaries. This is not achieved hence the failure.

(13) At the grossroot level the instructor is not given incentives but the other officials who do not have any contact with the illiterates are paid substantially. This is the main cause for the low level success.

(14) The instructors may be identified from among the unemployed educated youth and be given stipend. Their services should be recognised in the recruitment to jobs.

(15) One of the reasons for the slowness in the programme is the lack of proper systematic training and supervision inputs.

(16) The institutions identified for the purpose are not properly funded and strengthened.

(17) Literacy movement should have become a social action programme with total people's participation. But it is not so.

For the success of the programme the training and evaluation centres manned by qualified people with the required academic background should be established throughout the country at the district level. In the absence of this, national programme may last its direction and could not be implemented systematically.

SECTION 5
FOOD SECURITY — BASIC NEED FOR DEVELOPMENT

16

Food Security in Rural Andhra Pradesh through P.D.S.

—*D. Vasudeva Rao*

During great famine which had occurred in China (1958-61), an estimated 20 million people had died — which was wholly avoidable, for there was enough food within China then. There had been no drought or failure of crops. It was basically a matter of bad distribution[1].

Starvation is caused not by lack of food but by lack of purchasing power. Amartya Sen and J. Dreze showed that in the absence of Purchasing Power, food will travel even out of a starving nation (like potatoes for Ireland). On the other hand, if Purchasing Power is injected into a needy population, through employment schemes, there will be no starvation even in worst droughts.

Example : Maharastra and African Sahel suffered from severe drought in early 70's. The per capita food availability in Maharastra was much less than in African Sahel. In 1973, availability was 46 kg/PC in Maharastra as against 85 kg/PC in Sahel. Yet there was widespread starvation in Sahel and none in Maharastra.

India feeds a population twice as large as Africa's with only 13 per cent as much as arable land (with low yields). The blame for African starvation rests fairly, and squarely on governments neglected duty towards their citizens[2].

A policy that was relevant in the days of food shortage and availability of cheap supplies from abroad has lost its relevance. Now that we have not only plenty for our own consumption but also a significant amount of export surplus, we must think of streamlining the distribution system, such that everybody gets their food requirements, at reasonable rates.

Food grain production has increased from 51 million tonnes (1950-51) to about 194 million tonnes (1996-97). The yield of Wheat and Potato has increased nearly nine times since 1951 and Maize by six times. Grains output touched 192.12 million tonnes in 1996-97, which is 7.08 million tonnes more than the earlier year[3]. Rabi food grain production is expected to be 89.49 million tonnes plus Kharif 103.11 million tonnes. What we have not been able to ensure is its (food grains) economic access, the majority of the population not having adequate income to buy the food they need.

With the problem of plenty, we are saddled with an unwanted mountain of 35 million tonnes of buffer stock of rice and wheat. A controlled food sector stands out as an anachrorism amidst the policy of liberalisation and globalisation of economy.

Food availability per capita is a distinctly subsidiary element in the food security equation. On the other hand, food insecurity reflects the inequities of existing social and economic arrangements. Free market do not guarantee that adequate food production will translate directly into food security. The maldistribution of access, even to the limited supply is the principal cause of chronic hunger[4].

Building a sustainable food security system will be of no avail unless every individual in the country has physical, economic, social and environmental access to a balanced diet[5].

For a common man, even amidst of plenty of production, there is no assurance of deliverance from hunger, unless those charged with the task of governance take conscious and deliberate steps to channel that abundance in his direction so that he can absorb the little he needs[6]. Many planners mistook or misunderstood poverty as synonymous with hunger.

As per FAO, "Food security's ultimate objective should be to ensure that all people at all times, have both physical and economic access to the basic food they need." Food security aims at providing food grains requirement (at least partly), to each family below the poverty line, throughout the year. There are times at which the rural poor households don't have work leading to lack of purchasing power. During these periods, they approach private money lenders or their land lords for loans, to meet their consumption needs. They agree to unfavourable terms, under helpless conditions, and pledge their future services or their produce to the wholesaler. Thus, they are exploited and marginalisation perpetuates. Unless the vicious circle is broken, at one point, the poor have no respite. This can be done by the state with appropriate strategies and interventions.

HOUSEHOLD SURVEY ON FOOD SECURITY AND P.D.S.

In order to find out and quantify the food stocks and food requirements, at household level and the dependency and usefulness of the existing PDS, as a safety net against food insecurity, an elaborate household survey was conducted meticulously in two backward districts of Andhra Pradesh. The results are discussed, in detail.

Study Area

The Household survey was conducted in two districts, *viz*. in Vizianagaram district in 1122 households spread over 9 Mandals covering 32 villages. In Srikakulam district the coverage was 1357 households spread over 10 Mandals and 40 villages. Thus, in all 2479 Households were covered in 72 villages across 19 mandals in 2 districts of North Coastal Andhra Pradesh[7].

Methodology

The mandals were selected, based on 21 specific parameters for a separate exercise to identify and grade levels of poverty.

With probability proportional sampling, mandals were selected from "very poor", "poor" and "less poor" categories of mandals from each district, representing different levels of poverty and geographical dispersal. Out of the selected mandals, by adopting similar criteria, sample villages and households were selected. An interview schedule was prepared to collect the data on various aspects of living conditions. Of which details on food security are discussed, in detail, here in.

Results

The occupational pattern of the respondents (Table A) shows that nearly half of them are agriculture labour depending on daily wages. Cultivators are next in majority (28 per cent) but their landholding size is so meagre that at times they are worse off, than the agriculture labour. The average holding is just one acre, mostly under rainfed condition. They also depend on "wages".

The duration of employment of the respondents showed that for majority (59 per cent) 120-200 days work in an year is available (Table B). For another 13 per cent, work is available for 30-90 days in an year, whatever may be the wage per day. On an average, the number of days of work, available per head in an year is observed to be 186 days, *i.e.,* half the year they have no work.

Food Security

So far in the literature, there are very few studies reported at micro level (Household), on the problems faced by poor people regarding their food security. Most of the studies were at the state or district level, with aggregate estimates. But in this study apart from household survey, by adopting PRA methods, the perceptions of the poor on food security were captured. The results have suggested that the strategies and interventions to be adopted do not need new technology or knowledge but only a new approach — whereby half the problem can be solved, *i.e.,* maldistribution can be corrected.

The extent and nature of food security available for the poor and disadvantaged families is very saddening. Nearly 70 per cent of the households have no food stock *i.e.,* their survival is a day to day struggle for food (Table I). Even for the rest of the 30 per cent the position is not that rosy. For majority of the households the annual stock ranged between 250-750 kgs. (Table I).

As per the ICMR recommendation *i.e.,* @ 450 gms. cereals for consumption unit per day, it is assumed that each household requires 2 kgs. per day. Then only 9 per cent of the households have food stocks sufficient for one year (Table I).

Another 8 per cent each have stocks adequate for 4 months and less; 4-8 months, 8-12 months (Table II A).

TABLE II A

The effective percentage of households having food security for varying periods of time

Duration of Food Security	Percentage of Households
Up to 4 months	8.1
Between 4-8 months	8.0
Between 8-12 months	7.5
Beyond 13 months	8.6
	32.2

Thus, the real situation indicates that the food security has to be provided for at least 70 per cent of the Rural Poor households.

Food grain requirement

It is obvious that food grain requirement for consumption do vary depending on the size of their households. It is reflected from the field observation that for nearly 60 per cent of the households the annual requirement is nearly ten quintals or more. Another 35 per cent households require between 5-10 quintals. In general, the data has shown that for majority households a minimum of 10 quintals of food grain have to be provided for the 'Normative Consumption' (Table II).

Seasonality

The seasons in which the households feel the highest deficiency of food grains, has brought out very interesting revealation. For majority of the (56 per cent) households during rainy season, there is food grain deficiency (Table III). Only 13 per cent felt that the deficiency was during summer. For another 15 per cent winter was the deficient season. All through the year, a blessed few (16 per cent) did not feel any food grain deficiency. The reality is that, in all seasons there are households with food grain deficiency at varying degrees. Thus, the situation warrants that the food grain deficiency is the most during working season (rainy) and the least in idle (summer) season. There is a need for an appropriate strategy to be evolved to meet the food shortage, pointedly during the work season. This will give bargaining capacity to the working class. Otherwise they sell (pledge) their labour (in advance) cheaply, for a few measures of food grains to the landlord or contractor and work for countless hours, at the mercy of the middle men. Thus, their labour is exploited and they are marginalised. But if the State can provide adequate food security to the poor rural working class, during rainy season, they can fetch better wages.

Public Distribution System : A Bridge between requirement and availability

PDS is essential in a system like rural Andhra Pradesh, where people have poor incomes and open market prices of the essential food grains are beyond their reach.

Through PDS, Fair Price shops sell many items. But 83 per cent of the respondent households reported to be purchasing rice from Fair Price shops (Table IV). Next important question pertains, to the extent of lifting of stocks. Sixty per cent of the households are lifting between 10-20 kg. of rice from Fair Price shop. Only 12 per cent of the respondents (that too a meagre 4 kg./pm.) are lifting wheat, which is not an item in the food basket in these areas. But still as a policy wheat is supplied through Fair Price shops. Depending on the local food consumption habits and needs, wheat can be completely replaced by adequate quantities of millets, which will be lifted in full quantity by the poor.

Seventy Eight per cent of the households are not buying edible oil due to its irregular supply, huge-one time-investment-in bulk quantity (2 kgs. at a time) coupled with storage problem etc. But kerosene is bought by 93 per cent and sugar is bought by 91 per cent of the households. Thus, in all, it can be estimated that nearly 7-10 per cent of the families are so poor that they can't buy kerosene or sugar even from fair price shops. Ninety per cent of households buying kerosene, have bought less than 5 litres per month, and around 2 kgs. of sugar. The people not only don't feel the need for these items but also, they require more of rice (the staple food) or a millet like Ragi or Jowar.

As many as 60 per cent of the households are buying pulses from the open market (44 per cent buy Tur dal). Tamarind, soaps are also brought from the open market.

The prevailing situation warrants the need for expanding the scope of PDS to include other commodities essential for the households particularly pulses (on subsidy rates) on the lines of Girijan Cooperatives in the tribal areas. Also it is noticed that these people purchase their food requirement in small quantities, almost every day due to their 'daily wage' employment pattern. Hence, they pay more at the retailer's end in the open market. While selling their produce also, they get lesser prices. Thus, in both the counts erosion of the real value of already meagre incomes of the households is taking place. If this situation can be corrected by paying appropriate prices, it amounts to additional income and the marginalisation to majority of the poor can be averted.

A few suggestions have come from the respondents, as to how to strengthen the food security through help from government. Twenty one per cent of households wanted increased quantity of commodities from Fair Price shops at reduced prices. Another 23 per cent wanted assets like land and irrigation facilities, so that they can grow more food (Table V).

Majority of the respondents opined that PDS, even in its

present form of operation, has generated security among them. Incidentally their bargaining power has come to stay. Their fear of chronic hunger was greatly reduced because something is available, at the FP shops to mitigate their hunger, even though partially, if they can generate some income.

The need is to adjust the presently undifferentiated, generalised, urban oriented PDS (as the production of food grains is normal) to meet the fate of 40 per cent of the country's population, which is below poverty line. In the present context of acute hunger, poverty, unemployment, for millions of hungry people, subsidies are both inevitable and essential.

The scope of the existing PDS can be broadened, by including more items (like Girijan Cooperatives in ITDA areas) and making available the items throughout the month (at smaller quantities) will go a long way, in driving the wolf away from the door of the poor, throughout the year.

TABLE A

Occupational Aspects of Households

Occupational Aspects	Percentage of Households
Agriculture (Cultivator)	28.2
Agricultural Labour	49.6
Non-Agricultural Labour	1.0
Artisan	6.0
Business	4.0
Service	4.2
Fishing	0.5
Skilled Work	1.4
Job	3.1
A.H.	1.0
Others	1.0
Total	100.0

TABLE B

No. of months employed

No. of months employed	Percentage of Households
1-3	13.0
4-7	59.3
8-9	7.0
9-12	20.7
Total	100.0

HOUSEHOLD SURVEY TABLES

TABLE I

Pattern of Distribution of the Households according to the Availability of the Foodgrains

Foodgrains in Kgs.	Percentage of Households
Nil	67.8
1-250	8.1
251-500	8.0
501-750	7.5
751-1000	2.0
1001-1250	2.0
1251 above	4.6
Total	100.0

TABLE II

Distribution of Households according to the Requirements of the Foodgrains for a Year

Foodgrains in Kgs.	Percentage of Households
1-250	0.3
251-500	4.0
501-750	18.6
751-1000	17.0
1001-1250	22.5
1251+	37.6
Total	100.0

TABLE III

Distribution of Households against Seasonal Deficiency of Grains

Season	Percentage of Households
No Deficit	16.3
Winter	14.6
Rainy Season	55.7
Summer	13.4
Total	100.0

TABLE IV

Distribution of Households availing of PDS

	Particulars	Percentage
I.	Users	83.3
	Non Users	16.7
	Total	100.0
II.	**Rice (Kgs.)**	
	1-5	25.0
	6-10	9.0
	11-15	19.0
	16-20	40.0
	21-25	6.0
	26 above	1.0
	Total	100.0
III.	**Wheat (Kgs.)**	
	Nil	87.6
	1-2	5.2
	3-4	3.1
	4+	4.1
	Total	100.0

IV.	**Sugar (Kgs.)**	
	Nil	9.0
	1-2	85.3
	3-4	5.2
	4 Plus	0.5
	Total	100.0
V.	**Kerosene (Litres)**	
	Nil	7.5
	1-2	27.6
	3-4	59.4
	4 Plus	5.5
VI.	**Palmoline Oil**	
	Nil	78.3
	1-2	17.7
	3-4	4.0
	Total	100.0

TABLE V

Distribution of the Houscholds according to the Help they seek from the Government

S.No.	Nature of Assistance	Percentage of Households
1.	Increase in Quota, Reduction Price	21.2
2.	Monetary Help	27.3
3.	Land + Irrigation	23.2
4.	Tools	4.0
5.	No Response	11.4
6.	Storage Facilities	1.5
7.	Government Loan	3.0
8.	A.H. Help	2.0
9.	Any Help	0.4
10.	Not required	1.3
11.	White Card	0.4
12.	Business Investment	1.3
13.	Others	3.0
	Total	100.0

REFERENCES

1. Amartya Sen, 1997, "Hunger in the Contemporary World", Lecture at Delhi University (News item).
2. Killer Governments, 1996, *Indian Express*, November 19.
3. National Conference on Agriculture for Kharif Campaign, 1998, News item, *The Hindu*, April 10.
4. Mohan Rao, J., 1997, Food Security and Free Markets : Prospects and Policy Options University of Massachusetts at Amherst.
5. Swaminathan, M.S., 1996, Food Security Meaningless without Access — Lecture at National Academy of Agricultural Research and Management, Hyderabad, June 19, 1996.
6. Venugopal, K.R., 1992, Deliverance from Hunger — PDS in India, Sage Publications, New Delhi.
7. Vasudeva Rao, D (Co-author), 1997, Social Assessment Study District Poverty Initiative Project (Sponsored by World Bank), Council for Social Development, Hyderabad.

17

Changes in Cropping Pattern and Household Food security — Case Study of Dry Land South Indian Villages

—*P. Prabhakar Varma*

SECTION I

Introduction

The Universal Declaration of Human Rights of 1948 provides that 'everyone has the right to a standard of living adequate for the health and well-being of himself and his family, including food.' According to Amrtya Sen's "entitlement and deprivation thesis" (Sen, 1981 and Dreze and Sen, 1989) individual to be food secure when there is enough food in the system that he/she can buy (food availability), when he/she has the capacity to buy that food (ability to buy food), and when the food that the individual buys provides him/her with the requisite nutritional value (The World Bank, 1986). An extension to the sen's thesis emphasises that three additional conditions have to be met in order to ensure food security at the individual level. They are, role of institutional sanction to access available food, the exercise of choice to access the food that is available and presence secondary food system*.

More recently, The Committee on World Food Summit, which is going to take place in November 1996, articulated that, "Food Security means that food is available at all times,

---

*Mukherjee, Amitava (1996), ''Institutional Sanctions, Choice and Secondary Food System : Incompleteness of Sen's Entitlement and Deprivation Thesis As An Explanation for Hunger", *Indian Economic Review* (Forthcoming).

that all persons have means of access to it, that it is nutritionally adequate in terms of quantity, quality and variety, and that it is acceptable within the given culture."*

Food security is discussed in the policy discourse at two levels; at the global level, and at the household level. International bodies like the Food and Agriculture Organisation (FAO) and dominant literature on the food security treats the issue as one of balancing global production and consumption of food grains. Issues related to food entitlements and distribution is relegated to secondary priority in this approach. The second school of thought provides greater emphasis at the household level food security, which encompasses household level access and ability to food.

The present study documents that experiences of rural communities on food security at the household level, especially in relation to the changes in the cropping pattern in a dry land district of Andhra Pradesh. This study is important, as recent evidences from the state point out a substantial decline in area under food crops, especially that of area under paddy in the irrigated regions of the state. This decline is due to a shift towards export oriented cash crops and to aquaculture in the coastal districts of Andhra Pradesh. In this context, it would be of analytical interest to understand the changes in cropping pattern in dry land regions, which has traditionally subsistence farming among the small and marginal farmers, and its impact on the household food security.

The study is conducted in four selected villages of Neeradigonda Mandal (lowest administrative unit) of Adilabad district of Andhra Pradesh. These communities are tribals and dependent on agriculture and forest for their sustenance. Centre for Education and Agriculture Development (CEAD), a development NGO is working with these tribals in improving their productive capacities through interventions in agriculture development and other economic and social programmes. The selected four villages form part of 20 villages in which the NGO is working since 1993.

---

*From draft of a Policy Statement, Committee on World Food Security.

The study, it is hoped to develop greater understanding on implications of changes in the cropping pattern on food security at the household and at the community levels. It also helps in developing appropriate mechanisms to ensure food security especially during the scarce periods. The objectives of the study are to investigate and document.

(a) Changes in cropping pattern, its causes and impact on household level food security and the power to access food.

(b) Dependence of the communities on secondary food systems available from forests and common lands.

(c) Employment and earning opportunities in rural areas especially during the food scarcity periods.

(d) Availability and utilisation of food resources provided by the markets and government.

(e) Social, cultural and economic changes that affect the food habits and there by food security.

(f) Coping up mechanisms devised by the community to improve food security.

This report is divided into four Sections. Following this introduction, Section II discusses the theoretical and empirical issues related to food security and the current debate on the issue, Section III presents the study methodology, Section IV major findings and Section V, summary and policy implications.

SECTION II

ISSUES RELATED TO FOOD SECURITY

This Section provides analytical and empirical review on various perspective related to food security. This exercise is undertaken to contextualise the findings of the case study presented in the second part of this report.

1. Food Security — Fallacy in Global Approach. During the past few years, there has been a concern over declining world cereal production, stocks and food aid supplies as well as rising cereal prices. World cereal production in 1995 was estimated at 1,891 million tons, some 3 per cent below the

1994 volume and well below trend for the third consecutive year. Global production of staple foods, comprising the major cereals, roots and tubers, was also expected to be 3 per cent lower than in the previous year.*

While this is true, the issue of food security is looked from a different perspective., *i.e.* from the entitlements and distribution angle. A failure on this front would lead to food insecurity and famines. Examples of this are recent famines of many of the Sub Saharan Africa.

In the past and even now, food is used as a bargaining weapon in the global politics successfully by countries like United States. To illustrate how politics of food operate, there is no suitable example than the following statement from the Vice President of United States of 1960s. To quote; ".... I have heard that people may become dependent on us for food. I know that was not supposed to be good news. To me that was good news because before people can do anything they have got to eat and if you are looking for a way to get people lean on you and be dependent on you, in terms of their co-operation with you, it seems to me that food dependence is terrific" (Cited in Vyasula, 1995). Countries like India have learned this lesson through bitter experiences, after depending on United States for food during 1967 famine (under PL 480 of United States).

Another school of thought, which has influenced larger sections of policy makers especially those related to food production and distribution, argues that food production has to confine to few places (countries) which have comparative advantage in production. This view propagated under the present liberalised regime, has a basic premise that markets do function well for the welfare of the poor. As the experience with over fifteen years of structural adjustment programmes of many countries testify, liberalisation of agriculture commodity markets have not benefited the poor. This comparative advantage paradigm assumes that food production similar to any other commodity

*News Release. FAO Director-General Jacques Diouf Announces World Food Summit to be held at Organisation's Rome Headquarters from 13 to 17 November 1996. FAO document.

production. But in the case of food it forms basis for life itself. With internationalisation of capital, and free movement of capital across the nations, there is very danger of small and marginal farmers becoming vulnerable to food insecurity, if we apply comparative paradigm for food production. It would distort the domestic food grain prices and incentives and also lead to food dependency.

Michael Chossudovsky, Professor of Economics at the University of Ottawa, in fact, argues that global food oversupply in the era of globalisation actually undermines food security and causes famines. Chossudovsky points out that the peasantry is increasingly being transformed into landless workers, while small farmers are being driven out by larger farmers and international agro-business concerns. The prevalent economic paradigm, being promoted under structural adjustment, which emphasizes privatisation of common lands, commercialisation of water and production of high value added non-staple and processed foods, is actually detrimental to food security of the poor. Even as a number of developing countries pursue cash crop exports, a global surplus is created which depresses commodity prices and leads to a fall in incomes of the poor farmers. In many cases it is too late for them to return to the security offered by traditional subsistence farming.*

Thus, there is an urgent need to re-look into this dominant paradigm of food security which treats the whole issue in terms of matching the numbers of production and distribution. Also we need to test empirically certain hypothesis related to food security in countries like India, as many analysts would argue has relatively better distribution network and general infrastructure development which can meet any famine situation. It would be interesting to empirically test food security at the micro level, in the context of changes in the cropping pattern and commercialisation of agriculture in Dry land zones of India, which in habits most poverty stricken population who depend on subsistence agriculture. A study of food security of

*Michael Chossudovsky. The causes of global famine. Third World Resurgence. No. 64, December 1995.

these sections would throw new light on the validity of certain notions related to food production and availability to the poor.

2. Food Security At the Individual/Household Level

As mentioned earlier, literature on this front mainly emanates from Amrtya Sen's "Food Entitlementand Deprivation Thesis". According to Sen's thesis, food insecurity statements translate readily into statements of ownership of food by the person, and to understand food insecurity, therefore, one has to go into the structure of ownership of food. The ownership relations (or entitlement) can be based on trade, production, labour and transfer. Again, some of these can be treated as direct entitlements (Own) and some as indirect (Exchange) entitlements.

The exchange entitlement mapping is the relation that specifies the set of exchange entitlements for each ownership, which defines the possibilities that would be open to individuals corresponding to each ownership situation. Given an individual's ownership bundle (including labour power) Sen identified five factors which determine an individual's exchange entitlements, namely the following :

(1) The Individual's ability to find employment, the duration thereof and the wage rate at which the individual will be employed.

(2) The Individual's ability to earn by selling the relative individual's non-labour assets, and the costs to be incurred by the individual to buy whatever he or she may wish to buy.

(3) The commodities that the individual can produce with his/her own labour power and resources he/she can buy and manage.

(4) The cost, to the individual, of purchasing resources or resource services and the value of the products which he or she can sell.

(5) The social security benefits to which the respective individual is entitled to and the taxes etc., that he or she may be enjoined by law to pay.

The extent to which an individual can avoid food insecurity will depend upon both the individual's ownership of commodities and on the exchange entitlement mapping that the relative individual faces. A general decline in food supply may indeed cause an individual to be exposed to food insecurity through a rise in prices with an unfavourable impact upon the individual's exchange entitlement. Even where food insecurity of the person is thus caused by food shortage, the immediate reason for the individual's food insecurity will be decline in that individual's exchange entitlement.

A failure of these entitlements, according to Sen's thesis would result in food insecurity, though it can happen due to shortage of aggregate supply of food as well. This failure is termed as entitlement failure. Various factors would lead to this failure which means that an individual's failure to be entitled to a bundle of commodities with enough food. Those factors can be external to the individual's entitlements like, changes in economic policies, rise in prices, choice failure etc.

While the concept of entitlement so far focused on a person's legal rights of ownership, the entitlement and deprivation thesis accepts that there are some social relations that take the broader form of accepted legitimacy rather than legal rights that are justiciable. For instance, preferential treatment for male members of the households in provision of food can be one instance. Other cultural practices and restrictions imposed on consumption of certain typed of food would also lead to entitlement failure (Mukherjee, 1996).

These extended entitlements can be seen in three forms according to Mukherjee (1996), which determines food insecurity and has potential use in social analysis. They are, existence of institutional sanction, the issue of choice and existence of secondary food system. These three are important to understand food security in its entirely at the individual and household level apart from other entitlements discussed by Sen.

To summaries, we hold that while global food security is important in terms of increasing production to meet the growing population, but the comparative advantage paradigm of global food security would certainly threaten the individual food security through trade entitlement failure and would throw millions of subsistence farmers out of agriculture. This paradigm would also threaten the national food security of many countries and sovereignty and freedom of many nations. With free market economic paradigm sweeping across the developing world, individual/household food security is more important as markets exclude the poor from accessing food. There is a real threat to secondary food system available to the poor which play a crucial role in ensuring food security, especially during the scarce period with liberalisation of relevant laws which provide private access to common resources like forests, water and common lands.

SECTION III

STUDY METHODOLOGY

The methodology for this case study has evolved in consultation with the field staff of the NGO and other experts on the subject. Along with PRA techniques, group interviews and focused interviews with women and agriculture labour formed key methods of date collection. Group interviews and discussions were held with the sangha members present during the field work. Secondary data from CEAD records helped in describing the area profile and for substantiating some crucial observations from the field. Intensive interviews with few groups of households are conducted to arrive at quantification of some important data related to crop production and etc.

Selection of villages, preceded discussions with CEAD field staff and their opinion on the representativeness of the village has guided identification of villages. The study area is part of the Nooradigonda Mandal, which is classified as acute drought affected area of the district. This Mandal consists of 43 villages of which CEAD is operating in 25 villages. Four villages viz., Narayanpur, Yapalguda, Savargoan B and Rollmamda were selected for the study. Demographic features of these villages are presented in table 1.

TABLE 1
Village Profiles

	Yapalguda	Savargoan	Narayanpur*	Roolmamda	Total
Number of Households	59	52	90	63	264
Total Population	268	211	391	331	1201
SC population	0	57	124	1	182
ST population	268	154	43	330	795
Land (in Acres)					
Dry Cultivated	191	131	191	158	671
Dry Uncultivated	2	0	30	9	41
Wet Cultivated	7	0	3	5	15
Land ownership No. HH					
0. Acre	9	18	36	18	81
<5. Acre	49	34	49	44	176
No. HH having Irrigation					
Well	12	12	3	0	27
None	37	22	44	0	103
Household Occupation					
Cultivators	50	34	51	**	135
Agriculture labour	9	18	33		60
Others	0	0	2		2

*Others are backward caste population

**Data not available

Since the participating NGO, Centre for Education and Agriculture Development (CEAD) is working in the area for the past four years, there was no problem of familarising with the community. As a first step, the study team explained the objective of the study in the group meetings and solicited the response from the community. PRAs were conducted on social and economic status of the community by using social map. Group interviews were hold to collect data on agriculture practices, consumption pattern, dependence on secondary food system and wage employment potential.

SECTION IV

MAIN FINDINGS

Agriculture — Changes in Cropping Pattern

Historically most of the inhabitants used to cultivate land under 'Podu' (shift) cultivation, where they used to cut the forest and cultivate food crops. Settled cultivation in this area came into existence just prior to the Independence (1947). From earlier studies on the area, we understand that the main food crop grown in the area was jowar, followed by minor millet. During 1950s cotton was introduced in a limited scale, which picked up the momentum during the seventies. By 1980s cotton on an average reached 10-20 per cent of the total area under cultivation.

Presently cotton is a major cash crop of the area. The black alluvial soil is suitable for cultivation of cotton. Traditionally food crops like, Jowar, Bajra and pulses were grown during the Kharif season as mixed crops in this area. What we see presently is a shift towards cotton, in terms of larger area under cotton crop, compared to area under other food crops. Pie diagrams (charts I to III) of three villages studied, presented here would mid eighties, mainly at the cost of jowar crop. On an average, cotton now occupies 50 per cent of the area cultivated compared to an average of 20 per cent in mid eighties. *Prima facie* a shift in the cropping pattern to cash crops, does not necessarily make a peasant vulnerable, instead it allows the peasant to have cash in hand to purchase food grains. While this is theoretically true, the reality is something different. There is very limited enabling economic and social environment in this area in order to provide benefit of cash crops to the small and marginal peasants.

Prices seems to be one guiding factor determining the crop choice. If we see the wholesale price of different grains in the local market, it is clear that price inducement is primary factor and demonstration effect followed the suit, inducing small and marginal farmers to get into cotton crop production, which was earlier an arena of rich and middle peasants of the district. We have data from the local agriculture marketing society which handles wholesale trade of food grains of the surrounding areas. Between 1990-91 and 1995-96 the sale price of cotton and jowar per quintal has doubled. It was recorded a peak price of Rs. 955 per quintal during year 1990/91 and has reached to Rs. 1,950 during 1995/96. The rise in price of Jowar was from Rs. 190 to Rs. 389 during the same period. The price rise of other crops was somewhat modest. Maize has increased from Rs. 350 to Rs. 400, blackgram from Rs. 750 to Rs. 1120 per quintal during the same period. Some crops have recorded a decline in prices as well. Cases in point were Wheat, Bengal gram and sun flower etc. If the prices of both cotton and jowar has risen considerably, the shift from jowar to cotton is more guided by the anticipated high levels of income that accrue from cotton. Does this mean that the shift witnessed was due to prices? It appears so for many farmers, but they hasten to add that in real terms the net gain for the small and marginal farmer is most often negative. Tables presented below show the cost of periods. (Tables 2, 3 and 4). It can be seen that, compared to mid eighties, the peasant is now in a more vulnerable condition with respect to cotton. While on the whole there is surplus in jowar cultivation, the decline in aggregate area under jowar would have reduced the food availability at the household level.

The farmer tended to lose on both counts, one, crop failure and second, fluctuations in sale price, especially with exploitative middlemen and commission agents operating in the markets. For example, during 1994 the peak sale price of cotton during the season was Rs. 2,300 per quintal, which has come down to Rs.1,950 in the subsequent year. This kind of wide fluctuations would disappoint the calculations of the farmer by the time the crop comes to the market for sale. Linked with this, is the exploitative practice of traders/money lenders who give advances to the farmers for crop production and for consumption purposes and take the credit for crop inputs and exclusively for consumption purposes for at least four months in the year, after they consume the stored food grains. This means that farmers are facing both production and trade entitlement failures, which would induce them into food insecurity.

There was also a shift, from mixed crop to mono crop with large scale cultivation of cotton. This has resulted in decline in varieties of food grains available at the household. In the case of mixed crops, farmers used to get atleast part of the produce in the event of a failure of one or many of the crop(s). Now with mono cropping and high probability of failure due to uncertain rains, the vulnerability has increased. Along with this, the net benefit tended to be low or negative, because of the loss of by-products which used to be the case with traditional varieties of food grains like Jowar. The traditional variety of jowar stem used to be fed to livestock and it used to have pulp which provides nutrients and staple diet for cattle. With the HYV varieties, the stem tended to be shallow, which was not of much use a cattle feed (the cattle do not like this variety).

Yet another manifestation of change in cropping pattern and subsequent increase in vulnerability of the peasants can be seen from the amount of grain that farmers keep for self consumption. We come to know from the older farmers that till seventies, small farmers used to produce grains that are sufficient for 12 month period. This was not so in the recent past. For about four months from March to June, farmers are forced to make complete market purchase of food grains.

The decline in diversity in mixed crops also testify that more and more production is aimed at markets. Crops like green gram, black gram, Bengal gram are sown interspersing jowar which is the main food crop during the Kharif season. During the rabi season, wheat, sunflower, dhania are some of the crops grown by relatively better off farmers. From this it can be inferred that most of the produce goes to markets.

Not only a shift in choice of crops, but the cropping systems themselves have undergone a change. In all the four villages, during our group discussion with the community, it was revealed that, farmers are adopting high yielding varieties (HYV) of seeds, which would increase the yield levels. This is mainly through provision of seeds on relatively subsidised rates. But with the HYVs, villagers have complained, increased the use of fertilisers and pesticides. This sea change in cropping methods has come since the early seventies (according to them during Mrs. Indira Gandhi's regime). A historical transact of agriculture pattern as narrated by the villagers is presented in Chart IV for the village Savargoan B. The situation is similar in other three villages as well. From chart IV, it can be seen that mid seventies constituted the turning point, where in HYV seeds and chemical fertilisers were introduced in the area. From mid seventies a shift towards using more chemical fertilisers has set in, which has seen a progressive increase over the period.

This high input use and cropping methods has resulted in increase in cost of cultivation. Till the eighties, farmers used to prepare compost of natural manure and use it as fertiliser. The shift to chemical fertiliser and pesticides (HYVs are more prone to diseases) has led to increase in cost of cultivation. For example, in Narayanpur village, the fertiliser use has doubled between 1983 to 1991 and the cost has increased over 50 per cent during the same period. The average cost of pesticides used per acre is about Rs. 2000 in recent years. The data on cost of cultivation with respect to cotton in all the villages show that pesticides account for nearly half the cost.

This shift in cropping pattern along with use of HYV seeds, increase in use of fertiliser and pesticides has not increased the earnings and net profit to the farmers (Tables 2 to 4).

TABLE 2

Cost of Cultivation and Profitability of Cotton (per acre) Village : Roolmamda

	1995		1985	
	Quantity	Cost Rs.	Quantity	Cost Rs.
Total Cost of cultivation		4,012		160
Output	Quintal	2.5		0.5
Sale Price	@ Quintal	1,800		500
Net Profit		–488		90
Jowar				
Total cost of cultivation		ERR		ERR
Output	Quintal Jowar	5*		2
	Black gram	1		
Sale Price	@Quintal Jowar	400		500
	Black gram	1000		
Net Profit		1450		940

*Low output is due to crop failure (Normal output is about 10 q.).

TABLE 3

Cost of Cultivation and Profitability of Cotton (per acre) Village : Yapalguda

	1995		1985	
	Quantity	Cost Rs.	Quantity	Cost Rs.
Total Cost of cultivation		4,415		168
Output	Quintal	3		
Sale Price	@ Quintal	1,800		500
Net Profit		985		332
Jowar				
Total cost of cultivation		1,565		77
Output	Quintal Jowar	4*		7
	Black gram	80 Kg.		
Sale Price	@Quintal Jowar	400		560
	Black gram	1,400		
Net Profit		1,155		483

*Low output is due to crop failure (Normal output is about 10 q.).

TABLE 4

Cost of Cultivation and Profitability of Cotton (per acre) village : Savargoan B

	1995		1985	
	Quantity	Cost Rs.	Quantity	Cost Rs.
Total Cost of cultivation		4,175		134
Output	Quintal	1.5		0.4
Sale Price	@ Quintal	2,050		600
Net Profit		-1,100		106
Jowar				
Total cost of cultivation		1,450		100
Output	Quintal	3*		6
Sale Price	@Quintal	450		200
Net Profit		—100		1,100

* Low output is due to crop failure (Normal output is about 10 q.).

A closer examination of the data from the three villages show that the average rate of return on investment was high during 1985 compared to 1995. Fertiliser and pesticides together account for about 70 per cent of cost of cultivation in 1995, compared to a minimal use of natural manure during mid eighties. One feature observed from this data is the variation in average yield and the market prices which determines the profit and loss of the cultivation. While agriculture was profitable during mid eighties, farmers seems to be incurring losses in 1995, due to cultivation of even food crops like jowar. There seems to be some profit in cotton and jowar cultivation, when the latter is mixed with other cereals like black gram in Yapalguda. Nevertheless, one can come to a conclusion based on the discussions with the farmers that, the yield levels have gone up due to the introduction of HYV seeds. While a better managed farm gets about 12-15 quintals, a normal observation from many farmers is that the average yield for a small farmer would be about 10 quintals per acre in the case of jowar.

Farmers are either losing the crop due to natural disasters or able to barely meet the expenses incurred on the crop. This is especially the case with small and marginal farmers of the area, who are overwhelming majority in the tribal villages of this Mandal. The reasons for this situation are many. As many farmers and agriculture labour have testified, the periods of hunger has increased in spite of relatively better system of government Fair Price shops providing rice at the rate of Rs. 2 per kilo in this area.

This shift to cotton, has resulted in a reduced interest among farmers in cultivation of rabi crop. With cotton taking more time and investment, small and marginal farmers are either unable to raise the rabi crop or are not interested. This has also affected the production entitlement failure.

As discussed earlier, a major change witnessed since nineteen eighties in this region, is increase in use of HYV seeds, of food and non food crops. This has necessitated use of chemical fertiliser and pesticides, which according to farmers has resulted in losing soil fertility. This complaint, though had not been substantiated by the data, but a general observation among the old generation farmers was that, there was decline in soil fertility. One interesting observation was that many farmers have complained that there are "adulterated (duplicate)" fertiliser being sold in the market, which could be one reason for decline in soil fertility. Apart from this, another reason could be indiscriminate use of fertiliser, which would result in decline in soil fertility. If we see the trend usage of fertiliser, it is clear that farmers have increased the quantity of chemical fertiliser used over the period (see charts V and VI).

Coming to sources of credit, cooperative banks located at a nearby town and local money lenders are the main credit providers in the area. After CEAD has started its operations, some farmers are provided with agriculture credit. But this does not cover fully their crop operations. Hence, they continue to depend on the money lenders. The incidence of indebtedness, according to farmers is a necessary evil, as they would like to grow cotton and earn more money to repay and improve overall income levels. Occasionally this seems to be happening, but marginal and small farmers have not benefited from this shift to cash crops.

In summary, changes in cropping pattern to cash crops as against earlier preference for food crops has led to entitlement failure as far as production is concerned, which means that **food insecurity** has **increased** to a larger extent. The use of HYVs, higher dosage of fertilisers and pesticides, uncertain and uneven rainfall and subsequent increase in frequency of crop failure all these cumulatively led to vulnerable agriculture and this has certainly reduced the food availability and income to the farmer. We shall see the situation on the food consumption front at a later state of this report, which reinforces this view. It suffices to acknowledge here that production conditions in agriculture have changed substantially especially with respect to small and marginal farmers who are more vulnerable now compared to earlier period.

Wage Labour Situation

Predictably agriculture provides major employment in the four villages studied. Non agriculture work included, road construction, government public works and forest work (digging pits for saplings) etc. These works, according to the villagers are not regular. In Narayanpur, on an average a labourer gets 169 days of work in agriculture and non agriculture operations together. In Savargoan B, labourers get work for about 190 days. In Yapalguda the same was reported as 170 days.

We cannot make the assumption here that farmers work in their own fields and after that they hire themselves out in the labour market, especially for agriculture work as all the crop operations are time bound. What takes place, is hiring out of some members of the family, during the farm operation period, leaving the own operations to rest of the family members. The period between December to May, most of the households seek employment outside the agriculture. In December, about 10 days employment will be available in picking up cotton and about four days in the field during January for collecting late crops. The rest of the period ending May, employment is very scarce and the average number of days employed, reported by the respondents is about 8 per month. For securing this work, labourers have to go outside the village and often up to the nearby towns and district head quarters. During the month of

April, some people get employment in forest for about 8 days in the month.

Except during the period of harvest of crops like jowar, the wage payment is in cash. This is a marked contrast compared to earlier period, wherein labourers are paid partly kind wages at the end of the agriculture season.

Coming to wages, the usual wage rate is between Rs. 25-30 among men and Rs. 15 among women. These figures are far below from the minimum wages prescribed by the government and the gender disparity is also considerable. It is to be noted that during the eighties, the rates were still lower. But many respondents complained that a complete shift to cash wages, as they grow cash crops, for many agriculture operations, has reduced their accessibility to food and subsequently the food insecurity has increased. The price rise is one factor which was mentioned as a major factor in reducing the welfare of this class (A common phrase they use for this is "rupee has lost its value!!). There seems to be no seasonal variations in wage rates, which was the case with other areas which have irrigation. As a matter of fact, any employer who would give more wage than prescribed (agreed upon), would attract wrath of the village elders.

While many tribals have some land and they work as labourers apart from farming in their own lands, the case of scheduled caste group is quite different. Among the 28 families of scheduled caste in Narayanpur, only 8 of them have some land; the rest are landless labourers. With an average employment per year of 169 days, earning livelihood of this section is very difficult. In the group interview, these sections have complained that they face absolute scarcity of food between Dasara and Diwali festival (October-November). They have also complained that their wages are not commensurate to the rising prics of commodities. Most of them did not have ration cards for procuring subsidised food grains from the government run Fair Price shops. About 10 years ago, there used to be work available for this section, especially from government in laying the roads. Presently this was not available and work opportunities have reduced even though they are ready to work. This section of population, complain that wages in the agriculture sector are not paid regularly, as many small farmers postpone wage payment to the end of the agriculture season *i.e.*, harvesting period.

In Savargoan B absolute landless are very few. While most of the households work on their own fields, they do not engage in outside work unless it is absolutely necessary for them to earn more income for the family.

In summary it appears that many landless households face entitlement failure in terms of exchange of labour power along with failure of production front, which would put them in a severe condition of food insecurity. This situation is doubly uncomfortable for those who are marginal farmers and who have now turned to grow cash crops instead of food crops.

Food Consumption Pattern

We now turn to the discussion on consumption pattern, which determines the level of food security at the household level. The exercise to ascertain food calendar of the households was conducted exclusively with women members as respondents. These women have narrated the food consumption pattern and availability of food in different seasons of the year.

Cereals and vegetables formed staple food for the tribals of Roolmamda village. For staple food they depend on their own production and market purchase as well, since their own produce is often insufficient to meet all the food needs of a year. Most of the households reported having accessed rice and wheat from ration shops of the government. This dependence on government ration shops has been the practice since mid eighties when Rs. 2 a kilo rice scheme was started in Andhra Pradesh. Most of the households had ration cards with them. Rice, Jowar and vegetables are major food items they consume during the year. Dependence on forests for food items is seen in many villages, but not in all villages, as in some cases the forests are not very near. In Roolmamda, forest produce like ber fruits, Mahua flowers, tubers and other wild vegetables are consumed depending on their availability. Among the four villages, household of Narayanpur and Savargoan B are not using forest produce as forests are relatively far from their habitations. Many households reported that jowar produced from their own fields last for to about 3 to four months period. For the rest of the period they depend on market sources. As we see from the PRA data, most of the households purchase rice and wheat from the ration shops. To a certain extent government subsidised rice scheme has helped in procuring rice cheaply. For other commodities like wheat and jowar, they are forced to purchase from the markets. Many households of Narayanpur have reported that for about 3 months they have to purchase food grains by taking credit from landlords or money lenders.

Households of Yapalguda have reported consuming meat from animals caught in the forests during the months of May-June. During the other period, they depend on other forest produce like fruits and vegetables. A decline in availability of forest produce is reported in this village as well.

Women of Yapalguda have complained that due to price rise they were not able to purchase food sufficiently. They have maintained that during the earlier period, livestock products like milk are used for household consumption, now they are forced to sell milk outside instead of self consumption, due to economic compulsions. Overall livestock population also has declined over a period, due to the decline in fodder availability (due to the increase in cotton cultivation and a decline in CPRs) and sale of livestock to meet food requirements. They also have complained about decline in availability of animals like rabbits in the forests which used to provide protein during the earlier period. For the forest food villagers are forced to go into deep forests as the forests in their vicinity have disappeared rapidly during the last two decades.

For households of Savargoan B, forests are relatively at a far off distance, hence their dependence has reduced substantially. They complain that due to deforestation, they are deprived of forest foods like ber fruit, Mahua flowers and other fruits which were part of their diet earlier. According to the women of this village, HYV variety of jowar is not having nutrients as it used to be in the case of local varieties. They complain that the HYV variety is tasteless.

In Narayanpur, households had to purchase vegetables which was not the case earlier. They complain that due to deforestation, they are not getting any forest produce. With decline in soil fertility and uncertain rainfall, the villagers say they were not able to produce enough food for the family. Earlier period, more land used to be under jowar and less under cotton; now with the expectation of high incomes they are reversing this, which according to the women of this village, has resulted in scarcity of food grains.

For the women of Roolmamda, decline in forest produce is a major handicap in ensuring food availability at the household level. They have complained that with the expectation of high return, the farmers have switched over to cotton and they are increasingly entering into a debt trap. They are resorting to credit to purchase food grains from the market. Here also the women have reported a decline in livestock and that livestock products are being marketed instead of self consumption.

Seasonal calendar of food availability and ways of procurement reveal that the poor adopt various strategies to meet the consumption needs. For example, the poor of Roolmamda finds the period between April to July a period of scarcity, where in they have to resort to borrowing. As the seasonal calendar indicates, March and April are the only months the poor depend on forest produce like Mahua flower, Ippa parika and marri fruits. For the rest of the period they do not have any food available from the forests.

May and June are the periods in which they do not get any employment as well. Most of the farmers use their own family labour and start crop operations. In July poor farmers have to resort to borrowing for crop purposes and for good grains as well.

Crop harvesting starts from October and during this period, consumption of new crops (jowar and red gram) takes place in the house. Before this, during the month of September, some households get vegetables from their fields.

From the narrations of the women of these four villages, it is clear that they are vulnerable in terms of maintaining family consumption levels, compared to earlier period. Decline in access to forest produce, price rise and inability to produce enough food grains have led to this vulnerability.

Dependence on CPRs

We have enquired especially on the dependence on forests with the households in order to ascertain the role of forests in tribal food security. Traditionally forest produce are either used for self consumption or for sale, the proceeds of which are used for household level consumption. Forests provide employment avenues, like beedi collection, guarding the forests and afforestation etc.

Of the four villages studied, households of Narayanpur and Savargoan B depend least on forests for their food and employment. In Narayanpur and Savargoan B, men and women join in collection of Mahua flower, Beedi leaves and fuel wood during the months of March, April and May. For the rest of the period, their dependence on forests is negligible. The produce collected is sold in forest depots which are the authorised markets for sale of these products. Since dense forest is beyond 15 KMs. from their habitations these households do not venture into forests during the other periods. They also complain that, there is fierce competition on forest produce among the neighbouring villages which prevents them from venturing into forests, even if they want to go and get some products.

In the other two villages, *viz.*, Yapalguda and Roolmamda the dependence on forests is relatively high. This could be mainly due to the fact that forests are in their visibility. Forest produce lie Mahua flower, fuel wood, honey, gum and etc. are produced from forests in Roolmamda. Most of the collection of these products is done by women. They sell the products in the markets to government depots and to private traders. Part of these products are used at the household level, especially oil extracted from Mahua seed and fuel wood. To get food quality of products they have to travel up to five KMs. distance.

Gum is one product they get for about three months in a year. In Yapalguda, apart from minor forest produce, many households depend on forests for animals. They kill the animals like deer, peacock and rabbits and consume the meat.

A general observation made by many members is that the forest has declined and the variety of products available have subsequently declined over the past five years. They complain that now they have to travel deep inside the forest to get any products they can sell or consume. Deforestation is seen as main reason for this. One more reason could be the type of forests. Most of the forest of this area is mono species, it has teak as major species.

SECTION V
OVERALL OBSERVATIONS

This case study is an attempt to ascertain the extent of food insecurity the communities are facing in the interior tribal areas of South India. The study has used participatory methods to gather the opinions of the community on changes in cropping pattern, employment situation, food consumption pattern and dependence on forests for food and work.

From the responses it can be seen that over the past ten year period, more so during the last five years, there has been an increased insecurity in agriculture. A shift in cropping pattern, from subsistence food crops to cash crops by a majority of small and marginal farmers is seen during the past two decades which according to the villagers, has resulted in vulnerable household, economic position, compared to the earlier period. While theoretically there is no harm in moving towards cash crops, a large scale movement of small and marginal farmers to cash crops puts household food security at stake. As seen from the analysis, but for some support from the government in the form of subsidised rice scheme which provides on average 25 kilograms of rice per family per month, many families would have faced acute food shortages.

The outcome of such a shift in cropping pattern are many and complex as we have discussed in the earlier sections. To recapitulate,

(1) The competing interests of the farmers between food and cash crops has resulted in neglect of food crops, as cash crop requires more attention and investment. This has reduced the production of food grains.

(2) Availability of diverse variety of food grains has reduced due to increased mono crop (cotton) cultivation.

(3) Use of HYV seeds and consequently more chemical fertiliser and pesticides has resulted in unsustainable land use.

(4) The cost of cultivation has increased substantially as the farmers complain 'for higher output, we need to add more fertiliser'. The HYVs according to farmers are not pest resistant as it used to be the case with local varieties. This has increased the cost of cultivation. According to farmers, agriculture prices at the market is one inducement to shift to cash crops like cotton in a big way, but they soon get disappointed as the price fluctuations rob them of the profits.

(5) Decline in livestock rearing which has resulted in less additional income to the households. This means that there is a gradual entitlement failure among these sections as far as production of food grains is concerned.

(6) Indebtedness has increased due to the inability to meet the rising cost of inputs and for consumption purposes.

Though a majority of the tribals has land, most of them go out to do wage labour. They are willing to work, availability is hard to come by. According to landless labour, who are few in number, they on an average get about 170 days of work in a year. The wage rate, though increased over the past ten years, has not kept in pace with price rise. They are now more vulnerable, as the system of kind wage is slowly disappearing in the area and farmers are resorting to cash wage payment. There are limited avenues for non-farm employment. Most of the wage labourers seek employment in road construction by contractors, for which they have to move out of the village. Only able men and women enter into construction work.

On the consumption side, there is a decline in variety of foods that the rural people consume over the years. Women have complained that they are not getting adequate food for about four months a year. Increasingly households are resorting to credit to purchase food from the market. For their fortune, PDS is functioning in this area, but the limited quantity of food items are not sufficient for their survival. Farmers have told that due to more emphasis on cotton, they are not able to produce enough jowar for their year long needs. The produced jowar will last for about 3-4 months.

Villagers dependence on forests has declined over the period. This is due to deforestation which has resulted in shrinking of forests. In two villages forest dependence is limited to about 3 months because forests are far away beyond 15 KMs. from their habitations. In other areas, households complained that there is overall decline in variety of foods available in forests, due to deforestation. Decline in livestock has accentuated their miseries which is a direct outcome to shift to cotton and decline in CPRs.

It is clear from the data that, Rs. 2 a kilo rice scheme which is operating in the area for the past decade, seems to be the cushion on which most of the tribals depended for their food security. This could also be one of the reasons for the observed shift in the cropping pattern, where in farmers expected a continuous supply of food grains from the government run ration shops at cheaper rate. In this context, a steep rise in the price of the rice from Rs.2 to Rs. 3.50 a kilo, a recent decision of the state government would certainly reduce the purchasing power of the poor and leads to vulnerability with respect to access to the food at the household level.

From the above summary situation, it is clear that there is a overall decline in welfare of the tribal communities as far as their food security is concerned. While we did not find absolute hunger, going by the evidence, it can be concluded that the communities are more vulnerable to hunger at present compared to earlier period.

The coping up strategies

We have enquired about the coping up strategies for this situation. A shift towards local food self sufficiency was the main suggestion from the farmers.

We would like to use a judicious mix of natural manure and chemical fertiliser in order to retain soil fertility. (Presently most of the households sell natural manure to the people outside their villages). Efforts of CEAD in promoting sustainable agriculture practices seems to be the main guiding factor in farmer's appreciation towards using a combination of natural and chemical fertilisers. This according to some young farmers would ensure higher yield and protects their environment.

Improvements in agriculture through provision of irrigation water is one of the strategies farmers would like to adopt which would ensure availability of adequate land for food crops, improves their ability to raise second crop and work for landless and marginal farmers as well.

As a coping strategy, some villagers have come up with formation of grain banks which ensures food security during the scarce periods. This was supported by the tribal department of the government of Andhra Pradesh. Functioning of this has led to increased interest among other villages. Many households of the surveyed villages, have reported that they would like to see such grain banks, which are being promoted by the NGO working in that area.

SECTION 6
ENVIRONMENTAL IMPROVEMENT

18

Environmental Protection for Sustainable Development : The Role of Voluntary Agencies

—*Dr. (Mrs.) Susan Verghese* and *T.S. Rajakumari*

Introduction

Development is a well-accepted need of every nation and modernisation is adopted as the means to achieve the goals of development. Modernisation places great reliance on science and technology on the assumption that most human problems can be solved by injecting increasingly large dose of them. What if often forgotten is that by themselves science and technology cannot provide controls and correctives against their abuses. The tendency for ceaseless and uncontrolled modernisation has been challenged powerfully by environmentalists and conservationists. They point out that far from being an unmixed blessing, modernisation may prove to be the undoing of human race (Dube : 1988).

Non-renewable natural resources on which the edifice of modernisation is built are being rapidly depleted but adequate efficient substitutes are not in sight. Fumes and effluents from modern industries, indiscriminately used chemical fertilisers and pesticides, thoughtless exploitation of natural resources and injuries inflicted on flora and fauna are causing ecological imbalance and environmental pollution. To add to all these are the problems created by over urbanisation, growth of urban population without adequate civic amenities and the ever increasing vehicular traffic in cities. This calls for promotion of environmental consciousness among the population, so that we do not encounter problems of unmanageable proportions later, the emphasis should now be on sustainable development.

The term sustainable development brings together two basic principles underpinning the management of human activities. One concentrating on development goals, the other on limiting the harmful impact of human activities on natural environment. The first one is to meet the needs of present generation, the second component is about human activity that does not jeopardize the needs of the future generations.

Environment for sustainable development was the theme of the recent Earth Summit (June 1992) at which the UN adopted the historic Rio-Declaration and the Agenda 21 with a view to establish world peace and security through realisation of the goal of "Environment for Sustainable Development". In concrete and practical terms, sustainable development means a commitment to finding and using resources that are renewable and a more careful management of other resources that are non-renewable. It means choosing products and production processes that avoid adverse impact on the environment. One of the major achievements of the Earth Summit has been to establish universal consensus on the need for a holistic approach to development, bringing economic, social and ecological strategies into natural harmony.

Legislations to protect environment : The development of laws to protect environment has been slow in India. However, after the UN conference on human environment held in Stockholm in 1972 there has been a marked change in India's policies for environmental management. Suitable legislations were enacted to ensure environmental protection such as Wild Life Protection Act 1972, the Water Pollution (prevention and control) Act 1974, Air Pollution (prevention and control) Act 1981, and the Environmental Protection Act 1986 (EPA).

India was also a signatory to the Rio Declaration which reiterated the concept of sustainable development. Since then India has been playing a positive role by following vigorous plans for sustainable development. The National Environmental Tribunal Act 1995 (NETA) is an offspring of the Rio conference. Forest Conservation, afforestation, social forestry and wild life protection etc., have already been initiated by the Government. However law alone cannot help in restoring the ecological degradation. What is required is to awaken environmental awareness and the need for environmental protection among the people.

Today in India, environmental protection movement is gaining momentum and there has been an emergence of several voluntary groups rendering commendable service to create ecological and environmental awareness. Yet much remains to be done if the active participation of wider population is to be brought about. For example, today even the educated man does not realise that he is contributing to the pollution of the city by the over use of his motor vehicle.

Visakhapatnam is a fast growing industrial city in the Coastal Region of Andhra Pradesh, and is known as the industrial capital of the state. The population of the city per 1991 Census has crossed the million mark and the projections are that it will touch 2 million mark by 2000 A.D. Fast deterioration of environment and ecological imbalance has become a major threat to the city. Rapid urbanisation and industrialisation, population explosion, felling of trees, erosion of soil, chemical and biological pollution rapid depletion of ground water and ever increasing number of vehicles and factories are the main causes of these imbalances. The enormous amount of garbage (500 tonnes a day) and mushrooming of slums are also causing serious concern.

As observed by Sharma (1992) the upsurge of grassroots action groups in the last two decades is a trend of profound sociological significance. It signified the emergence of new initiatives on the part of sensitised people and a new sensibility for concrete social transformation in localised settings. The present paper will focus on the voluntary efforts based on the initiatives of a single individual in bringing about environmental awareness among younger generation.

In response to the environmental threat many grassroots level activists and organisations have emerged in Visakhapatnam and are trying to arouse environmental awareness, and to bring about change in attitudes and practices of the people.

Green Vision

In 1992, Jyothishmathi, a dynamic young arts graduate, organised, like minded young people into a group to work towards creating environmental awareness among the citizens of Visakhapatnam and this group came to be known under the name of "Green Vision". Since then the group has been engaged in various environmental protection activities such as creation of environmental awareness among residential communities and students, motivating people to participate in social forestry programmes dissuading people from clogging drains and clearing garbage from vegetable markets to make vermi compost and net working with more established NGOs in the field. The present paper has examined the impact of one of their main activities namely imparting environmental education to school children. The study selected two schools in Visakhapatnam, one exposed to environmental education efforts of Green Vision and the other not exposed. By comparing the level of awareness of the students of the two schools the study aimed to measure the impact of this voluntary group on environmental awareness of the younger generation. The sample : The sample of the study was drawn from two schools in the suburbs of Visakhapatnam city. One was grammar school, Pendurthi and other public school Pendurthi. Both are private English medium, co-educational schools, drawing children from the same Socio Economic backgrounds. The only difference between their schools was that the grammar school was exposed to environmental education imparted by Jyothishmati and her group while the public school was not.

The 8th and 9th grade students of both schools constituted the sample of the study. The entire students in each of these grades were included in the sample. There were 63 students from Grammar School and 61 from Public School. A questionnaire was prepared to assess the awareness of these students on selected environmental issues such as standards of cleanliness, air, water, noise and food pollution, protection of flora and fauna and the need to conserve renewable and non-renewable resources.

A total of 71 questions were asked on the above issues. A maximum score of 2 was given for high environmental awareness, a score of 1 was given for medium awareness and 0 for wrong answers. On the basis of this the score of each student was compared. The following table shows the scores obtained by the students.

The awareness levels on environmental issues of students by school/grade/gender

	8th and 9th grade percentage of total score	9th grade percentage of total score	8th grade percentage of total score	Boys of 8th and 9th grade percentage of total score	Girls of 8th and 9th grade percentage of total score
Grammar School	41.95	51.52	32.29	42.71	38.98
Public	25.70	36.59	23.32	25.47	26.73

The table indicates clearly that the grammar school which is exposed to the environmental education imparted by Green Vision has secured higher scores in environmental awareness. Not only have they secured higher scores school-wise, but they are also found to have higher scores when examined grade-wise and gender-wise. Although exposure to environmental education is a crucial variable in determining the levels of awareness, education levels and gender of the student also seem to independently influence the scores.

Further the fact that public school which has not been exposed to "Green Vision" is not totally lacking in environmental awareness indicates that the modern curriculum and the influence of mass media particularly, the television is imparting certain degree of environmental awareness. This indicates that the school curriculum and mass media can further enhance the environmental education input in their contents.

In view of the several environmental problems faced by the city today it is hoped that the initiatives of an action group like the green vision will go a long way to bring about the desired change in attitudes and practices of communities with regard to environmental protection.

In conclusion it may be said that the grass roots level action groups are playing a very significant role in bringing about environmental awareness among the people of Visakhapatnam City. Although there is still much to be done to awaken environmental consciousness among the public credit has to be given to the green vision group for the priority given by them in sensitising school children. By doing so they are bringing about a steady but silent social revolution. Further, instead of working in isolation from other larger NGOs, the group has displayed a willingness to network with them in the larger interest of the cause they are supporting. Such willingness surely pave the way for the movement to grow into a macro force.

REFERENCES

Dune, S.C., *Modernisation and Development Search for Alternative Paradigms*, Vistar publications, 1998, New Delhi.

Sharma S.L., Social Action Groups as Harbingers 1992 of silent revolution, *Economic and Political weekly*, November 21, 1992, pp. 2557-61.

19

Environment and Development : The Future Scenario

—Dr. (Mrs.) S. Uma Devi

Introduction

The relationship between man and nature changes unfailingly in accordance with the development of human society. With the improvement of productional means and technique, the scale and degree of human transformation of nature are enlarging, and the relation between man and nature is getting closer (Chuanjun, 1992 : 91).

The perception that man lives in close relationship with all living things, plants and animals, is quite old. Ancient and medieval philosophers have often emphasized the inter-relatedness of the entire living world. But a new dimension had begun to appear as the impact of man and his activities on nature came to be noted. The word 'environment' was given an additional meaning since 1960s, to express the broader concept of interaction of human activities on the ecological system and the impact of the ecosystem changes on man himself.

When primitive man lived as a part of the ecological system, he was one of the many species of animals which interacted with one another and with the physical world. Thus, he lived in harmony with nature. Whereas the civilised man, with the growth of modern technology, gained the ability to interfere with or even damage nature.

The civilisation of man is built around two of his greatest inventions — the plough and the wheel. The plough gave man freedom from hunger and wheel, a means of quick transport.

These two inventions have been refined so much that within a few thousand years, man has come to monopolize the management of all natural resources. But this managerial monopoly has brought him to the brink of an ecological disaster, which in its sweep is endangering his own survival. For too long we have been blinded by the positive side of technology and ignored the emerging dark side, because in infancy it was not discernible. In 1895, the introduction of automobile was hailed as the remedy for city pollution from such sources as horse manure. Now we decry the automobile's contribution to acid rain, blood lead content and carbon dioxide buildup. CFCs (Chloroflorocarbons) used in air conditioning and spray cans destroy stratospheric ozone that protects from cancer causing ultra violet radiation.

The destructive impact of such developments has come, with their surge in popularity, in world's bulging population and consequently their increased use. Thus, the industrial revolution proved to be a vital factor in the upgradation of consumerism and consequent degradation of environment. Disposal of the bitter fruits of high consumption, trash and toxic wastes, has become an unimaginable and unmanageable problem. Thus, we are victims of our own success, bogged down in our own garbage (Kayastha : 1992 : 50).

Besides technology, the growth of human population also had led to the profound alternations of our environment. Man is largely dependent on his environment for the resources that sustain him and give him various products. Sustaining large population requires greater availability of goods and services through the process of development. This developmental process requires utilization of natural resources. The use of these resources should not degrade the remaining resources for future use. Extracting these resources in the name of development without due concern for the resource base leads to disturbances in the ecosystems. In the long term these imbalances threaten the future of our planet.

Growth can be physically destructive — laying waste to forests, polluting rivers, depleting natural resources. While these effects are undesirable enough for people living today, they are even greater concerns for future generations — based on a fear that this form of growth cannot last (Human Development Report : 1996 : 63). There is mountainous evidence to show that huge projects, irrigational and industrial, provide man only a very short lived relief. In the long run they disturb the ecology of that area so much that clean water, air and healthy food cannot be taken for granted.

(a) One billion people do not have access to clean water.

(b) 1.7 billion people have no access to sanitation.

(c) These two figures together result in two to three million imminently avoidable infant deaths a year.

With the understanding today of the interdependence of all life on earth with each other and accumulated scientific evidence about various phenomena impacting on earth's atmosphere, a new holistic approach to management of all natural resources is being vigorously advocated. Environment and development are two sides of the same coin.

A paradigm shift in the approach to development is called for to avoid development becoming environmentally destructive and socially disruptive (Swaminathan, 1995). The growing awareness of the importance of maintaining environmental quality in man's own interest and the mounting concern on human progress at what cost, has led to a marked change in development strategies over the past half century.

It used to be that development was seen as simply increasing GDP. Today we have a broader set of objectives including egalitarian development, sustainable development and higher living standards. It is recognized that there is more to living standards than is typically captured in GDP accounting. Improvements in education or health are not means to an end of increased output, but are ends in themselves. Growth by itself does not ensure that the fruits will be equitably shared. We no longer take for granted our environment and we recognize that in the struggle to increase GDP, the air in many developing country cities became so polluted as to make them almost unlivable. We know that cutting down an irreplaceable hard wood forest provides an increase in measured GDP that is probably not sustainable (Stiglitz : 1997 : 19-20).

Development is needed for a better standard of life, but it has to be sustainable, otherwise it would be a self-defeating process transgressing the outer limits, which lead to ecocide. Development which is not equitable is not sustainable and development which is not ecologically sound will be self destructive (Swaminathan, 1994). Populist economic policies will have to yield place from economic growth at all costs to sustainable growth and environmental protection. Therefore, environment and development issues and the links between them are of vital significance. It is essential to have a close understanding of the interrelationship between environment and development for the formulation and implementation of any strategy that safeguards all concerned aspects.

Today, there is an overwhelming concern with respect to global and national environmental degradation caused by both, the forces of development in one group of countries and lack of development by most others some of whom have millions of people living in poverty struggling to survive. Most of them live directly off the natural environment — unable because of poverty and growing numbers, to replenish the earth or temper their demands on limited, fragile ecosystems. The increasing environmental degradation is adversely affecting not only the physical environment, but also the quality of life. "The rapid pace of resource exploitation without due regard for sustainable development has led to this environment development crisis" (Kayastha, 1988). This environmental degradation also threatens the economic and social progress of any country. The future generations may discover that life support systems (*i.e.*, the natural world of animals, plants, soils, waters and air, upon which the whole complex structure of human society and welfare is built) have been damaged beyond repair.

Interdependence has become the environmental as well as the economic reality. This interdependence refers to the interdependence of man and nature, between generations and also between nations because most of the environmental problems are trans-national.

Ecological danger signals in places as different and far apart as Scandinavia and Africa, Nepal and the Caribbean Islands have caused environmentalists to turn their attention to the wise management of earth's renewable resources and to the global effects of industrial pollution and the disposal of the deadly by-products of industrial processes. If the survival of man's life support systems is to be assured, conservation and economic development have to go together (Ellington, 1984 : 204).

Thus, the thrust of the global approach to environmental problems is on how environment development can include the essential aspects of sound environmental stewardship and sustainable economic development.

Broadly threats to natural environment are of three types : pollution, overuse and destruction (Eighth Five Year Plan, 1992-97 : 93). Pollution is a major source of environmental degradation. Much of the water resources and the air continue to be polluted, affecting human health.

(a) 1.3 billion people mostly in cities in developing worlds are breathing air below the standards consideration acceptable by WHO.

(b) 700 million people mostly women and children suffer from indoor air pollution due to biomass burning stoves that is equivalent to smoking three packs of cigarettes a day.

Besides, traditional domestic pollutants, there is increasing contamination by chemicals, heavy metals and other toxic substances, which are thrown into the rivers and the sea due to careless industrial and agricultural practices. Unplanned urban growth and industrialization are also increasing the level of pollution.

Mass consumption and throw away culture reflect overuse of the resources. Both the renewable and non-renewable resources are being exploited without similar stress on their conservation. What we want directly goes against what we need and that is the crux of the problem. People should consume resources according to their needs rather than their wants. There is, in

Gandhi's famous words, 'enough for man's needs, but not for his greed.'

Destruction is another serious threat to the environment.

(a) 70 per cent of the European forests are gone. Many of them were cut down for firewood and this land has been taken over by the expanding population and their need for agriculture products.

(b) About 100 acres of tropical forests are cut every minute. At this rate, in 40 years there will be no more tropical forest left.

The destruction and the degradation of the forests are taking a heavy toll of the soil and water resources. Our enhanced ability to clear forests, building roads and dams, drain wet lands and excavate minerals is destroying natural habitats on a scale never before experienced by out planet.

Any strategy to meet these threats to the natural environment should include raising the levels of education, enforcement of laws and above all increasing awareness among the public and the political leaders to rectify the situation.

Environment and Development

The primary motivation for development is human welfare, which is also the primary motivation for environmental quality. The two motivations coverage and not conflict, thereby rejecting the false dichotomy between environment and development. This should, therefore, encourage the search for optimal harmonious relationship between environment and development. When we speak of environment and development, some of the basic issues which need to looked at, are poverty, population, international inequality and sustainability, of development.

Environmental problems are not new but the accelerating pace and changing character of human impact on environment is alarming. For nearly a century of the industrial revolution and gallop of technology, the issues of environmental degradation and its implication for human welfare did not become apparent. This was partly due to the slowness of biological processes and manifestation of damages to them and partly due to the advantages gained by the development countries (Rajamani, 1995 : 171). But now there is wide-ranging and accumulating evidence that many types of human activity especially since 1960s, are contributing to long term adverse impacts on environment. Particularly notable among them are soil erosion, desertification, deforestation, ecosystem degradation and destruction and extinction of several varieties and species of fauna and flora.

As these environmental effects of the industrial revolution became apparent, scientists, and private individuals had begun to build the organisations which are the foundations of the present environment movement. The drive for prosperity in the aftermath of World War II led to a massive expansion of world trade and a rate of technological development that multiplied man's harmful impact on the environment many times over. Inevitably, this led to a further response from concerned people (Burke, 1984 : 190).

The environmental problems faced by individual counties are components of a global problem. The effects of many of the environmental problems like acid rain, deforestation, desertification, loss of wild species and the serious degradation of the coastal marine environment cannot be contained within national boundaries, nor can they be dealt with exclusively at the national level. Trees cut from steep hill slopes in one country cause folds in another. Toxic wastes eliminated from power stations in Britain fall as acid rain destroying fish and trees in Sweden (Burke, 1984 : 191-192). Cooperative, international effort is required to limit the global impact of serious natural resource depletion and unsustainable economic growth, the growing concern about environment and development is shared in various ways by most countries of the world.

This worldwide concern for accelerated exploitation of resources for development led to the holding of United Nations Conference on Human Environment in Stockholm in 1972. It marked the meeting of minds for global thinking on environmental phenomena and issues that were having their impact on people. Even prior to the Stockholm conference, in the U-Thant Report on "Man and His Environment" published in 1969, there was a clarion call to humanity which stated in the introduction : "For the first time in the history of humanity a crisis of worldwide scope has come into existence, including both the developed as well as the developing countries-concerning the relation of man to his environment. Threatening signs were visible long ago, the demographic explosion, the inadequate integration of technology with the requirements of the environment, the destruction of cultivated lands, the unplanned development of urban areas, the diminishing of open spaces and the ever growing danger of the extinction of many forms of animal and plant life. There is no doubt that if this process will continue future life on earth will be threatened" (Rajamani : 1995 : 172-173).

What the conference marked was not just the recognition that the environment was facing serious problems but also that solving them was a political question which could not be left to private individuals and experts. There was also a recognition that governments must act and act together to stop mankind from destroying the basis of life. The result of the Stockholm conference was thus to establish, for the first time, the place of environment on the political agenda.

The Stockholm Conference brought into focus differing points of view of the industrialised North and the developing South. There was recognition that developing countries faced environmental problems, which had their roots in poverty and under-development. These prevailing conditions of poverty and under-development themselves create a situation where people are forced to live in squalor and further degrade their environment. On the other hand, in the industrialised countries the process of development itself damaged the environment, when not properly managed. The viewpoint of the South was forcefully put across by India's Prime Minister Mrs. Indira Gandhi. According to her, "the environmental problems of the developing countries are not the side effects of excessive industrialisation but reflect the inadequacy of development" (Rajamani, 1995 : 174). She observed that environment cannot be improved in conditions of poverty and that ecology and conservation should not work against the interest of the poor but bring improvement (Kayastha, 1992 : 39-40). The poor suffer the first and most painfully from environmental degradation in rural and urban areas. Although agriculture is still the main source of income for the world's poor, most of them have very little land or are complete landless. In their struggle for survival they plough unsuitable land, cut bushes and trees and overgraze pastures. It is the poor who are also the most vulnerable to the natural catastrophes, particularly droughts, floods and famines. So the poor of the world are both the victims and the perpetrators of a deteriorating environment (Sdasyuk, 1992 : 76).

Poverty and high population growth are closely related. The poor are unaware of the means of controlling pregnancies and are often too poorly educated to use those means even if they are available. Besides this, they see more children as an insurance against high rates of child mortality, and as a provision for their old age.

Rapid population growth is an impediment to development and protection of environment. The population explosion sustained by science and technology is causing almost insoluble problems for the future generations. Unchecked population growth is accelerating the imbalance between human needs and the sustainable use of land. "Degradation of the world's environment, income and equality, and potential for conflict exist today because of over-consumption and over-population. If the unprecedented population growth continues, future generations of children will not have adequate food, housing, medical care, education, earth resources, and employment opportunities" ('Statement on Population Stabilization by World Leaders', presented to the United Nations in 1985).

There exist serious imbalances between the developed and the developing countries of the world with regard to the availability of natural resources and their utilisation. Some countries have an excess of development symbolizing an assault on earth's life support system. There are many cases wherein the less developed countries are endowed with more resources, their level of production is also high but the final consumption therein is much less than in the more developed countries.

The consumption per capita in the industrialized countries is more than twenty times than that in the less developed countries (Raza : 1992 : 62). While the developing countries severely tax their environment, the population of rich countries have a vastly disproportionate mark on the planet.

(a) The birth of a baby in U.S.A. imposes more than a hundred times the stress on world resources and environment as the birth of a baby in poor development countries.

(b) For every hectare of land a citizen of Holland uses within in his own country, he uses the resources of 40 hectares of land elsewhere.

(c) Every year Latin America exports more than 250 million pounds of beef to U.S.A. This amount of meat requires more than 5,00,000 cows to be raised. For every cow that is raised about 1000 trees are cut down. This loss of trees for hamburgers is staggering.

Several programmes were triggered off by the Stockholm Conference on Human Environment. One such was the creation of 'The World Commission on Environment and Development' (also known as Brundtland Commission) by the UN General Assembly in 1983, which produced an unanimous report called 'Our Common Future'. The Commission (1987) called for a new sense of urgency in promoting harmony between mankind and the biosphere.

Since people are the only cause of ecological devastation on a global scale, they are the only source of its recovery. The environment cannot be defended by mere laws, no matter how strict the laws or powerful and rigorous the governments that enforce them. As Burke has rightly said, "it is only by the positive affirmation of the mutual dependence of ecology and economy, of man and nature, by individuals ..... that we can hope to achieve the equilibrium necessary to avoid the looming catastrophe".

The unity, interconnectedness and interdependence of all phenomena on the planet earth was suggested even in our own ancient texts. Thus, the Yajur Veda speaks of "peace of air, peace of earth, peace of waters, peace of plants and peace of trees". The earth as the source of life-human as well as non-human has been considered to be an object of awe, love and reverence and worshipped as the mother goddess since the advent of agriculture (Raza : 1984). The Gaia (mother earth) doctrine which states that the biosphere has been in homeostatic equilibrium with its global environment for millions of years stresses the fundamental interdependence of elements on planet earth. All things are useful for humans and, therefore, should live in harmony with non-human nature as well (Rajamani, 1995 : 170). The Sufi and Bhakti saint poets (Kabir, Tukaram, Ramdas, etc.) sang of the unity and oneness of all phenomena so that a wound inflicted on any element hurts the total system. This system of interdependence is our ecosystem. The wisdom of our ancients has become the imperative of our own troubled times wherein the very survival of the human race and its home — the planet earth — is at stake (Raza, 1992 : 57-58). Barbara Ward, recognised as the pioneer of the ecology movement points out "the vision of unity shared by so many of the great philosophers and so central to all great religions is recognised now as an inescapable scientific fact" (Forward to Down to Earth by Eric Eckholm, 1982).

In the case of India, as early as the Fourth Five — Year Plan, a fairly clear understanding about the relationship between ecology and development was discernible. It was stated therein "The Physical environment is a dynamic, complex and interconnected system in which any action in one part affects others. There is also the interdependence of living things and their relationships with land, air and water. Planning for harmonious development recognises this unity of nature and man. Such planning is possible only on the basis of a comprehensive appraisal of issues particularly economic and ecological. It was necessary, therefore, to introduce the environmental aspects into our planning and development. Along with effective conservation and rational use of natural resources, protection and improvement of human environment is vital for national well being. It is particularly important that long term basic considerations, the social costs and benefits be used as yardstick rather than private gains and losses". Thus, sustainability is a crucially important concept in the context of both ecology and development (Raza, 1992 : 62-63).

The Brundtland Commission Report defined sustainable development as that which "meets the needs of the present without compromising the ability of the future generations to meet their own needs". In the context of ecology sustainable eco-development calls for a sane strategy of conservation of natural resources. Conservation does not mean only the preservation of the wilderness but also and more importantly the rational management of natural resources so that it may yield the greatest sustainable benefit to the present generation while enriching or atleast maintaining its potential to meet the needs of the future generations. Conservation and development may appear to be incompatible but they are not so. While development aims at achieving human goals largely through the current utilisation of natural resources, conservation aims at ensuring the endless continuance of such utilisation (Raza, 1992 : 63). Hence, the concept of eco-development stresses the unity of system of interdependencies through the mechanism of social man and non-human nature.

Future Scenario

If mankind's greatest advances occurred in the twentieth century perhaps, the greatest challenges lie in the twenty first century. The greatest imperatives will be to find ways and means of protecting our habitat, the environment of planet of earth, (Grosvenor, 1988). Basic knowledge of environmental processes has increased greatly during the last half century. However, the main conclusion to be drawn is that more attention should be paid to the problem of preparing for surprise and the future.

Hence, one of the highest stake debates in human history is currently taking place on the future of environment. The usual of array of scenarios runs from the very draconian to the nothing to worry about perspective to the middle — through scenario, with a range of alternatives in between. What is at risk is no less than the future of the whole globe. The question for the future is how serious are the environmental issues facing us, and what are their solutions? The debate, even in scientific circles, ultimately reduces itself to a battle of educated guesses in answer to important questions : what is the earth's carrying capacity and what is the absorptive capacity of the ocean and earth? Will population stablize on its own and even if it does can earth support even a stablized but very large population at a decent standard of living? (Lamm, 1992 : 58).

By the 1980's the international character of many environmental problems had become clear. Warning of the long implications of the present environmental trends contained in reports like "Global 2000 Report" and the "World Conservation Strategy" both published in 1980. These reports made it clear that in man's battle against nature not only was nature losing, so was man (Ellington, 1984 : 205). They made an effort to project the impact on the world of the then current trends in population, resource use and the environment.

In terms of population growth and resource use, humankind is living on the upper slopes of some awesome geometric curves. "Current growth rates have certain areas of the world doubling their population every 25 years. The world is growing 1.8 per cent every year and adds approximately 93 million people a year to those of us already here, 92 per cent of these additions are in the Third World" (Lamm, 1992 : 58). The growing population of these third world countries are, in the words of environmentalist Erik Eekholm (In Down to Earth 1982) "caught in endless cycles of hunger, illiteracy exploitation and disease (and) have no time to worry about global environmental trends. Many are forced by circumstances beyond their control to destroy the very resources from which they must scrape their living". Helping these poor people of the Third World will remain a piece of rhetoric unless the affluent sections of the global population adopt sustainable life styles. Reduced consumption of natural resources is essential for ensuring that the human carrying capacity of supporting ecosystems is not exceeded (Swaminathan, 1994).

Geometric population growth requires geometric growth in

amounts of food, minerals, forest products and other resources and causes increasing stress on the environment. While the population increases by geometrical progression, productive capacities increase only in arithmetical progression. Therefore, social upheaval and instability are the predetermined future predicament of mankind (Seminar, 474, December 1998 : 12).

While biotechnology has made great strides in increasing the food supply, all of the experts warn us that these will only give us breathing room to stabilize population. We are loosing the diversity of genetic material in our new food species as a result they are much more vulnerable to pests, blight and drought. It would see, likely that at some point, the fragile food systems that now feed the world will be interrupted and large-scale famine will result. Water shortages, in some parts of world, aggravated by population will likely cause new tensions. In such conditions environmental refugees will leave deteriorated areas and create pressures on their neighbours. Demographic pressures will likely cause large-scale migration and urbanization and tax the ability of many countries to provide political stability. The key factor of this scenario is "the inability to change reproductive habits in time to avoid overtaxing an area's carrying capacity" (Lamm, 1992 : 61).

There is a significant lag time between taking an environmental problem seriously and effecting a solution. The challenge that faces us is to correctly identify the magnitude of the various environmental threats and adopt appropriate remedies in time. Hence, the global problems of the twenty first century, which we should be beginning to solve now, will require more foresight, coordination, trust and mutual understanding by more people than has been previously displayed in human history

There is a new note of urgency in current warnings about the environment. Twenty-five years ago environmental problems were immediately tangible and visible and they affected people's health or quality of life. Whereas today the environmental problems are less immediately perceptible (acid rain, global warning and loss of ozone layer are less dramatic but have more of an impact) but, as mentioned before, they threaten our very survival.

Then, the environmental problems were most often addressed by engineering solutions which were imposed on corporations but today solutions demand life style changes — changes in how we recycle and reuse things and in what we buy and these solutions are increasingly sought to be imposed upon individuals. Under these conditions, it is hard to form a consensus. There is yet an additional concern : how do we motivate people or nations to make sacrifices today what will avoid a catastrophe which will manifest itself in the future (Lamm, 1992 : 62).

There can be no doubt that the combination of growing population, rising expectations and the enhanced capacity to transform the environment has set us in a path leading to collapse. There is much argument about how far along the path we are and how fast we are travelling but the direction is not in question. It seems likely that some environmental trauma or disaster lies in our future. It is impossible to cover all possible scenarios. "There are so many things that could go wrong that one or more probably will" (Lamm, 1992 : 65). The possibilities are infinite, and as Kenneth Boulding has observed, "the human dilemma is that all our experience is in the past while all our decisions deal with the future". Hence, we are left to speculate on so many variables.

All crisis have opportunity as the other side of the coin. This is as true of the ecological crisis as of others. Hence, the future presents both a challenge and an opportunity. Never have the scientific community and thoughtful policy makers been more united in their warnings that if environmental disaster in the future is to be averted that humankind must change its ways. "No generation has a free hold on this earth. All we have is a life tenancy with a full repairing lease" (Margaret Thatcher : 1990).

Thus, armed with vastly increased knowledge about dangerously ecological trends, environmentalists have been turning their attention to the centres of political power in both the rich countries of the North and the poor countries of the South. It is here, in countries still poles apart geographically and culturally but economically and environmentally linked that support for concerted national and international action has to come (Ellington, 1984 : 207). Many areas of meaningful cooperation emerge with a meeting of minds that share a common concern on environment and development (White 1974, 1986, Clarke *et al.*, 1989). Therefore, "think globally and act locally" has been the slogan which gained currency now in the environmental context (Rajamani, 1995 : 169). It implies that the nature of the subject and its complexities in the world of today are such that the most feasible option is of global thinking and local or regional action to correct environmental imbalances or weld environmental considerations into the process of development.

The need of the hour is for more humans especially the decision makers who are better trained to make responsible choices among alternative futures. Thus, we must locally and globally train more people and select more leaders "who are able to think holistically, who are concerned about violating the biosphere they have inherited and who have the dedication and competence to strengthen international cooperation and organisation to help ensure a decent quality of life for the present and future generations" (Kayastha, 1992 : 54).

We have the tools and technology for bringing improvements in the environment. There is evidence of growing scientific and technological research designed to recycle resources and reduce pollutant emissions. However, the increased scale, diversification and higher costs of research call for a fruitful mutual exchange of research experience such as through UNEP. We can push for myriad public policies where the environmental protection will be incorporated into the price of goods, which will help promote conservation such as a higher tax on petroleum. We can also work for the enhancement of human caring and sharing capacity. For instance, "an investment by one billion people currently living in great affluence in all countries of 1000 dollar per capita could help to form a trillion dollar fund to create a world without poverty" (Swaminathan, 1994). The models are there, but the hurdles are immense. Maurice Strong, head of the 1992 UN Conference on the Human Environment put it succinctly : "Brotherhood, caring, sharing, working together are no longer simply pious ideals divorced from realities of life, but the indispensable ingredients for human survival".

Understanding a problem and its solution is one thing actually solving it is entirely another. We need political and private will, supported by an appropriate environmental policy and environmental ethics to solve them. As Barbara Ward put it, "for an increasing number of environmental issues the difficulty is not to identify the remedy, because the remedy is now well understood. The problems are rooted in the society and the economy — and in the end in the political structures. Foresters know how to plant trees, but not how to device methods whereby villagers in India, the Andes or the Sahel can manage a plantation for themselves. Biologists know where to draw boundaries for nature reserves, but cannot keep landless peasants from invading them to grow food or cut fuel. The solutions to such problems are increasingly seen to involve reforms in land tenures and economic strategy and the involvement of communities in shaping their own lives".

We must stabilize our population, we must achieve the sustainable use of the biological resources, and we must eliminate waste from our use of the non-renewable resources. We already know how to do all of these things. What we lack are the personal commitments that translate into the political will to bring our knowledge, our inventiveness to bear on the crisis in which we find ourselves. We are faced with a choice of direction. In other words we have a choice, the outcome does not depend on the blind forces of nature or the impersonal working of the economy. It depends on how each one of us chooses to live our life..... What we choose to teach our children. Our personal choices, no matter how apparently trivial, when aggregated together are what determines the fate of the planet. A sustainable world in which the economy is in equilibrium with the ecology, in which mankind is in harmony with nature is not out of reach. It is within our power to do everything necessary to reach that world, if each one of us so chooses (Burke, 1984 : 241).

It is increasingly being recognized that environmental policies should be based as far as possible on the consensus between political leadership and the people or the community. True equilibrium and true improvement in the quality of our lives will happen only when an informed and dedicated public wants it to happen. We must educate the people to create an awareness and response in them, who have to be at the heart of it all. People cannot push for action unless they know what the problems are. Individuals and groups relate to the environment through their perception. "Without understanding the bases of perception and behaviour, environmental planning becomes a mere academic exercise doomed to failure because it is unrelated to the terms in which people think and the goals they set (Lowenthal : 1967). The people cooperate only when they get benefit from various developments and policies of the government. The leadership should be able to motivate people and their cooperation by actual participation whenever possible.

Down the whole environmental agenda, a growing awareness of the problem has spurred human inventiveness and ingenuity towards technological innovation and the social transformation which goes hand in hand with it, for developing new approaches for humanity to adopt. Presented with a clear choice, given good information about its implications, some incentive to choose and a small amount of positive leadership, most people are prepared to change their attitudes and behaviour necessary to build a sustainable society. Today we still have a choice of direction because we have not yet passed the point of irrecoverability for most of our degraded ecosystems. If we choose to invest our capital, our minds, and our skills on restoring and sustaining the ecosystem, on opening up the several roads to a sustainable society, then the prospect will be one which offers each succeeding generation the hope that life will get better.

REFERENCES

Burke Tom, "The Politics of Ecology" in Sir Edmund Hillary (ed.), Ecology 2000 — The Changing Face of the Earth. Michael Joseph. London. 189-202, 1984.

Burke Tom, "The Future" in Sir Edmund Hillary (ed.), Ecology 2000 — The Changing Face of the Earth, Michael Joseph, London, 227-241, 1984

Boulding Kenneth, "The Fallacy of Trends", National Forum, 64(3), 19-20, 1984

Chuanjun Wu, "Utilization and Production of Natural Resources in National Economic Development" in Mehdi Raza (ed.), Development and Ecology, Rawat Publications, New Delhi, 91-95, 1992.

Clarke, J.I., Curson, P., Kayastha, S.L., and Nag, P., "Population and Disaster", Basil Blackwell, Oxford, 1989.

Ellington Athleen, "Environmental Hot Spots" in Sir Edmund Hillary (ed.), Ecology 2000 — The Changing Face of the Earth, Michael Joseph, London, 204-226, 1984.

Grosvenor, Gilbert M., "Will We Mend Our Earth?", National Geographic, Washington D.C., 766-771, 1988.

Kayastha, S.L., "Frontiers in Environment : Re-Appraisal Of Environmental Problems And Policies in India", Presidential Address, Geology and Geography Section, Indian Science Congress, Platinum Jubilee Session, Pune, 1988.

Kayastha, S.L., "Environment and Development Emerging Perspectives and Imperatives", in Mehdi Raza (ed.), Development and Ecology, Rawat Publications, New Delhi, 39-56, 1992.

Lamm, Richard D., "The Future Of The Environment", Annals, American Academy of Political and Social Science, 522, July, 57-66, 1992.

Lowenthal, D., "Environmental Perception and Behaviour", University of Chicago, Chicago, 1967.

Planning Commission, "Environment and Forests", Eighth Five Year Plan, Government of India, New Delhi, 92-103, 1992-1997.

Rajamani, R., "The United Nations and Environment" in Satish Kumar (ed.), The United Nations at 50 : An Indian View, UBSPED, New Delhi, 169-188, 1995.

Raza Moonis, "Some Reflections On the Concept of Sustainability in Development" in Mehdi Raza (ed.), Development and Ecology, Rawat Publications, New Delhi, 57-68, 1962.

Sdasyuk Galina, "Critical Environmental Regions : Scope for International Geographical Cooperation in Research" in Mehdi Raza (ed.), Development and Ecology, Rawat Publications, New Delhi, 69-86, 1992.

Stiglitz Joseph, E., "An Agenda for Development in the Twenty First Century" in Boris Pleskovie & Joseph E. Stiglitz (ed.), Annual World Bank Conference on Development Economics, Washington D.C., 17-31, 1997.

Swaminathan, M.S., Foreword to "Promoting Sustainable Development : Towards a New Paradigm", Ismail Seragaldin, RGICS, Paper No. 12, 1994.

UNDP, "Human Development Report", Oxford University Press, New York, 1996.

White Gilbert, F., "National Hazards", Oxford University Press, London, 1974.

White Gilbert, F., Foreword to "Nature of the Rampage : Our Violent Earth", National Geographic Society, 1986.